—— THE ——
FIREARMS
LAW
HANDBOOK

◆

EIGHTH EDITION

First published as *The British Firearms Law Handbook* in 2011.
Incorporating the work previously published as *Gun Law*, by
the late Godfrey Sandys-Winsch, Solicitor.

Sixth edition – 1999

Fifth edition – 1990

Fourth edition – 1985

Third edition – 1979

Second edition – 1973

First published – 1969

THE

FIREARMS
LAW

HANDBOOK

◆

EIGHTH EDITION

LAURA SAUNSBURY, LLB
Consultant Solicitor, Honorary Solicitor and Shotgun Licensing
Advisor to the Clay Pigeon Shooting Association and Honorary
Solicitor to the Deactivated Weapons Association

and

NICK DOHERTY, LLB
of Lincoln's Inn and the Inner Temple, Barrister, Legal Advisor to
the CIC, the International Council for Game and Wildlife
Conservation

Wildy, Simmonds & Hill Publishing

Contains public sector information licensed under the Open Government Licence v3.0

ISBN: 9780854902736

British Library Cataloguing in Publication Data

A catalogue record for this book is available from the British Library

This edition published in 2019 by

Wildy, Simmonds & Hill Publishing
Wildy & Sons Ltd
Lincoln's Inn Archway
Carey Street
London WC2A 2JD
www.wildy.com

Typeset by Heather Jones, North Petherton, Somerset.
Printed in Great Britain by CPI Antony Rowe, Chippenham, Wiltshire.

Contents

Preface

This is the second edition of *The Firearms Law Handbook*, and therefore the eighth edition of *Gun Law*, last published in July 1999, which this work incorporates. It has grown with every succeeding edition as the legislation regarding the ownership and use of guns in Britain becomes ever more onerous and complicated. The aim of this book, and its predecessor, is simple; to help the ordinary reader understand the complexities of firearms legislation in Britain.

As the late Godfrey Sandys-Winsch observed in the Preface to his first edition of *Gun Law* in 1969, it had been his intention to write a simple book, but 'it soon became apparent that the complications of the law would not allow the attainment of that objective'. Those familiar with this subject will agree with our view that the 'complications of the law' have increased many times in the intervening 50 years.

This work is concerned with the law as it stands today, which we have attempted to explain in terms as concise and easily understood as possible given the complexities that exist in this area. We are not concerned with the various policies behind the legislation currently on the statute book, although there is certainly scope for the view that if the overriding objective was a reduction in armed crime, it has achieved little, whilst leading to the abolition of some shooting sports and causing additional inconvenience for many hundreds of thousands of other law-abiding shooters. The administrative burden and cost on the police who have to license the activities of those lawful shooters is enormous. This is particularly so when one considers that according to the government's own figures, published in the briefing paper in relation to the Offensive Weapons Bill 2018, firearms were only used in 0.2 per cent of recorded crime and 0.8 per cent of violence against the person offences in 2016/2017.

Since the previous edition of this book was published in 2011 there have been major changes in the legislation regarding firearms, most importantly the provisions contained within the Policing and Crime Act 2017 (P&CA 2017) which have changed the definitions of 'firearm', 'component part', 'deactivated weapon' and 'antique firearm'. In addition, there have in recent years been significant amendments to the Home Office, *Guide on Firearms Licensing Law*

(*Guide*), for example the introduction in 2016 of the requirement for the police to make enquiries with the doctor of every applicant for a firearm or a shotgun certificate. All of these developments are considered in detail in this new edition.

The decision of the United Kingdom to leave the European Union will inevitably have an impact on a number of the laws and regulations covered in this work. How much difference Brexit will make in practice largely depends on whether it is a 'deal' or 'no deal'. We have tried to anticipate the likely effects as best we can in the relevant sections.

The Offensive Weapons Bill 2018/19 currently before Parliament contains provisions relating to certain types of firearms. These include prohibiting firearms which produce over 13,600 joules of energy at the muzzle and certain types of lever release and 'MARS' rifles. 'Bump stocks' are also to become prohibited, with the application of the minimum sentences provisions for such items. Given that almost all parliamentary time is currently concerned with the issue mentioned in the paragraph above, if, or when, such provisions become law remains to be seen. A late amendment was proposed to repeal the section 11(4) exemption for miniature rifle ranges. This would have a major impact on new entrants taking up shooting sports, for example through schools, cadets, scouts groups and the like.

The *Guide* is always referred to by the police to assist them in interpreting and administering firearms law and licensing. The current edition is available on the web and dated April 2016, but has in fact been revised several times since then. This *Guide* has been placed on a statutory footing by the P&CA 2017, and the police and courts now have to take account of it when making decisions with regards to firearms licensing decisions.

The Firearms Law Handbook covers Scotland, for the simple reason that the principal legislation applies there as it does further south. As Scottish readers will know, although the law in this area is the same, the practice and procedure in the Scottish courts is quite different to that in England and Wales. We have reflected this to a limited extent in Chapter 5 relating to appeals. We have also included the new licensing regime for air weapons in Scotland.

We would like to express our gratitude to all those who have helped us with this work. There are many and so we apologise now if you have not been given an individual mention here. Nonetheless, we trust you know who you are and that your various contributions are appreciated. The well-known firearms expert David Dyson has again been a source of great knowledge and help to us in all of the areas covered by this book. We must also thank David Barrington Barnes and Theresa Gibbs of Shooting Law; Joe Beatham of The Gunshop in East Barnet; Andrew Broome at VHS Fletchers Solicitors; David Frost the shooting journalist;

Barry Johnson, Chairman of the Deactivated Weapons Association; Richard Law, Secretary to the Shooters' Rights Association; Richard Mabbitt, the Proof Master at the Worshipful Company of Gunmakers; David Penn, Secretary to the British Shooting Sports Council; Ian Robertson and James Harris, respectively the Safety, Legal and Technical Officer and the Target Shotgun Representative at the National Rifle Association; and Savvas Toufexis, the firearms and section 5 dealer, for giving us the benefit of all their respective wisdom, experience and advice.

Lastly, we must thank barrister Sophie Chaplin for kindly agreeing, as with the previous edition, to undertake once again the onerous task of proofreading the manuscript. As they say, the errors that remain are all ours.

Firearms licensing is ultimately a mechanism for managing risk. Creating a body of law which fulfils that objective, whilst balancing the rights of law-abiding shooters and collectors of firearms, is complex and difficult. Explaining that body of law is an equally difficult path to navigate. This is an attempt to do that in a clear and approachable manner for the non-lawyer and lawyer alike. We hope that we have taken on the task started by Godfrey Sandys-Winsch in 1969 with a reasonable degree of success and have managed to continue that tradition, so that all who read this book will find it useful. We have attempted to state the law correctly up to 31 January 2019.

References in this book to the masculine represent both masculine and feminine.

Laura Saunsbury
Nick Doherty
London, January 2019

Table of Cases

Table of Statutes

Table of Statutory Instruments

References are to page numbers.

Table of European Material

References are to page numbers.

Table of Other Material

List of Abbreviations

AA 1947	Agriculture Act 1947
ACP	Automatic Colt Pistol
ACPO	Association of Chief Police Officers
ACPO FELWG	Association of Chief Police Officers Firearms and Explosives Licensing Working Group
ATT	Arms Trade Treaty
AWC	Air Weapon Certificate
BASC	British Association for Shooting & Conservation
BMA	British Medical Association
BWSS	British Western Shooting Society
CCA 1847	Cemeteries Clauses Act 1847
CDA 1971	Criminal Damage Act 1971
CJA 1967	Criminal Justice Act 1967
CJA 1988	Criminal Justice Act 1988
CLA 1977	Criminal Law Act 1977
CPR	Criminal Procedure Rules 2015
CSA 1970	Conservation of Seals Act 1970
DA 1991	Deer Act 1991
DDW	defectively deactivated weapon
DVLA	Driver and Vehicle Licensing Authority
EU	European Union
European Weapons Directive	European Council Directive No 91/477/EEC
FA 1968	Firearms Act 1968
FA 1982	Firearms Act 1982
F(A)A 1988	Firearms (Amendment) Act 1988
F(A)A 1992	Firearms (Amendment) Act 1992
F(A)A 1994	Firearms (Amendment) Act 1994
F(A)A 1997	Firearms (Amendment) Act 1997
FEO	Firearms Enquiry Officer
FSS	Forensic Science Service

GA 1831   Game Act 1831
GGA 1880   Ground Game Act 1880
GL(A)A 1960   Game Laws (Amendment) Act 1960
Good Practice Guide   *Good Practice Guide for Registered Firearms Dealers*:
                            https://basc.org.uk/wp-content/uploads/2013/02/Good-
                            Practice-Guide-for-Registered-Firearms-Dealers.pdf
G(S)A 1772   Game (Scotland) Act 1772
GTA   Gun Trade Association
Guide, or *Guidance*   Home Office, *Guide on Firearms Licensing Law*, still
                            referred to widely by its former title, *Firearms Law,*
                            Guidance to the Police, latest edition published April 2016,
                            but amended from time to time on the internet:
                            www.gov.uk/government/publications/
                            firearms-law-guidance-to-the-police-2012

HA 1980   Highways Act 1980
Habitats Directive   European Council Directive No 92/43/EEC
HPA 1892   Hare Preservation Act 1892

IA 1978   Interpretation Act 1978

LGA 1972   Local Government Act 1972

MOD   Ministry of Defence
MPA 1839   Metropolitan Police Act 1839
M(S)A 2010   Marine (Scotland) Act 2010

NABIS   National Ballistics Intelligence Service
N(C)SA 2004   Nature Conservation (Scotland) Act 2004
NFLMS   National Firearms Licensing Management System (a
                            computerised record of all certificate holders and firearms
                            held on certificate in Great Britain)
NPA 1828   Night Poaching Act 1828
NPA 1844   Night Poaching Act 1844
NRA   National Rifle Association (in this book always the NRA of
                            Great Britain, not the United States)

P&CA 2017   Policing and Crime Act 2017
PACE 1984   Police and Criminal Evidence Act 1984
PBA 1992   Protection of Badgers Act 1992
PCA 1953   Prevention of Crime Act 1953
PCP   pre-charged pneumatic
PPA 1862   Poaching Prevention Act 1862

RFD   Registered Firearms Dealer
RR(G)O 2007   Regulatory Reform (Game) Order 2007

TA 1968	Theft Act 1968
TPCA 1847	Town Police Clauses Act 1847
UK	United Kingdom
UKPSA	United Kingdom Practical Shooting Association
UN	United Nations
VCRA 2006	Violent Crime Reduction Act 2006
WCA 1981	Wildlife and Countryside Act 1981
WM(P)A 1996	Wild Mammals (Protection) Act 1996

Chapter 1

General Definitions

INTRODUCTION

1.01   Firearms law in Great Britain is neither simple nor straightforward. The aim of this book is not to produce a highly technical legal textbook but rather to unravel the complexities with which this field of law is so frequently peppered and to make it as approachable to the average layman as possible. That said, there are times where it is difficult to avoid being legalistic. To understand the fundamental principles that are the foundations of firearms law in Britain, we must begin with definitions of the key terms, some of which are inevitably rather technical in their nature. These definitions are, perhaps for obvious reasons, dealt with at the beginning of the book, although the reader who has an enquiry regarding a particular type of weapon or topic may find it helpful to consult the Table of Contents and the Index, and then revert back to this chapter where necessary.

1.02   The main body of the law regulating the use of firearms and ammunition is contained in the Firearms Acts (FA) of 1968 (the principal Act) and 1982, as amended by the Firearms (Amendment) Acts (F(A)A) of 1988, 1992 and 1994, plus two amending Acts of 1997, the Firearms (Amendment) Act 1997 and the Firearms (Amendment) (No 2) Act 1997. In addition, the Firearms Acts (Amendment) Regulations 1992[1] were made to implement European legislation. There are further relevant provisions in the Criminal Justice Act 2003, the Violent Crime Reduction Act 2006 (VCRA 2006), the Criminal Justice and Immigration Act 2008 and the Crime and Security Act 2010. Important changes were made to the definition of a number of the key terms in earlier legislation by sections 125 to 133 of the Policing and Crime Act 2017 (P&CA 2017). Most, although not all, of these changes came into force in May 2017.

1.03   The major parts of this book that deal with the words 'firearm' and 'ammunition' are Chapters 2 to 9, 14, 15 and 16. While the meanings of these words are very wide and will cover all ordinary cases, it is appropriate, at the

---

[1]   SI 1992/2823.

outset, to examine their precise meanings. For certain purposes particular kinds of weapons are defined in the law. This is the case with prohibited weapons, section 1 firearms, shotguns and slaughtering instruments. These definitions are dealt with later in the relevant chapters.

1.04   As with all laws, there are exceptions, and the general rules which are set out in this chapter do not apply for the purposes of firearms being proved, nor do they apply to 'antiques', which are dealt with in this chapter. It must be appreciated that the law relating to firearms is a mixture of law and fact and that while the definitions given here have general application, there will always be items which for various reasons cannot easily be classified.

DEFINITION OF 'FIREARM'

1.05   The word 'firearm' is lengthily defined in the Firearms Act 1968 (FA 1968), and the ingredients of this definition must be examined with the help of a number of court decisions. The definition falls into two parts: the core of the definition, and the particular additions to it.

The core of the definition

1.06   The expression 'firearm' is defined in the amended section 57(1)[2] of the FA 1968 (the definition section) as follows:

(1)   In this Act, the expression 'firearm' means—

   (a)   a lethal barrelled weapon (see subsection (1B));
   ...

(1B)   In subsection (1)(a), 'lethal barrelled weapon' means a barrelled weapon of any description from which a shot, bullet or other missile, with kinetic energy of more than one joule at the muzzle of the weapon, can be discharged.

(1C)   Subsection (1) is subject to section 57A (exception for airsoft guns).

The words in this part of the definition mean as follows.

Lethal

1.07   Even before the FA 1968 was passed the term 'lethal' has been associated with the definition of a firearm. Curiously, however, until as recently as 2017 there was no statutory definition of that term and it was left to case law to come

---

2   P&CA 2017, s 125, amending FA 1968, s 57.

up with a test of lethality. Now any firearm, except an airsoft gun, which produces a kinetic energy at the muzzle of more than 1 joule is defined as 'lethal'. The intentions of the designer or manufacturer of the weapon are immaterial;[3] the sole test is does the weapon produce energy in excess of 1 joule? It is important to keep in mind that air weapons which are not 'specially dangerous' are exempt from this definition in accordance with the wording of section 1 of the FA 1968, despite the fact that the least powerful type of air gun, which normally would cause only trivial injury, is nevertheless 'lethal' as they exceed the energy limit. In one case an air weapon producing 3.7 foot pounds caused death.[4] The energy limit for air rifles is 12 foot pounds.[5]

Barrelled

1.08   The relevant dictionary definition of 'barrel' is: 'cylindrical body or trunk of an object; metal tube of gun'. Thus, a barrel must at least be cylindrical; it would not be sufficient for the missile to be discharged along a groove or channel which was unenclosed for any part of its circumference. Despite the second part of the definition, it is suggested that the barrel may be made of any substance.

1.09   The length of the barrel is immaterial in this context, although as we will see for other reasons the length may affect the classification of a firearm under the legislation.[6]

Weapon

1.10   The dictionary defines a 'weapon' as a material thing designed or used (or usable) as an instrument for inflicting bodily harm on humans or animals.[7] There will be cases where a genuine issue arises as to whether the item in question is a 'weapon'. Signalling and line-throwing equipment for example, while no doubt potentially lethal, is intended to save lives, not take them, and cannot properly be so described.

1.11   It must be remembered that while a firearm is described as a 'weapon', the Firearms Acts also refer to 'prohibited weapons', a term which includes not only firearms but also certain other types of devices such as stun guns and CS gas

---

3   *Read v Donovan* [1947] 1 All ER 37.

4   *Moore v Gooderham* [1960] 3 All ER 575 and *R v Thorpe* [1987] 2 All ER 108. 3.7 foot pounds has been known to cause death when an air weapon was fired into the side of a small child.

5   1 foot pound = 1.355 joules, so a legal air weapon can be up to 16.26 joules.

6   E.g. for the definition of a shotgun, see para 4.01 *et seq*, and as to a 'small firearm', see paras 2.10 and 2.20.

7   An electric stunning device is a prohibited weapon (*Flack v Baldry* [1988] 1 All ER 673), as is an item which discharges CS or other noxious liquids or gasses: FA 1968, s 5(1)(b).

canisters which do not fall within the definition of a 'firearm', as (in those cases) they do not have a barrel. See further Chapter 2.

A shot, bullet or other missile

1.12   Following the general rule for construing Acts of Parliament, the meaning of the words 'or other missile' must be confined to things of the same kind as shot and bullet. This leads to the probable conclusion that the missile must be a solid object; thus a dart from an air gun would be included, but not liquid or gas.[8]

Can be discharged

1.13   Here, also, the normal meaning of these words has been expanded by decisions of the courts and by legislation.

1.14   It should be noted, for completeness, that there is no limitation on the means of propulsion of the missile. The explosive charge is most common, and compressed air and liquid carbon dioxide are used for air weapons, but the use of other forces, for example, springs, elastic or tension as used in a bow, is acceptable.[9]

Airsoft guns

1.15   By virtue of section 57A of the FA 1968 an airsoft gun is not to be considered a firearm for the purposes of the Act. An airsoft gun is one which is designed to discharge only small spherical plastic missiles, not exceeding 8 mm in diameter; and does not exceed a muzzle energy of 1.3 joules if it is capable of firing two or more missiles without repeated pressure on the trigger ('full auto'), or in any other case does not exceed 2.5 joules.[10]

Particular additions to the definition

1.16   After the core of the definition, 'lethal barrelled weapon', as set out above, section 57(1) of the FA 1968 goes on to indicate that the expression 'firearm' also includes:

---

[8]   For guns and ammunition discharging a noxious liquid, gas or other thing, see prohibited weapons in Chapter 2.

[9]   Although query to what extent a barrel is necessary for some of these methods?

[10]   FA 1968, s 57A as inserted by P&CA 2017, s 125(5).

(b) a prohibited weapon;

(c) a relevant component part in relation to a lethal barrelled weapon or a prohibited weapon (see subsection (1D));

(d) an accessory to a lethal barrelled weapon or a prohibited weapon where the accessory is designed or adapted to diminish the noise or flash caused by firing the weapon;

and so much of section 1 of this Act as excludes any description of firearm from the category of firearms to which that section applies shall be construed as also excluding component parts of, and accessories to, firearms of that description.

1.17   This exclusion means that component parts of, and accessories to, shotguns and air weapons do not fall to be classified within the definition of 'firearm'.

1.18   We now consider each of these additions to the definition of what constitutes a 'firearm' in turn.

1.19   The meaning of 'prohibited weapon' is discussed fully in Chapter 2.

Component parts of firearms

1.20   Section 57(1) of the FA 1968 sets out the definition as:

(c) a relevant component part in relation to a lethal barrelled weapon or a prohibited weapon (see subsection (1D));

(1D) For the purposes of subsection (1)(c), each of the following items is a relevant component part in relation to a lethal barrelled weapon or a prohibited weapon—

(a) a barrel, chamber or cylinder,

(b) a frame, body or receiver,

(c) a breech block, bolt or other mechanism for containing the pressure of discharge at the rear of a chamber,

but only where the item is capable of being used as a part of a lethal barrelled weapon or a prohibited weapon.

1.21   'Component part' is another key term in firearms law which is frequently used and yet strangely was not defined anywhere in legislation until very recently. As we discovered from cases we have dealt with, this left firearms dealers and others exposed to the risk of prosecution in the past based on how their local police force interpreted this expression. However, as can be seen from the above, with the passing of the P&CA 2017, we finally have a definitive list of what constitutes a controlled component part of a firearm.

1.22   The final part of this new statutory definition at section 57(1D) merits some consideration. Despite commencing with the words 'but only ...', the inclusion of the phrase 'where the item is capable of being used' represents an expansion of the previous legal position. In the past there was a line of authorities in case law which, with one or two notable exceptions, effectively established that whether an item was to be classified as a component part of a firearm, or prohibited weapon, depended on whether that item was indeed part of a firearm or prohibited weapon at the time of seizure from the accused or other relevant time in question. However, now the law has shifted to a position where the mere fact that an item is capable of being used as one of the specified component parts of a firearm or prohibited weapon will be sufficient for it to be classified as such, notwithstanding the fact that the part may at the relevant time have been fitted to something which could not be considered a lethal barrelled weapon or prohibited weapon.

1.23   It will always be a question of fact in each case as to whether a particular item falls within this statutory list, and this will usually be decided on expert evidence. If a part is contained within something which is not itself a firearm, it may be a component part of that weapon or other item, but a further question now arises: can that part be removed from whatever it is within and placed in a working firearm? Many deactivated weapons (see para 1.30 *et seq*, 'Deactivated firearms') are welded up. It would therefore be wrong to suggest that parts within such an item are controlled component parts as it would not normally be possible to remove them. Conversely, if one of the specified components can simply be removed or unscrewed and used in a firearm, then it is now controlled, and so possession is dealt with in the same way as possession of the complete firearm. Also note that component parts of prohibited weapons are covered by this provision; see Chapter 2 for further details.

1.24   With this clarification of 'component parts' it follows that all other items which form parts of a firearm, such as the firing pin, magazines (detachable or not), sights and other parts and 'furniture', are not component parts, and therefore possession of them is not controlled.

1.25   The Secretary of State has power to amend the list of controlled component parts,[11] giving scope to the possibility of adding further items to that list.

Accessories to firearms

1.26   Section 57(1) of the FA 1968 sets out the definition as:

(d)   any accessory to any such weapon designed or adapted to diminish the noise or flash caused by firing the weapon.

---

[11]   FA 1968, s 57B.

1.27 This covers what are usually described as sound moderators and flash hiders. These are fitted to the end of the barrel and can usually be unscrewed. It is clear from the concluding words of section 57(1) of the FA 1968 that component parts of, and accessories to, a firearm are only controlled if it is a firearm or prohibited weapon within section 1 or section 5. It should be noted that while Parliament has taken the opportunity in the P&CA 2017 to clarify that an item is classified as a 'component part' 'where the item is capable of being used as a part of a lethal barrelled weapon or a prohibited weapon', it did not choose to include similar wording at the end of section 57(1)(d) regarding accessories.

1.28 Consequently, a legal anomaly remains with sound moderators which are not permanently fixed to the firearms in question; they need to be removed to clean the gun, for example. Such items must be on the firearm certificate if they indeed come within section 57(1)(d) by virtue of the fact they are accessories of a section 1 firearm. However, as the final part of section 57(1) makes clear, if they are accessories for a shotgun or an air weapon, they fall outside any control. A sound moderator for a .22″ section 1 rifle or for a .22″ air rifle can often be identical and interchangeable. If you do not have it on your firearm certificate, whether you are prosecuted for possession of the sound moderator may depend on what weapons you have in your possession. We submit that an accessory of this nature is what should properly still be considered a 'mixed use item'. This was considered by the Court of Appeal in 2015 in the case of *Yong*,[12] where it was stated that if there was evidence for an item having a mixed use it should be determined by the jury as a question of fact whether indeed it was an accessory to a section 1 firearm or a prohibited weapon.

1.29 A flash hider on the end of an airsoft gun to complete the appearance of the item, for example, would not be a controlled accessory, as it is an accessory to an airsoft gun, which is not a firearm, and even if it could be unscrewed the 'mixed use' argument would apply.

DEACTIVATED FIREARMS

1.30 Any discussion of the legal definition of 'firearm', and what that term includes, would not be complete without consideration of another expression, 'deactivated firearm'. A firearm shall be considered deactivated if it has been rendered 'incapable of discharging any shot, bullet or other missile and has consequently ceased to be a firearm within the definition of that word'.[13]

---

[12] *R v Yong* [2015] EWCA Crim 852, [2015] 2 Cr App R 15.

[13] F(A)A 1988, s 8.

1.31   There have been substantial changes to the law relating to deactivated firearms since the last edition of this work was published in 2011 such that this topic requires detailed consideration. To assist readers in their interpretation of the new legal provisions contained in the P&CA 2017, and the discussion that follows, the relevant sections are produced here in full.

1.32   Since the Firearms (Amendment) Act 1988 (F(A)A 1988) there has been a procedure by which a firearm can be deactivated to an approved standard. The standards ('Specifications') to which any particular type of gun has been required to be deactivated have changed over the years. Specifications were published in 1989, 1995, 2010 and 2015, increasing in every case the amount of work that needed to be done. The previous regime was not retrospective, so guns deactivated to the 1989 specifications were still lawful to possess and transfer. This previous scheme, which could have been described as voluntary, has now been replaced by a scheme set out in the P&CA 2017 which is mandatory. Section 128 inserts section 8A into the F(A)A 1988:

8A Controls on defectively deactivated weapons
(1)   It is an offence for a person who owns or claims to own a defectively deactivated weapon—

    (a)   to make the weapon available for sale or as a gift to another person, or
    (b)   to sell it or give it (as a gift) to another person.

(2)   Subsection (1)(a) does not apply if—

    (a)   the weapon is made available for sale or as a gift only to a person who is outside the EU (or to persons all of whom are outside the EU), and
    (b)   it is made so available on the basis that, if a sale or gift were to take place, the weapon would be transferred to a place outside the EU.

(3)   Subsection (1)(b) does not apply if—

    (a)   the weapon is sold or given to a person who is outside the EU (or to persons all of whom are outside the EU), and
    (b)   in consequence of the sale or gift, it is (or is to be) transferred to a place outside the EU.

1.33   Therefore any transfer of a defectively deactivated weapon (DDW) within the United Kingdom (UK) is an offence, punishable by up to 5 years' imprisonment.[14]

---

[14]   F(A)A 1988, s 8A(11), or at least it will be when the Secretary of State has published the 'technical specification document' in accordance with subsection (5).

(4)   For the purpose of this section, something is a 'defectively deactivated weapon' if—

    (a)   it was at any time a firearm,

    (b)   it has been rendered incapable of discharging any shot, bullet or other missile (and, accordingly, has either ceased to be a firearm or is a firearm only by virtue of the Firearms Act 1982), but

    (c)   it has not been rendered so incapable in a way that meets the technical specifications for the deactivation of the weapon that apply at the time when the weapon is made available for sale or as a gift or (as the case may be) when it is sold or given as a gift.

1.34   A DDW is therefore any item which has at any stage been a firearm, but is now incapable of functioning as a firearm, and does not comply with the published specifications at the time of transfer. Section 8A further provides:

(5)   The Secretary of State must publish a document setting out the technical specifications that apply for the purposes of subsection (4)(c) ('the technical specifications document').

(6)   The technical specifications document may set out different technical specifications for different kinds of weapon.

(7)   The Secretary of State—

    (a)   may from time to time revise the technical specifications document, and

    (b)   where it is revised—

        (i)   must publish the document as revised, and

        (ii)   specify in it the date on which any changes to the technical specifications that apply for the purposes of subsection (4)(c) take effect.

1.35   The net effect of these provisions is that a person who has a deactivated weapon, including those deactivated under the previous scheme, as well as the new scheme, may continue to possess it. He cannot transfer it to another person unless that person is outside the European Union (EU). Further, even if a person acquires a gun which has been deactivated under the new scheme, he will not be able to transfer it if the Secretary of State has seen fit to revise the specifications in respect of that type of gun. The weapon has to comply with the specifications current at the time of transfer. It is the seller/transferor who commits the offence, not the receiver. Simple possession of a DDW is not an offence, and you are not in possession of a firearm. What will the police do on the death of someone who possessed deactivated weapons: prosecute their executors when they distribute the estate?

1.36   Questions of fact will remain:

(a)   Is it an item that was ever a firearm?
(b)   Is it now not a firearm, or only a firearm by virtue of being 'readily convertible' in accordance with the FA 1982?
(c)   Was it at the time of transfer an item which came within (a) and (b) but is not deactivated to the current specifications?

1.37   In reality all of these questions are only going to be capable of being answered by experts. In addition, a successful prosecution will have to prove that a transfer took place, and the date that it happened.

1.38   These provisions follow EU Regulation 2015/2403, and passed into European law following concerns that some recent terrorist atrocities carried out in Europe had used previously deactivated weapons. The UK had the strictest European regulations on such items before the directive came into force. This change in the law will render all guns previously deactivated worthless, and in the majority of cases it will not be possible to bring items up to the new specifications because they will already have been welded up, and would necessitate destruction of most of the external parts if it were to be attempted. Although these measures were passed in order to improve public safety, by restricting the availability of guns that might 'easily' be 're-activated', the reason that simple possession is still permitted is to avoid large-scale compensation claims against the government. In the UK the existing deactivation standards were sufficient to ensure that there could be no realistic prospect of reactivation, which, taken together with the fact that existing owners are free to retain all such items, might make the reader wonder what will be achieved by this legislation, apart from rendering many people's property worthless.

1.39   The only exception to the prohibition on transfer of a DDW is where an item is transferred to a museum which holds a 'museum firearms licence' issued by the Home Office.[15] In the case of a weapon rendered incapable as mentioned in subsection (4)(b) of section 8A of the F(A)A 1988, as amended, before 8 April 2016, subsection (1)(a) or (b) of the same section does not apply if the weapon is made available for sale or as a gift, or (as the case may be) sold or given, by or on behalf of a museum in respect of which a museum firearms licence is in force to another museum in respect of which such a licence is in force.

1.40   Whether a deactivated weapon complies with the Specifications that will be published by the Secretary of State will be confirmed by one of the two Proof Houses, as is done now. Indeed, the Proof Houses have been applying the most up-to-date version of the European Specifications since they were published in 2016.

---

[15]   F(A)A 1988, s 8A(8).

1.41   We currently await the Specifications, as or when published by the Home Office. When those Specifications are published in accordance with the Act, the offences set out above will come in to force.

DEFINITION OF 'AMMUNITION'

1.42   Section 57(2) of the FA 1968 provides:

> (2)   In this Act, the expression 'ammunition' means ammunition for any firearm and includes grenades, bombs and other like missiles, whether capable of use with a firearm or not, and also includes prohibited ammunition.

1.43   There are three points in this which require examination.

Ammunition for any firearm

1.44   The use of the words 'any firearm' indicates that the definition includes ammunition for a firearm which does not fall within the definition of 'firearm' as earlier discussed; in other words, the precise legal definition of 'firearm' does not apply in this context.[16] Consequently, 'ammunition' also includes blank ammunition for use in a blank firing gun.

Parts of ammunition

1.45   Unlike the definition of 'firearm', there is no reference to a component part, and therefore the ingredients or component parts of a piece of ammunition are not caught by the definition. However the sale of primers, other than to those with an appropriate certificate, is restricted.[17] Simple possession of component parts of ammunition is not controlled, nor is possession of complete shotgun ammunition.[18]

---

[16]   This view is reinforced by the fact that in the FA 1937 the wording of the first part of the definition was: ammunition for any firearm *as hereinafter defined.* The inference is therefore that in the FA 1968 the definition of 'firearm' does not apply. Some prohibited weapons are not 'lethal barrelled weapons'.

[17]   VCRA 2006, s 35.

[18]   FA 1968, s 1(4).

Prohibited ammunition

1.46   The meaning of 'prohibited ammunition' is discussed fully in Chapter 2, although note that expanding ammunition is no longer prohibited for some purposes.[19]

1.47   The Court of Appeal have decided that to constitute ammunition, it must be capable of causing some effect, so a primed case constitutes ammunition, but a spent case does not.[20]

1.48   Beware that the ammunition frequently seen for sale at militaria fairs, boot sales and the like is *supposed* to have been rendered inert. Our experience shows that a small percentage has not been rendered inert and is still live. Check it carefully and if you do decide to buy it, take the seller's name and address. If he is happy to provide his details he's probably confident it is inert.

COMPONENT PARTS OF AMMUNITION

1.49   There is no definition of this in the Firearms Acts, but those who reload their own ammunition will be aware that there are restrictions on the sale and purchase of primers. The prohibition relates to the sale or purchase of 'cap-type primers for use in metallic ammunition' unless the seller is a registered firearms dealer (RFD), or in business selling such ammunition, and the buyer holds a certificate 'authorising him to possess a firearm of a relevant kind'.[21] As with shotgun ammunition, simple possession of primers is not an offence, and neither is the possession of other component parts of ammunition.

GENERAL EXCEPTIONS TO THE CONTROL OF FIREARMS

1.50   There are three exceptions to the provisions in the Firearms Acts which take all types of firearm outside the requirements of the Acts.

Proving firearms

1.51   The FA 1968 provides:

---

[19]   P&CA 2017, s 129, amending FA 1968, s 5(1A)(f).

[20]   *Stubbings v The Queen* [1990] Crim LR 811.

[21]   VCRA 2006, s 35.

Nothing in this Act shall apply to the proof houses of the Master, Wardens and Society of the Mystery of Gunmakers of the City of London and the Guardians of the Birmingham Proof House or the rifle range at Small Heath in Birmingham where firearms are sighted and tested, so as to interfere in any way with the operations of those two companies in proving firearms under the provisions of the Gun Barrel Proof Act 1868 or any other Acts for the time being in force, or to any person carrying firearms to or from any such proof house when being taken to such proof house for the purposes of proof or being removed therefrom after proof.[22]

1.52   Any person can take a gun to the Proof House to have it proved, or be in possession of it for purposes connected with it being proved, and, as the above confirms, that individual will not be committing any offence by having that firearm in his possession even if he does not hold a firearm certificate.

Antique firearms

1.53   The provisions of the Act do not apply to an antique firearm which is sold, transferred,[23] purchased, acquired[24] or possessed[25] as a curiosity or ornament.[26] However, crime statistics in recent years indicate the use of 'antique' firearms in crime has increased because of the relative ease with which they can be acquired, since they do not need to be licensed. The Law Commission considered this problem in some detail in their 2015 review of firearms law. The solution they identified as part of their proposals for reform of the law was to create a new statutory definition of *antique firearm*, where none had existed before. As a result, a new definition has been introduced by section 126 of the P&CA 2017, although these provisions are not in force at the time of writing. Section 126 inserts subsection 2A as follows into section 58 of the FA 1968:

(2A) For the purposes of subsection (2), a firearm is an 'antique firearm' if—

    (a)   either the conditions in subsection (2B) are met or the condition in subsection (2C) is met, and

    (b)   if an additional condition is specified in regulations under subsection (2D), that condition is also met.

(2B) The conditions in this subsection are that—

---

[22]   FA 1968, s 58(1).

[23]   'Transfer' is defined to include let on hire, give, lend and part with possession (FA 1968, s 57(4)).

[24]   'Acquire' is defined to mean hire, accept as a gift or borrow (FA 1968, s 57(4)).

[25]   For commentary on the meaning of 'possessed', see para 3.13 *et seq*, 'When do I need a firearm certificate?'.

[26]   FA 1968, s 58(2).

     (a)   the firearm's chamber or, if the firearm has more than one chamber, each of its chambers is either—

          (i)   a chamber that the firearm had when it was manufactured, or
          (ii) a replacement for such a chamber that is identical to it in all material respects;

     (b)   the firearm's chamber or (as the case may be) each of the firearm's chambers is designed for use with a cartridge of a description specified in regulations made by statutory instrument by the Secretary of State (whether or not it is also capable of being used with other cartridges).

(2C) The condition in this subsection is that the firearm's propulsion system is of a description specified in regulations made by statutory instrument by the Secretary of State.

(2D) The Secretary of State may by regulations made by statutory instrument specify either of the following conditions for the purposes of subsection (2A)(b)—

     (a)   a condition that a number of years specified in the regulations has elapsed since the date on which the firearm was manufactured;
     (b)   a condition that the firearm was manufactured before a date specified in the regulations.

(2E) In its application to Scotland, subsection (2C) does not apply in relation to a firearm that is an air weapon.

(2F) Regulations under subsection (2B), (2C) or (2D) may make different provision for different purposes.

(2G) Subject to subsection (2H), a statutory instrument containing regulations under subsection (2B), (2C) or (2D) may not be made unless a draft of the instrument has been laid before and approved by a resolution of each House of Parliament.

(2H) A statutory instrument containing regulations under subsection (2B) or (2C) which contain only provision amending regulations previously made under that subsection so as to remove a description of cartridge or a description of propulsion system from the descriptions specified in those regulations is subject to annulment in pursuance of a resolution of either House of Parliament.

1.54   The Regulations referred to in subsections 2B, 2C and 2D have yet to be published. There is a consultation process under way. We are confident however that the Regulations when published will define an antique by a number of characteristics. It is possible that any firearm which operates with a centre-fire cartridge will not be permitted, although pin-fire, for example, will still be considered an antique. The concept of 'obsolete' cartridges and calibres is likely to be retained. There will be a certain 'cut-off point' in terms of age, perhaps 1939 or perhaps 1945. Whatever criteria are set, there will be a tightening of the types of firearms that can be classified as antiques.

1.55   This change in the law will preserve as antique firearms, free from any control, those firearms which are genuinely obsolete, and for which no ammunition is realistically available. Those guns which were previously considered to be antiques, but for which ammunition was sometimes available, and were occasionally used in armed crime, are now going to require certification.

1.56   The amended section 58(2A) continues:

> (3)   In subsection (2)—
>
> > (a)   in paragraph (a), for 'section 21' substitute 'sections 19, 20 and 21';
> > (b)   in paragraph (b), for 'section 21' substitute 'section 19, 20 or 21'.

This includes antique firearms within offences relating to having a firearm in a public place without a reasonable excuse (section 19) and trespassing with a firearm (section 20). Since 2014, a person prohibited from possessing firearms under section 21 has not been permitted to possess an antique firearm.[27]

1.57   The requirement for a certificate for certain types of antique firearms is as follows:

> (4)   Subsections (5) to (7) apply where—
>
> > (a)   immediately before the coming into force of regulations under section 58(2B), (2C) or (2D) of the Firearms Act 1968 (as inserted by subsection (2) above), a person has in his or her possession a firearm that is an antique firearm for the purposes of section 58(2) of that Act, and
> > (b)   in consequence of the coming into force of the regulations, the firearm ceases to be an antique firearm for those purposes.
>
> (5)   Section 5 of the Firearms Act 1968 does not apply in relation to the possession of the firearm by the person unless—
>
> > (a)   the person carries on a business as a firearms dealer, and
> > (b)   the firearm is in his or her possession for the purpose of the business.
>
> (6)   An application by the person for a certificate under section 1 or 2 of that Act in respect of possession of the firearm may not be refused on the ground that the person does not have a good reason for having the firearm in his or her possession.
> (7)   An application by the person for the renewal of a certificate issued under section 1 or 2 of that Act in respect of possession of the firearm may not be refused on the ground that the person does not have a good reason for having the firearm in his or her possession.

---

[27]   Anti-social Behaviour, Crime and Policing Act 2014, s 110(2).

(8) The provision made by subsections (4) to (7) does not prevent additional transitional provision being made (under the power conferred by section 183(9)) in connection with the coming into force of this section (including provision for enabling certificates and authorisations under the Firearms Act 1968 to be issued or granted before this section comes fully into force).

1.58   As with the provisions in relation to deactivated firearms, the government realised that any attempt to prohibit possession of antique firearms which had previously been free of control would result in huge compensation claims. However, the claims may have been larger with antiques and so those who already have possession of such items can now have a free firearm certificate. This mirrors the measures taken in 2004 in relation to Brococks, self-contained air-cartridge guns; see para 2.05, fn 13. The difference between deactivated weapons and antiques is that transfer is prohibited with deactivated weapons, para 1.30 *et seq*, but those who possess antiques will be able to dispose of them, at least to a dealer. Consequently, there should still be a market in antique firearms. A discussion as to why a similar measure could not have been applied to deactivated firearms is outside the scope of this work.

1.59   An individual in possession of an antique firearm when the new law comes into effect will be granted a free certificate, and a 'lack of good reason' is not a ground for refusal or non-renewal of the certificate. This applies even if the item in question (now it is classified as a firearm) would fall within section 5 of the Act. This will often be because it is a 'small firearm', a handgun. Note, however, that all the other usual criteria for the grant of a firearm certificate will apply. In particular, the police will no doubt apply the usual tests in relation to whether a person can be permitted to possess firearms without danger to public safety or the peace, and whether that person is 'unfitted' to possess firearms. This will be of some importance, as large numbers of people who would never previously have applied for a firearm certificate will now be required to apply for one. An issue may arise in some cases as to whether an item possessed by a person is an antique at all. Can the police simply say, 'that is not an antique and you can't have a certificate for it'? Presumably, that will be subject to a firearms licensing appeal.

1.60   As with the similar provisions in respect of Brococks, we suggest that those subsequently found in possession of an antique firearm falling within section 5 of the Act should in fact be dealt with as if they had committed an offence under section 1.[28] This is on the basis that they should have obtained, and were entitled to, a certificate under section 1 of the Act, the real criterion being

---

[28] 'Self-contained air cartridge' weapons – Anti-social Behaviour Act 2003, s 39 and *R v Goldsborough* [2015] EWCA Crim 1278, [2015] 2 Cr App R 29.

whether they can prove they were in possession of the weapon before the new law came in to effect.

1.61   There is now a statutory definition of what is an antique firearm. As with other issues covered by the Firearms Acts, many of these questions can either only be, or should be, dealt with by expert evidence. It should be noted that antique firearms are only excluded from the operation of the FA 1968 when possessed or handled *as a curiosity or ornament.*[29] Using them in any other way, for example by firing them, removes this exemption. It follows from this that the fact a weapon is capable of firing does not necessarily prevent it from being classified as an antique. However, possession of ammunition suitable for use in the weapon will be taken by the police as a strong indication that the item was not possessed as a curiosity, unless there is some other good reason to have such ammunition. We anticipate that those antiques which will now be held on certificate will be held with a 'not to be fired' condition attached to them.

1.62   The principle in *Howells*[30] that a modern reproduction of an antique was not an antique and that the belief of the holder, even though honestly and reasonably held as to the age of the item, is irrelevant, will still apply. The appropriate charge will be under either section 1, 2 or 5, depending on the classification of the weapon, with the caveat that if a section 5 item had been possessed when the law changed, it might be that an offence is committed under section 1, rather than section 5.

1.63   A firearm can change status as an antique. One person may possess it as a curiosity and then sell it to someone else who wishes to use it. Both the first and the second owner may, or may not, require a certificate. The same applies to a single owner who, over time, changes his mind as to the reasons for which he keeps it. Previous guidance suggests a letter to the licensing authority to notify the change of status is sufficient.

1.64   Once the issue of antiquity has been raised, it is for the prosecution to prove that it is not an antique at all, or that it is an antique, but one which should be held on certificate. These are all questions of fact for the jury, not a question of law for the judge.[31]

1.65   The question of whether a firearm is an antique is not to be confused with the provisions in the Firearms (Amendment) Act 1997 (F(A)A 1997) regarding 'historic' handguns.[32] These provisions are dealt with in point (g) of the list at

---

[29]   FA 1968, s 58(2).

[30]   *R v Howells* [1977] 3 All ER 417.

[31]   *R v Burke* [1978] 67 Cr App R 220, CA.

[32]   F(A)A 1997, s 7.

para 2.20. See the comments at point (h) in the same list as to the circumstances where a firearm certificate might be required for a firearm which would also qualify as an antique.

1.66   The issue of antiquity applies to firearms but is not considered to apply to ammunition. Those who wish to collect ammunition will need to obtain a certificate.

'Persons in the service of Her Majesty'

1.67   While dealing with general exceptions it should be pointed out that 'Persons in the service of Her Majesty' are exempt for all purposes from firearms controls.[33] This includes not only the armed forces (including the Territorial Army and Cadet Corps) and the police, but also other law enforcement agencies such as the National Crime Agency and the Border Force. The Channel Tunnel Act 1987 and the regulations under it added 'Officers of the French Republic' to the list. For obvious reasons, this exemption only applies to official duties and not to such employees' activities in a private capacity. This exemption obviously applies to all firearms and not just those that are prohibited by virtue of section 5, but includes all of those items within sections 1, 2 and 5.

1.68   It is under these powers that police officers can seize firearms and ammunition, as well as carry them.

EXPERT EVIDENCE

1.69   Reference has already been made on a number of occasions in this chapter to evidence being given by experts in the examination of firearms. A suitable expert will be able to give an opinion on whether an item is a firearm, whether it discharges a projectile with an energy of more than 1 joule, whether it is capable of automatic fire and so on. Experts can also help with questions such as antiquity, convertibility, type of mechanism, and many other issues which arise in this area.

1.70   In criminal cases relating to firearms classification, the experts are in the unique position of giving evidence about the facts *and* the law. In order to give an opinion in this field an expert may have to say 'as a result of the facts I found on examination, this is a prohibited weapon within section 5(1)(b) of the Act', or as appropriate. It is only by giving an assessment of the factual background within the context of the Act that the expert can reach a conclusion. The Court of Appeal recently voiced concerns that when doing so in firearms cases, 'they are expressing a view on the law and thereby usurping the function of the judge, and

---

[33]   See FA 1968, s 54 for more precise details.

when they give views on the facts they are usurping the functions of the jury'.[34] This is correct, although how most criminal cases would proceed with the experts only being allowed to say 'I got it to fire' is an interesting question. These are often complex issues outside of the experience of most lawyers and judges, let alone juries, and both sides, and the court, often appreciate the help that is available. Suffice it to say, if a case turns to any extent on the classification of an item, get an expert. There will very often be points that the shooter, and the lawyer, may have missed.

1.71   It is said with frequency in the criminal courts these days that 'a defendant knows whether he has committed the offence or not', this observation usually being made when the court is deciding how much credit to give a defendant who has pleaded guilty. While that comment may well apply to a number of criminal offences, it often does not apply to offences relating to firearms, particularly those concerning the classification or capability of an item. A person may be in possession of an item, but quite unaware of the capability or correct classification of it. Not only can an expert help with these matters, but he may also be able to give evidence about whether the alleged attribute of the item, even if correct, would have been apparent to the owner, for example.

1.72   There has been a tendency for police/prosecution experts to apply what they see as an accepted view or policy and 'sing from the same hymn sheet'. Occasionally these policies do not fit the specific facts of a given case. Assumptions are sometimes being made which the facts do not support. Not surprisingly, the Forensic Science Service (FSS), when it existed, had 'public safety and policy' uppermost in its mind when considering the classification of any given allegedly dangerous item. Most police forces now tend to use force armourers, or they instruct an outside forensic examiner, most of whom are former FSS personnel. Whether either of these situations leads to completely independent thought is sometimes open to question. One further consideration for lawyers: if you are minded to instruct an expert who is a former employee of the FSS, you may well run into the problem that he could not now say something different to what he would have said in his previous employment. He would be susceptible to cross-examination on it.

1.73   A recent example of the application of this type of policy consideration is the case of *Bewley*.[35] This concerned a 'Kimar 85 blank firer', which the Crown contended was a firearm (and by virtue of its size prohibited, so whoever had it would receive a minimum mandatory 5-year sentence) on the basis that an 'expert' managed to make it fire using a mallet and a punch and a great deal of

[34]   Discussion between Treacy LJ and counsel in *Paul Heddell v The Queen* [2016] EWCA Crim 443.

[35]   *Bewley v Regina* [2012] EWCA Crim 1457, [2013] 1 All ER 1.

expertise. The FA 1982 created an offence of having possession of items which are 'readily convertible' to being firearms. However, those offences are only committed if the conversion can be done with ordinary household tools, with no specialist knowledge, and the person in possession is shown to be aware that the item is capable of such a conversion. The prosecution were never very keen on having to jump through those hoops, so simply charged possession of a firearm under the FA 1968. In *Bewley* the Court of Appeal disapproved of this approach, pointing out that the defence were being deprived of the 'safeguards' set out in the FA 1982. Moses LJ observed:

> It would be absurd to allow the prosecution to sidestep the safeguards within the 1982 Act merely by construing 'firearm' as meaning an item which could 'easily' be converted into a lethal-barrelled weapon, capable of discharging a missile, in the application of the principle in *Freeman*.

1.74 The Court went on to say, in robust terms, that it was impossible to say that the item in question, in its current condition, constituted a firearm under the Act. They were similarly dismissive of the Crown's argument that in any event the defendant must have component parts of a prohibited weapon:

> The question then arises as to whether the starting pistol could be regarded as a component part of 'such a lethal or prohibited weapon'. The Divisional Court in *Cafferata* would, no doubt, have concluded that it could be so regarded. That seems to us to be an impossible construction of s.57(1)(b). The definition of firearm cannot include a component part of a lethal-barrelled weapon of any description from which any shot, bullet or other missile can *not* be discharged.

1.75 This issue of 'readily convertible' firearms was revisited again in *Heddell*, referred to in para 1.70, with a slightly different outcome, but the point regarding expert evidence remains valid.

1.76 Like all of us, experts can make mistakes. The dangers of accepting prosecution evidence without getting a defence expert were dramatically demonstrated in the case of *Lawrence*.[36] This was a case that had proceeded under the 'early guilty plea scheme'. The prosecution had provided a 'fast track' expert's report, which wrongly asserted the shotgun she had was a section 5 prohibited firearm, when in fact it was, and always had been, a section 1 firearm. For some reason it took the defence solicitor 89 days to spot that the defendant had pleaded guilty to an offence which she did not commit, and for which she had received a sentence of 5 years' imprisonment. The Court of Appeal refused to order a retrial, although she could have been charged with the offence under section 1. As the last lines of the judgment state:

---

[36] *R v Nyira Lawrence* [2013] EWCA Crim 1054, [2014] 1 WLR 106.

This case serves to highlight that in relation to 'streamlined' procedures directed at encouraging early guilty pleas it is important that all involved are alert to check that the necessary elements of what will sometimes be relatively specific offences are in fact provable.

Precisely.

Chapter 2

Prohibited Weapons and Ammunition

GENERAL OVERVIEW

2.01   Let us begin by saying we would be the first to concede this is the most difficult chapter in the book to digest. (Heaven knows it was certainly the most difficult to write!) The terms 'prohibited weapon' and 'prohibited ammunition' are fundamental in the Firearms Acts. They cover a very wide range of different things and whether or not a particular firearm, other weapon or ammunition is deemed prohibited can have serious implications.

2.02   In very broad terms, 'prohibited weapons' are handguns and automatic weapons, while 'prohibited ammunition' is ammunition which is designed to explode, expand or ignite on or immediately before impact. However, it should be said this is a considerable over-simplification of a very complex area of law which even the most experienced lawyers or police officers can struggle to get to grips with. As will be seen shortly at paras 2.05 *et seq* and 2.12 *et seq*, in a vain attempt to reduce violent gun crime, there have been a number of Acts of Parliament which have each in succession extended the scope of the terms 'prohibited weapon' and 'prohibited ammunition' to include further categories of item within their definitions. We are now left with a long and unwieldy list of categories of item, each of which requires defining.

2.03   As is also discussed later at paras 2.05 *et seq* and 2.12 *et seq*, possession of prohibited weapons or prohibited ammunition without proper lawful authority is a serious criminal offence for which there can be very grave consequences. We have represented enough people who have inadvertently fallen foul of this area of law to know that you cannot be too careful about checking whether an item in your possession might potentially be classified as a prohibited firearm or ammunition. Therefore, while this does not make for easy reading, we considered it our duty to fully explore in this work the finer details of what is included in the terms 'prohibited weapons' and 'prohibited ammunition'.

DEFINITION OF PROHIBITED WEAPONS

2.04 'Prohibited weapons' are those considered by the legislature to be so dangerous that the special authority of the Home Office is needed before their possession or use becomes lawful. In the FA 1968 as originally enacted, which remains the basis of modern firearms legislation, prohibited weapons included only automatic weapons and those discharging noxious liquids and other things. The violent incidents at Hungerford in 1987 and at Dunblane in 1996 have caused Parliament to add several other types of weapon to the list. In addition, European legislation[1] has required Parliament to make further amendments.

2.05 The following is the current list of prohibited weapons using the section numbers in the FA 1968 for ease of reference:

section 5(1)(a)	Any firearm which is so designed or adapted that two or more missiles can be successively discharged without repeated pressure on the trigger.[2]
section 5(1)(ab)	Any self-loading[3] or pump-action[4] rifled[5] gun, other than one which is chambered for .22 rim-fire cartridges.
section 5(1)(aba)	Any firearm which *either* has a barrel less than 30cm (about 11.8 inches) long *or* is less than 60cm (about 23.6 inches) in length overall, other than an air weapon, a muzzle-loading gun or a firearm designed as signalling apparatus.[6]
section 5(1)(ac)	Any self-loading or pump-action smooth-bore gun which is not an air weapon or chambered for .22 rim-fire cartridges *and either* has a barrel less than 24 inches long[7] *or* is less than 40 inches in length overall.[8]

---

[1] European Council Directive No 91/477/EEC (European Weapons Directive) which was introduced into English law by the Firearms Acts (Amendment) Regulations 1992, and others, which attempt to 'harmonise' firearms legislation across the Union. Directive 2008/51/EC and Regulation 2015/2403 have amended the earlier Directive and have also been incorporated in to UK domestic law and relate to firearms. Note, the 1992 Regulations have included prohibited weapons which are not firearms, so include a disguised stun gun or CS canister, as well as disguised firearms. This is not what the Council Directive says, and so English law has gone further than was required in this respect.

[2] This includes burst-fire weapons.

[3] This means a weapon designed or adapted so that it is automatically re-loaded (FA 1968, s 57(2A); F(A)A 1988, s 25(2)).

[4] This means a weapon so designed or adapted that it is re-loaded by the manual operation of the fore-end or forestock of the weapon (FA 1968, s 57(2A)).

[5] I.e. not smooth bored.

[6] For the purposes of section 5(1)(aba) and (1)(ac) any detachable, folding, retractable or other moveable butt-stock shall be disregarded in measuring the length of any firearm (FA 1968, s 5(8); F(A)A 1997, s 1(6)). Items in this category are often referred to as 'small firearms'.

[7] Measurement is from the muzzle to the point at which the charge is exploded (FA 1968, s 57(6)(a); F(A)A 1988, s 25(1)).

[8] See fn 7 with regard to measuring the overall length of the gun.

section 5(1)(ad)	Any smooth-bore revolver gun[9] other than one which is chambered for 9mm rim-fire cartridges or a muzzle-loading[10] gun.
section 5(1)(ae)	Any rocket launcher, or any mortar, for projecting a stabilised missile, other than a launcher or mortar designed for line-throwing[11] or pyrotechnic[12] purposes, or as signalling apparatus.
section 5(1)(af)	Any air rifle, air gun or air pistol which uses, or is designed or adapted for use with, a self-contained gas cartridge system.[13]
section 5(1)(b)	Any weapon of whatever description designed or adapted for the discharge of any noxious liquid, gas or other thing.[14]
section 5(1A)(a)	Any firearm which is disguised as another object.[15]
section 5(1A)(c)	Any launcher or other projecting apparatus not falling within 5(1)(ae) above which is designed to be used with any rocket or ammunition falling within 5(1A)(b), or with ammunition which would fall within that subsection, but for it being ammunition falling within subsection 5(1)(c).[16]

The Home Office may, within limitations, add other firearms, except air weapons, to the foregoing list.[17]

2.06   As to section 5(1)(b) above, the words 'weapon of whatever description' show that the weapon need not be any sort of gun or in any way resemble a gun.[18] A dictionary definition of a weapon is 'a material thing designed or used or usable as an instrument for inflicting bodily harm'.

---

[9]   'Revolver' in relation to a smooth-bore gun means a gun containing a series of chambers which revolve when the gun is fired (FA 1968, s 57(2B); F(A)A 1988, s 25(2)).

[10]   A muzzle-loading gun is a gun which is designed to be loaded at the muzzle end of the barrel or chamber with a loose charge and a separate ball (or other missile) (FA 1968, s 5(9); F(A)A 1997, s 1(6)).

[11]   E.g. for coastguard rescue purposes.

[12]   I.e. for firework displays.

[13]   Anti-social Behaviour Act 2003, s 39(3). Although not the only type, these are predominantly known as 'Brococks'.

[14]   This has wide application, but by far the most common in practice are items which discharge CS gas, freely available in Europe. Electricity is a noxious thing and its discharge by means of an electric stunning device is a discharge within the meaning of that word. Such a device is therefore a prohibited weapon (*Flack v Baldry* [1988] 1 All ER 673). Cattle prods are not. Likewise, weapons specially designed or adapted to discharge tranquillising darts are prohibited weapons.

[15]   This is to comply with European criteria. Firearms and swords that look like umbrellas or walking sticks are common examples.

[16]   For discussion of items falling under this category and the associated ammunition under FA 1968, s 5(1A)(b) and (1)(c), see para 2.12 *et seq*, 'Definition of prohibited ammunition'.

[17]   F(A)A 1988, s 1(4).

[18]   This is demonstrated by a 'Taser' being classified as a prohibited weapon.

2.07   The word 'noxious', meaning 'harmful or unwholesome', is thought to apply to the words 'gas' and 'other thing' as well as to 'liquid'. The words 'other thing' should be interpreted, it is suggested, as meaning 'any other thing of any kind', i.e. their meaning is not restricted to a thing which is of the same kind as liquid or gas.[19] Thus it appears that the last seven words in section 5(1)(b) could be written as 'any noxious liquid, any noxious gas, or any noxious thing of any kind'.[20] It is interesting to note that, as already stated, the most common item in practice in this category is CS gas. This is carried by police forces throughout this country for the very reason that it causes no lasting damage to the body. Is it therefore 'noxious' within the above meaning? Arguably not, but the courts have always tended to readily accept CS gas is 'noxious' and have therefore classified as a prohibited weapon any item designed for the discharge of CS gas.

2.08   As to items in section 5(1)(a) above, there are three court decisions concerned with automatic weapons which had been modified or adapted or were incomplete. It has been held that a sub-machine gun which had been modified to prevent it from being fired when the automatic mode was selected was not a prohibited weapon,[21] but an adaptation to the trigger mechanism of an automatic weapon making the firing of single shots easier did not prevent the weapon from being an automatic weapon and therefore prohibited.[22] The third case concerned a sub-machine gun lacking three parts which could easily be replaced so as to make it fire normally; the court decided that the gun was a prohibited weapon.[23] In only the first of these decisions did the court rule that the weapon was not prohibited. As already mentioned, it has become increasingly important to ascertain whether an item is indeed a 'prohibited' weapon as possession, etc of such weapons now carries a mandatory minimum term of 5 years' imprisonment.

2.09   In the past, attempts were sometimes made to take firearms out of the prohibited category by 'converting' them to a weapon in a lower category, perhaps the most obvious example being to smooth bore a machine gun or rifle and thereby (under the previous legislation) removing it from section 5, or section 1, and placing it into section 2, as a smooth-bore gun. Parliament has

---

[19]   This construction is different from that applied to the words 'any shot, bullet or other missile' (see Chapter 1) because the words 'liquid' and 'gas' do not constitute a category or class of thing (*Halsbury's Laws of England*, LexisNexis Butterworths, 4th Edition, Vol 44, para 877).

[20]   In the absence of any court decisions on the point, this interpretation can be tentative only.

[21]   *R v Jobling* [1981] Crim LR 625.

[22]   *R v Pannell* (1983) 76 Crim App R 53, CA.

[23]   *R v Clarke (Frederick)* [1986] 1 All ER 846. The court also decided that, in any case, the incomplete gun constituted component parts of a prohibited weapon which fell within the definition of that kind of weapon by virtue of FA 1968, s 57(1)(b).

attempted to stop this practice. The conversion of a prohibited weapon into a weapon not classified as prohibited may therefore now fail. A weapon which:

(a) has at any time been a weapon of a kind described in sections 5(1)(a) to 5(1A)(a) above or in section 5(1A)(c) above; and

(b) is not a self-loading or pump-action[24] smooth-bore gun which has at any time been a weapon of the type described at (a) above by reason only of having had a barrel less than 24 inches long,[25]

is to be treated as a prohibited weapon notwithstanding anything done to convert it into a different kind of weapon.[26]

COMPONENT PARTS OF PROHIBITED WEAPONS

2.10 There is now a statutory definition of 'component parts' of firearms,[27] and in most cases this applies equally to component parts of prohibited weapons. However, current Home Office guidance[28] states that it is only component parts of items within sections 5(1)(a) (fully automatic weapons), 5(1A)(a) (weapons disguised as another object) and 5(1)(aba) (small firearms) that are themselves controlled by section 5 of the FA 1968. It has been accepted for many years that component parts of self-loading ('semi-automatic') rifles (section 5(1)(ab)); large capacity shotguns with barrels less than 24 inches (section 5(1)(ac)); smooth-bored revolver guns, except 9 mm (section 5(1)(ad)); rocket launchers and mortars (section 5(1)(ae)); and self-contained air cartridge weapons (section 5(1)(af)) fall to be classified under section 1 or section 2, as appropriate. This is because in many cases the component parts could be from a firearm within that category and therefore applying general principles of criminal law the prosecution should be on the basis of the lesser charge.

2.11 The writers of this book suggest that this principle should be retained, if only because it is often difficult as a question of fact to determine from what type of gun a part came, even if it is a relevant component part. It also occurs to us, however, that on a plain reading of the new definition in section 57(1D):

---

[24] This means a weapon so designed or adapted that it is re-loaded by the manual operation of the fore-end or forestock of the weapon (FA 1968, s 57(2A)).

[25] Measurement is from the muzzle to the point at which the charge is exploded (FA 1968, s 57(6)(a); F(A)A 1988, s 25(1)).

[26] F(A)A 1988, s 7(1).

[27] See para 1.20 *et seq*, 'Component parts of firearms'.

[28] Home Office, *Guide on Firearms Licensing Law*, April 2016 (*Guide*), para 3.3.

For the purposes of subsection (1)(c), each of the following items is a relevant component part in relation to a lethal barrelled weapon or a prohibited weapon—

(a)   a barrel, chamber or cylinder,
(b)   a frame, body or receiver,
(c)   a breech block, bolt or other mechanism for containing the pressure of discharge at the rear of a chamber,

but only where the item is capable of being used as a part of a lethal barrelled weapon or a prohibited weapon.

it could be argued that this new definition includes those parts found in *any* type of prohibited weapon. Parts included in (a) and (c) do not materially alter the existing position. But what about the body of a stun gun controlled under section 5(1)(b)? It is a prohibited weapon, so is a person in possession of a non-working stun gun (which would not have been an offence under the previous guidance) now committing an offence by possessing a component part (the body) of such a weapon? The anomaly was due to the fact that section 5(1)(b) items are prohibited weapons, but not barrelled weapons. The prosecution would have to prove that it could be used in another such weapon, which might not be that easy, as a plastic body might be broken in the process of dismantling it. We should bear in mind that, as indicated elsewhere, despite the introduction of the P&CA 2017, the Home Office have only introduced minor changes to the *Guide on Firearms Licensing Law*[29] (*Guide*), and none since April 2016. Until there is updated guidance or a decision of the Court of Appeal it is difficult to predict how this issue will be resolved.

DEFINITION OF PROHIBITED AMMUNITION

2.12   As with prohibited weapons, the classification of prohibited ammunition has been much widened since the earlier definition in the FA 1968, which only covered ammunition containing, or designed or adapted to contain, any noxious liquid, gas or other thing. The following is the current list of prohibited ammunition using the section numbers in the FA 1968, as amended:

section 5(1)(c)   Any cartridge with a bullet designed to explode on or immediately before impact,[30] any ammunition containing or designed or adapted to contain any noxious thing as is mentioned in 5(1)(b) above and, if capable of being used with

---

[29]   Available at www.gov.uk/government/publications/firearms-law-guidance-to-the-police-2012.
[30]   Hollow-point and soft-point bullets ('expanding ammunition') are not within this definition, they come within s 5(1A)(f).

a firearm of any description,[31] any grenade, bomb (or other like missile), or rocket or shell designed to explode as aforesaid.

section 5(1A)(b)	Any rocket or ammunition not falling within items 5(1)(c) above which consists in or incorporates a missile designed to explode on or immediately before impact, and is for military use.[32]
section 5(1A)(c)	Any launcher or other projecting apparatus not falling within 5(1)(ae) of that subsection which is designed to be used with any rocket or ammunition falling within paragraph 5(1A)(b) above or with ammunition which would fall within that paragraph but for it being ammunition falling within 5(1)(c).[33]
section 5(1A)(d)	Any ammunition for military use which consists in or incorporates a missile designed so that a substance contained in the missile will ignite on or immediately before impact.[34]
section 5(1A)(e)	Any ammunition for military use which consists in or incorporates a missile designed, on account of its having a jacket and hard-core, to penetrate armour plating, armour screening or body armour.
section 5(1A)(f)	Any ammunition which incorporates a missile designed or adapted to expand on impact.[35]
section 5(1A)(g)	Anything which is designed to be projected as a missile from any weapon and is designed to be, or has been, incorporated in:

    (i) any ammunition falling within any of the preceding paragraphs; or

    (ii) any ammunition which would fall within those items but for its being specified in subsection (1) of this section.

The Home Office may, by order, add specially dangerous ammunition of other descriptions to the foregoing list.[36]

---

[31] I.e. including a firearm which does not fall within the definition of that term as discussed in Chapter 1.

[32] Any rocket or ammunition which is designed to be capable of being used with a military weapon shall be taken to be for military use (FA 1968, s 5(7)(a)).

[33] This is intended to cover items such as rocket launch tubes fitted to aircraft. Launch rails are not included unless they provide initial guidance to the rocket. It is submitted that it does not cover items such as the spent launcher tube from a LAW 66 rocket; these are 'one use only' items and cannot be reused.

[34] References to a missile designed as described in this item will include references to any missile containing a substance that ignites on exposure to air (FA 1968, s 5(7)(b)). Napalm is an example. This does not include tracer or spotter ammunition.

[35] References to a missile expanding on impact include references to its deforming in any predictable manner on or immediately after impact (FA 1968, s 5(7)(c)).

[36] F(A)A 1988, s 1(4).

2.13   Some of these definitions are somewhat tortuous to say the least, particularly in relation to prohibited ammunition. An item may fall into more than one category of prohibition but, following the normal rules of statutory interpretation, the list should be looked at as being in sequential order and you should consider which section an item is prohibited by first. It would be an incorrect approach to prosecute someone for having an item contrary to section 5(1)(aba) when in fact it is a fully automatic weapon covered by section 5(1)(a), although the item might actually fall into both classifications. This may clearly have an effect in relation to the level of punishment for any unlawful possession but will also be relevant when considering the many exemptions which apply to section 5.

2.14   Those readers who have managed the significant achievement of remaining alert after reading the last few pages may have noticed that section 5(1A)(c) appears listed as both a category of prohibited weapon and also a category of prohibited ammunition. This repetition was deliberate. Even the relatively uninformed reader will be aware that a wide variety of munitions has been designed and developed in recent years. Depending on your point of view, some of these rockets, grenades and similar items which are intended to be encompassed by the various subsections of section 5(1A) might themselves be considered to be prohibited weapons, or alternatively prohibited ammunition for use in such weapons. The inclusion of the words 'for military use' in a number of the subsections of section 5(1A) makes it clear that items which create a similar effect but are designed for other purposes, such as for use in the film industry or large fireworks displays, will not be classified as prohibited.

2.15   In reality, items falling within the various categories of prohibited ammunition covered by section 5(1A) probably only amount to a very small quantity of items in private hands. We therefore do not propose to dwell any further on this topic within this work. We simply add that anyone who has an issue with any item potentially falling into any of these categories really does need to seek expert help and advice.

DEALINGS WITH PROHIBITED WEAPONS AND PROHIBITED AMMUNITION

2.16   Authority to deal with prohibited weapons and ammunition is usually known as a 'section 5 authority' and is issued by the Home Office following consultation with the police. It will normally only be granted to those who can show a need to possess such items for business purposes, for trading within the UK or abroad, or for other purposes such as theatrical or film hire. It is normal for such authority to be issued subject to conditions specified therein.

2.17   With the exceptions mentioned below, you will commit an offence if you have in your possession,[37] purchase, acquire,[38] manufacture, sell or transfer[39] any prohibited weapon or ammunition. These offences are considered very seriously by the courts and most now carry a mandatory minimum sentence of 5 years.[40] The maximum is usually 10 years. These developments in the law can lead to what some might view as draconian penalties. For example, self-contained gas cartridge air weapons (Brococks) were freely available until 2006 and had been widely sold since the early 1980s. They are air weapons of much lower power than most other types. There are doubtless many which once belonged to father or grandfather still in lofts, cellars and garages across the country. Those widows and children who inherit such items are automatically facing a prison sentence for an offence of which we would suggest most of the public is unaware. An existing owner would be liable to be prosecuted for an offence under section 1,[41] but those who inherit such items later were not the owners at the time and in law do not benefit from that decision as they would never have been entitled to have held it on a certificate.

2.18   The courts do have the power to find 'exceptional circumstances' not to impose the mandatory minimum punishment, and it is to be hoped that in these cases such circumstances would be found, but it is a daunting prospect to go to court hoping that the normal rule of the law will be overturned in your case.[42] Brococks were banned because they were easy to convert to fire live .22″ ammunition and had gained popularity amongst criminal gangs.

2.19   If an authority from the Secretary of State is not held, there are a number of other exceptions to the general rule that those items in section 5 are prohibited. This was necessary as, in addition to the sport of target shooting, there are a number of other legitimate uses for handguns in circumstances where they are the only realistic option.

2.20   In relation to section 5(1)(aba) ('small firearms') the exceptions are:

---

[37]   For guidance on the meaning of 'possession', see para 3.13 *et seq*, 'When do I need a firearm certificate?'.

[38]   'Acquire' is defined to mean hire, accept as a gift or borrow (FA 1968, s 57(4)).

[39]   'Transfer' is defined to mean let on hire, give, lend or part with possession (FA 1968, s 57(4)).

[40]   Criminal Justice Act 2003, s 287, inserting s 51A into the FA 1968.

[41]   Following the decision in *R v Goldsborough* [2015] EWCA Crim 1278, [2015] 2 Cr App R 29.

[42]   A comprehensive analysis of the penalties available for possession of prohibited weapons is beyond the scope of this work, but in summary it is a 5-year minimum mandatory sentence (and a 10-year maximum) for all prohibited weapons except for s 5(1)(b) items (stun guns and CS gas). Firearms disguised as other objects are subject to the mandatory 5 years, but some types of prohibited ammunition (including expanding) are not. We have indicated the relevant penalties for most offences in this book in the footnotes.

(a)   When your handling of weapons or ammunition is covered by a museum firearms licence.[43]

(b)   When you are killing livestock for human consumption if you are a licensed *slaughterman* you do not need a firearm certificate[44] to possess a slaughtering instrument[45] and suitable ammunition for use in any slaughterhouse or knacker's yard, and this also applies to your employees. Further you do not need the authority of the Secretary of State to possess what would otherwise be a prohibited weapon by virtue of section 5(1)(aba), if you do not require a firearm certificate for the instrument by virtue of section 10 of the FA 1968.[46] This would also cover 'prohibited' ammunition.

(c)   If you have a firearm certificate authorising your possession of a firearm conditioned for use in connection with the *humane killing of animals*, you do not need the authority of the Secretary of State to possess what would otherwise be a prohibited weapon by virtue of section 5(1)(aba).[47] This applies to vets,[48] huntsmen and hunt servants, hunters who may have to dispatch injured deer and the like, and RSPCA Inspectors. It might also apply to those who farm wild boar and other large animals where it would be desirable and necessary to have a handgun to dispatch large and dangerous animals at close quarters. The current *Guide* suggests that a 2-shot .32″ calibre revolver is adequate for this,[49] but with larger animals most practitioners would take the view that it is wholly inadequate, in terms of both muzzle energy and the number of rounds available. In a number of cases in recent years licensing departments have tried to claim that this exemption only applies to revolvers which have been restricted to two shots. This is not what the law states. The exemption applies to any handgun, of any calibre, any type of action and any magazine capacity. The applicant needs to show good reason, but if, for example, a .45″ self-loading pistol with an unrestricted magazine is the best tool for the job, that is what should be granted.

(d)   If you have a firearm certificate authorising your possession of a *shot pistol* conditioned for use in connection with the *shooting of vermin*, you do not need the authority of the Secretary of State to possess what would otherwise

---

[43]   See Chapter 17 and Appendix B for this kind of licence.

[44]   FA 1968, s 10.

[45]   'Slaughtering instrument' is defined to mean a firearm which is specifically designed or adapted for the instantaneous slaughter of animals or for the instantaneous stunning of animals with a view to slaughtering them (FA 1968, s 57(4)).

[46]   F(A)A 1997, s 2.

[47]   F(A)A 1997, s 3.

[48]   Vets at racecourses are the only persons who are considered appropriate to have a silencer for a handgun; not to prevent them frightening the horses, but the crowd. *Guide*, para 13.39.

[49]   *Guide*, para 13.38.

be a prohibited weapon by virtue of section 5(1)(aba).[50] Such a shot pistol can only be in .410", or 9 mm rim-fire calibre.[51] This is for persons who control vermin (perhaps in confined spaces) where a shotgun would be too cumbersome.

(e) If you have a firearm certificate authorising your possession of a firearm conditioned for use in connection with the *starting of races at athletics meetings*, you do not need the authority of the Secretary of State to possess what would otherwise be a prohibited weapon by virtue of section 5(1)(aba).[52]

(f) If you have a firearm certificate authorising your possession of a firearm which is a *trophy of war*,[53] the item must have been acquired before 1 January 1946. No ammunition will be permitted, and there is no charge for the certificate.[54] Trophies of war can be inherited, so it is possible to keep that Luger your grandfather liberated in Berlin at the end of the war, on certificate.

(g) *Firearms of historic interest.* The authority of the Secretary of State is not required to have a firearm in your possession, or to purchase or acquire it, where you are authorised by a firearm certificate to have in your possession or buy, acquire, sell or transfer a firearm if:

(i)   it was manufactured before 1 January 1919; and

(ii) such firearms were manufactured before that date and no ammunition is readily available for them,

subject to a condition that you do so only for the purpose of their being kept or exhibited as part of a collection.[55]

This provision (a section 7(1) authority) allows collectors to keep such historic handguns at home, without ammunition. The Secretary of State has by Statutory Instrument[56] issued a list of calibres which are considered to be readily available and therefore firearms in those calibres are not permitted under this provision. Commonly available calibres such as .22" rim-fire, 9 mm and .45" Automatic Colt Pistol (ACP) are all excluded. The relevant calibres are set out in Appendix A. No sale or transfer may be made under these provisions except to a person who produces an appropriate authority to acquire the weapon.

---

[50] F(A)A 1997, s 4.

[51] F(A)A 1997, s 4(2).

[52] F(A)A 1997, s 5.

[53] F(A)A 1997, s 6.

[54] *Guide*, para 13.67.

[55] F(A)A 1997, s 7(1).

[56] Firearms (Amendment) Act 1997 (Firearms of Historic Interest) Order 1997 (SI 1997/1537).

(h)   The authority of the Secretary of State is also not required to possess, buy, acquire, sell or transfer a firearm which is of:

    (i)   particular rarity, aesthetic quality or technical interest, or,
    (ii)   is of historical importance,

if you are authorised by a firearm certificate or a visitor's firearm permit to have it in your possession subject to a condition requiring it to be kept and used only at a place designated by the Home Office.[57]

This provision (a section 7(3) authority) allows owners to keep and shoot firearms which qualify at a limited number of locations in this country. They may be used at those authorised locations but may not be kept at home. An entire book could be written on the criteria to be met for a firearm to enjoy this exemption from prohibition, and there may well be differences of opinion, for example, as to 'aesthetic qualities'. Rarity and technical interest might be easier to resolve, but in all cases the police would expect to see evidence of the claimed exemption. 'Historical importance' would normally include the use of the firearm by a famous person, or evidence of it being used in a famous battle.

Section 7 'has effect without prejudice to section 58(2) of the 1968 Act';[58] in other words it does not affect the classification of a firearm as an antique, dealt with in Chapter 1, and will not directly affect the new definition of antique firearms. We would suggest that a large number, if not all, firearms which meet the criteria in section 7(1) would also benefit from the exemption relating to antiques, provided they are held as a 'curiosity or ornament'. Given that those held under section 7(1) cannot be fired, this is likely to be so. Under the new provisions for antiques it is likely that a number not now held under section 7(1) will have to be brought within certification control. Another anomaly is that under section 7(3) they can be fired, and so would not qualify as antiques, but this provision relates to firearms of real rarity or historical interest where one might imagine the owner would wish to fire them only very occasionally, if at all, in order to preserve their pristine condition.

(i)   The authority of the Secretary of State is also not required to possess, buy, acquire, sell or transfer any firearm, weapon or ammunition which falls within the provisions of section 5(1)(aba), (b) or (c) which is designed or adapted for the purpose of tranquillising or otherwise *treating any animal* if you are authorised by a firearm certificate or a visitor's firearm permit to possess, buy or acquire it subject to a condition restricting its use to use in connection with the treatment of animals.[59]

---

[57]   F(A)A 1997, ss 1(8), 7(3). There are now a number of such centres across the country.

[58]   F(A)A 1997, s 7(4).

[59]   F(A)A 1997, s 8.

This applies to vets and those who run zoos and safari parks where there is a need to deal humanely with large and dangerous animals. It may also be appropriate for those who farm deer and wild boar.

(j)   Section 9 of the FA(A) 1997 introduced a general prohibition on *expanding ammunition*, but this has been repealed[60] and section 5(1A)(f) now only places in the prohibited category any ammunition which is 'designed to be used with a pistol and incorporates a missile designed or adapted to expand on impact'. This amendment is welcome; there was no public safety benefit to restricting such ammunition. However, the authors consider that the wording of this amendment is rather meaningless. Nearly every round of ammunition ever made has been used in a pistol at some point,[61] and so one might think one would need to look at the intentions of the original designer. This could be difficult to establish as some designers of common cartridges have now been dead for many years. Further, this approach has been discouraged and the Court of Appeal have on a number of occasions stated that the intentions of the designers are not relevant, it is objective capability that matters.[62]

We take the view that parliamentary draftsmen should avoid the use of the term 'designed to' in firearms legislation. The only persons such drafting helps are lawyers and experts. It certainly doesn't help the police or the public. In a recent Court of Appeal decision[63] it was decided that a forward-venting blank firer was 'designed' to emit a noxious substance (CS gas) because such cartridges are available in Europe, and such items are sometimes advertised as self-defence weapons there on that basis. The Court decided that 'design equals capability', so if it is capable of doing it, it was designed to do so. It seems to have been accepted that the type of blank firing gun in question had been designed before the invention of CS gas, but they had still been designed to utilise it. Putting aside the potential illogicality of that decision, it means, to take but one example, that everyone who owns a shotgun in Britain is in unlawful possession of a prohibited weapon contrary to section 5(1)(b), as it is possible to obtain 12-gauge shotgun cartridges which discharge CS gas. All 12-gauge shotguns are capable of firing such cartridges, and as capability is now the test, all such owners should arguably

---

[60] P&CA 2017, s 129.

[61] According to one experienced firearms dealer, Joe Beatham of Gunshop in East Barnet, the only two pistol cartridges that have never been used in a rifle are .25″ ACP and 5.45 x 18 mm Russian. There has been a version of the Thompson Contender pistol made chambered for virtually every modern cartridge. The National Ballistics Intelligence Service (NABIS) take the view that .32″ S&W, .32″ Colt, .320″ Revolver, .380″ Revolver, .45″ Auto Rim, .44″ Automag and .50″ Action Express were 'designed to be used with a pistol' and so should remain prohibited ammunition if the bullet is designed to expand on impact. This is likely to be the police view despite the problems with the case of *Rhodes*, below.

[62] See *R v Law* [1999] Crim LR 837, CA, followed in *Rhodes*, below.

[63] *R v Rhodes* [2015] EWCA Crim 155, [2015] 2 Cr App R 16, 2015 WL 640837.

hand themselves in. To return to the subject of expanding ammunition, there will probably be, somewhere in the world, a pistol which has utilised virtually every rifle round used in this country. So, applying the *ratio* in *Rhodes*, it is still prohibited ammunition. We do not imagine this is what Parliament intended.

Expanding ammunition is generally considered to be 'semi-jacketed soft point' or 'hollow point'. These types are designed to expand on impact causing a larger amount of the kinetic energy to stop in the body of the animal and thus ensuring a humane kill. Target or 'match' ammunition which sometimes has a small hole in the front and flat nosed 'wadcutter' ammunition do not fall within this definition.

It remains to be seen how the repeal of section 9 of the F(A)A 1997 will be applied in practice. We anticipate that the police will take the view that the specific authority for expanding ammunition previously placed on the certificates of those who use firearms for stalking, vermin destruction, humane killing, slaughter, etc will no longer be required.

It should be noted that if there are any prohibited calibres of ammunition remaining, section 5(1A)(f) covers the missiles themselves, so shooters who reload have to include the number of bullet heads in their possession in their total to ensure that they are within the limit of their allowance for that calibre on their certificate. This is a common mistake as non-expanding (i.e. section 1) bullet heads do not count towards your total. Expanding ammunition can only be sold or transferred to those with appropriate authority.[64]

Those who run slaughterhouses and have an exemption under section 10 of the FA 1968 have a similar exemption for expanding ammunition.[65]

(k)   When you carry on the business of a firearms dealer, you or your employees may have in your possession, buy, acquire, sell or transfer any expanding ammunition or the missile for any such ammunition in the ordinary course of that business.[66]

(l)   The authority of the Secretary of State shall not be required by virtue of section 5(1A) for any person to have in his possession, or to purchase, acquire, sell or transfer, any prohibited weapon or ammunition if he is authorised by a certificate under this Act to possess, purchase or acquire that weapon or ammunition subject to a condition that he does so only for the purpose of its being kept or exhibited as *part of a collection*.[67] Similar provisions are made for collectors recognised in other EU countries.[68] There

---

[64]   FA 1968, s 5A(6).

[65]   FA 1968 5A(5).

[66]   FA 1968, s 5A(7).

[67]   FA 1968, s 5A(1).

[68]   FA 1968, s 5A(3).

are restrictions upon the transfer of such items by the certificate holder.[69] Essentially, they can only be transferred to other individuals or museums authorised to acquire and possess them as part of a collection.

---

[69] FA 1968, s 5A(2) and (3).

Chapter 3

The Licensing of Section 1 Firearms and Ammunition

DEFINITION OF SECTION 1 FIREARMS

3.01   The term 'section 1 firearm' is commonly applied to those guns which are caught by the definition in section 1 of the FA 1968 and which, in general, require a firearm certificate for lawful possession or use. In practice, most section 1 firearms held on certificate now are rifles, muzzle-loading pistols, long-barrelled pistols or large capacity shotguns.

3.02   These firearms are mainly defined by exception,[1] but include one type of gun which can be positively identified. Rules made by the Home Office have declared certain kinds of air weapons to be specially dangerous. These are:

(a)   An air rifle or air gun capable of discharging a missile so that the missile has, on discharge from the muzzle, kinetic energy exceeding 12 foot pounds, except a weapon as described below.

(b)   An air pistol discharging a missile as above but with a kinetic energy exceeding 6 foot pounds, except a weapon as described below.
The exceptions from items (a) and (b) above are weapons designed for use only under water.

(c)   Any air rifle, air gun or air pistol which is disguised as another object.[2]

Air weapons include weapons powered by compressed carbon dioxide.[3]

---

[1]   FA 1968, s 1(3).

[2]   Firearms (Dangerous Air Weapons) Rules 1969 (SI 1969/47). Item (c) was added to the list on 1 July 1993 by amending rules. Note that air weapons within item (c) are declared to be specially dangerous irrespective of their kinetic energy performance.

[3]   F(A)A 1997, s 48.

3.03   In total, section 1 firearms consist of:

(a)   Air weapons declared to be specially dangerous as above.

(b)   All other kinds of firearms[4] except:

    (i)   air weapons not declared to be specially dangerous as above; and

    (ii)   smooth-bore guns[5] (not being air guns) which:

        (1)   have barrels not less than 24 inches long[6] and do not have any barrel with a bore exceeding 2 inches; and

        (2)   either have no magazine or have a non-detachable magazine incapable of holding more than two cartridges; and

        (3)   are not revolver guns.[7]

3.04   The effect of paragraph (b) (ii) above is that a shotgun with a magazine capable of holding more than two cartridges will be classified as a section 1 firearm rather than as a section 2 shotgun. The exemption in paragraph (2) above for limited capacity magazines does not apply unless the magazine:

(a)   bears an approved[8] mark denoting that it so limited; and

(b)   that mark has been made, and the adaptation certified in writing as having been carried out in an approved[9] manner, by the Worshipful Company of Gunmakers of London, by the Birmingham Proof House or by another approved[10] person.[11]

In other words, a two-shot capacity magazine shotgun does not qualify as a section 2 shotgun unless the magazine has the appropriate stamp from the Proof House. If not, it will be classified as a section 1 firearm (for which you need a firearm certificate), even if the magazine is in fact two-shot only.

---

[4]   For the full scope of meaning of the term 'firearm', see Chapter 1.

[5]   For shotguns generally see Chapter 4.

[6]   Measurement is from the muzzle to the point at which the charge is exploded (FA 1968, s 57(6)(a)).

[7]   FA 1968, s 1(1)(a), (3)(a); F(A)A 1988, s 2(1), (2). 'Revolver gun' in relation to a smooth-bore gun means a gun containing a series of chambers which revolve when the gun is fired (FA 1968, s 57(2B)).

[8]   'Approved' means approved by the Secretary of State for the Home Department. The approved marks and the approved manner of adaptation may be found in 'Firearms Law: Specifications for the Adaptation of Shotgun Magazines and the De-activation of Firearms', available on the government website www.gov.uk.

[9]   As above.

[10]   As above. Only the two Proof Houses have been approved.

[11]   FA 1968, ss 1(3A), 58(1); F(A)A 1988, s 2(3).

3.05   In addition, a weapon which:

(a)   has at any time since 1 July 1989[12] been a weapon of a kind described at items (a) and (b) in paragraph 3.03 above, or

(b)   would at any time before that date have been treated as a section 1 firearm if the present legislation had then been in force,

shall, if it has or at any time has had, a rifled barrel less than 24 inches long,[13] be treated as a section 1 firearm notwithstanding anything done to convert it into a shotgun or an air weapon.[14] But, for the foregoing purposes, the shortening of a barrel by an RFD[15] solely to replace part of it so as to produce a barrel not less than 24 inches long shall be disregarded.[16]

Air weapons

3.06   Air rifles which are only 'capable' of producing muzzle velocities below 12 foot pounds and air pistols below 6 foot pounds[17] do not require a certificate and can be freely held,[18] although there are now age limits as to possession and purchase, see Chapter 14. Be aware, however, that the owner and user of an air weapon obviously cannot tell the power of the weapon from firing it. This can only be determined with a chronograph which measures the muzzle velocity. Almost all firearms dealers own such a device and will check your air weapon and give you a certificate with the results for a modest fee. We thoroughly recommend that this is done when an air weapon is acquired and perhaps at 3-yearly intervals thereafter. We may sound paranoid, but most police forces now have air weapons checked if they come to their notice and there are a large number of prosecutions every year of persons whose air weapon (unbeknownst to them) developed, for example, 14 foot pounds. They are then in possession of a section 1 firearm without a certificate, an offence which attracts up to 5 years' imprisonment as a maximum, and there are guidelines suggesting the penalty should usually be a custodial sentence! Being able to produce a certificate to show you had the air weapon's power tested might avoid a prosecution, and, in any

---

[12]   The date on which F(A)A 1988, s 2 came into force (Firearms (Amendment) Act 1988 (Commencement No 2) Order 1989, Article 3(a) and Sch, Part I).

[13]   Measurement is from the muzzle to the point at which the charge is exploded, FA 1968, s 57(6)(a).

[14]   F(A)A 1988, s 7(2). 'Air weapons' are defined as air rifles, air guns and air pistols (FA 1968, ss 1(3)(b), 57(4)).

[15]   As to the registration of firearms dealers, see Chapter 16.

[16]   F(A)A 1988, s 7(3).

[17]   Firearms (Dangerous Air Weapons) Rules 1969, r 2(b).

[18]   Readers in Scotland will be aware that a certificate is required for an air weapon in that country: Air Weapons and Licensing (Scotland) Act 2015. See para 3.10 *et seq*, 'Scotland – Air Weapon Certificate'.

event, even if the certificate proves to be inaccurate, it might reduce the penalty to a conditional discharge. Possession of a firearm is an offence of 'strict liability', in other words what the owner thought about the weapon is irrelevant. You have been warned.

3.07   Some air rifles which are usually below the limit can exceed the limits prescribed in the 1969 Rules, either by having oil placed in the barrel ('dieselling') or by making adjustments to the gun, sometimes by the use of an external screw. In the last decade or so 'pre-charged pneumatic' (PCP) air weapons have become widely available. These use a small cylinder of compressed air to provide the force to propel the pellet. A number of such air rifles are quite easily adjustable, some by use of an external knob. The manufacturers add this feature to enable these rifles to be adjusted to keep them within the limit. However, in our experience, some of this type can equally be adjusted to exceed the permitted limits. The test in the Firearms (Dangerous Air Weapons) Rules 1969 is whether the gun is 'capable' of exceeding the limit. Does that apply as found, or after adjustment by a forensic scientist instructed by the police? Almost all firearms are 'capable' of being placed into a higher category within the Act. As one example, the removal of a stock from a rifle might reduce it to under 60cm overall length, and so raise it to section 5 classification. That operation will often only require the turn of one screw, just as is the case on a PCP air rifle to adjust the power.

3.08   Does the law say such items are 'capable' of being in the higher category, or is the proper test to look at the condition and capability of the item as found in the owner's possession? The difficulty is that the law has not been updated since PCP air rifles were introduced. As a general rule, most ordinary air weapons are only capable of adjustment to increase the power output by changing the spring or by altering some other physical aspect of the gun. However, given that the manufacturers of PCP air rifles incorporate an adjustment feature, this indicates an acknowledgement on their part that these rifles require adjustment from time to time in order to keep them within the legal limit, and thus that as designed and sold they are also potentially 'capable' of exceeding the limit. This begs the question whether it is appropriate to prosecute an individual who is found with an air weapon of this type which in his possession was set within the legal limit. In the absence of any evidence of a deliberate attempt to circumvent the rules, we take the view that if they are below the limit in your possession then you are not breaking the law, although there has so far not been a decided case on this issue.

3.09   As stated above, 'air weapons' include those powered by compressed carbon dioxide.[19] Guns used for paintballing games are not normally considered

---

[19]   F(A)A 1997, s 48.

to be controlled under the Firearms Acts. Air weapons disguised as another object are deemed to be 'specially dangerous'[20] and a certificate would be required.

Scotland – Air Weapon Certificate

3.10   In Scotland, the Air Weapons and Licensing (Scotland) Act 2015, section 2 now requires a person to have an 'Air Weapon Certificate' (AWC) to be in possession of an air weapon in that jurisdiction. To obtain a certificate the person must be over 14 and, if under 18, he requires the consent of his parent or guardian. The applicant for an AWC must demonstrate a good reason for possessing such a weapon. A statutory condition for all AWCs for those under 18 is that the holder may not purchase, hire, accept a gift of or own, an air weapon, and there are six conditions which have to be attached to such a certificate; see Chapter 14 for more details regarding young people and air weapons in Scotland. For those over 18, an applicant has to show a 'good reason', and we suggest that the same principles apply as with an application for a firearm certificate. The test of possession being without danger to public safety or the peace is applied.[21] A referee, referred to as 'a verifier', who has known the applicant for at least 2 years is required. An AWC is valid for 5 years. For a person who holds a firearm or shotgun certificate it is assumed that he is a fit person to hold an AWC, and that his possession of an air weapon would not pose a danger to public safety or the peace. An AWC licenses the person to possess an unlimited number of air weapons. Airsoft guns or those used in paintballing will not be covered by this regime, nor weapons designed to be used under water. A person who possesses a firearm or shotgun certificate in Scotland, or the rest of Britain, will not require an AWC until the expiry of any current certificate, at which point he should apply for an AWC to run concurrently with his existing certificate. Following this transitional period, a person who resides outside Scotland, but visits frequently, can apply for an AWC, and if Police Scotland are satisfied of the need for one, it shall be granted. Otherwise, if you reside in England and Wales be careful not to drive north of the border with an air weapon unless you have a visitor's permit for it.

3.11   An AWC is not available to those under 14, and there are special conditions on an AWC for those under 18, see Chapter 14 for more details.

---

[20] Firearms (Dangerous Air Weapons) Rules 1969, r 2(b).
[21] Air Weapons and Licensing (Scotland) Act 2015, s 5.

DEFINITION OF SECTION 1 AMMUNITION

3.12   This classification is totally defined by exception. Section 1 applies to any ammunition for a firearm[22] except:

(a)   cartridges containing five or more shot, none of which exceeds 0.36 inch in diameter;
(b)   ammunition for an air gun, air rifle or air pistol;
(c)   blank cartridges not more than one inch in diameter.[23]

It should be mentioned here that the sale or purchase of primers for metallic ammunition must be to or by a person who holds a relevant certificate authorising possession of ammunition or a firearm 'of a relevant kind'. This does not include blanks, primers for shotgun ammunition, or rim-fire ammunition. RFDs, those who trade in such components and others who do not need a certificate are exempt from this requirement.[24] This places primers in a similar position to shotgun ammunition; simple possession is not an offence, but a certificate is needed to purchase. Others can purchase on your behalf by presenting your certificate and a suitable letter of authorisation from you.

WHEN DO I NEED A FIREARM CERTIFICATE?

3.13   Subject to the many exceptions mentioned below, you need a firearm certificate if you purchase, hire, accept as a gift, borrow or have in your possession a section 1 firearm or section 1 ammunition.[25]

3.14   Before dealing with the specific exceptions below, three matters of general application need to be noted.

---

[22]   For the full scope of meaning of the term 'firearm' see Chapter 1.

[23]   FA 1968, s 1(4). The one-inch measurement is to be made immediately in front of the rim or cannelure of the base of the cartridge (FA 1968, s 1(4)(c)).

[24]   VCRA 2006, s 35.

[25]   FA 1968, ss 1(1), 57(4). The maximum punishment for non-compliance, on summary conviction, is imprisonment for 6 months or an unlimited fine or both; or, on indictment, 5 years' imprisonment, or an unlimited fine, or both, unless the offence is committed in an aggravated form within the meaning of FA 1968, s 4(4), when the maximum term is 7 years (FA 1968, s 51(1), (2) and Sch 6, Part I). For special provisions about buying firearms in a country which is a Member State of the European Community, see F(A)A 1988, s 18A and Chapter 7.

3.15   The proving of firearms and the handling of antique firearms,[26] which are described more fully in Chapter 1, do not require firearm certificates.

3.16   As detailed in Chapter 1, the definition of a firearm includes its component parts and accessories for diminishing noise or flash so therefore these need a certificate as much as the firearm itself.

3.17   The extent of the meaning of the word 'possession' in the requirement to hold a certificate has long been an important and contentious subject in this area of law and it may be helpful here to attempt some explanation of the word in this context. The law itself would have to admit that it has not yet been able to evolve a satisfactory definition of the term. For example, it is now decided that the word has a slightly different (and less draconian) meaning when considered in relation to controlled drugs than it does in relation to firearms! However, cases decided in the last 50 years have produced some guidance.

3.18   The words should be construed in a popular and not a narrow sense; a person has possession of an object, not only when carrying it, but also when the object is in some place, for example, a building or a vehicle, over which that person has control, unless he does not realise that the object is, or may be, in that place.[27] Even control of the place where the object is may not be necessary; in a case concerning the need for a firearm certificate it was decided that the owner of firearms kept at his mother's flat in a different part of the country was still in possession of the firearms, even though he did not have physical custody of them.[28] This is correct as long as you equate 'possession' with 'control'. Are you able to say to someone 'can you go in to my spare room and bring that thing to the restaurant for me'? If you can, you are in control of it, and possess it for these purposes.

3.19   In another case it was decided, perhaps predictably, that a person, whose only interest in a firearm was to convey it from one person to another, nonetheless had possession of it during that time.[29] It is also important to bear in mind that the

---

[26]   There are now two categories of antique firearm, those for which you need a firearm certificate, and those that are free of control.

[27]   *Lockyer v Gibb* [1966] 2 All ER 653; *Warner v Metropolitan Police Commissioner* [1968] 2 All ER 356.

[28]   *Sullivan v Earl of Caithness* [1976] 1 All ER 844.

[29]   *Woodage v Moss* [1974] 1 All ER 584. Note that if the person conveying the firearm had been a carrier in business as such or an RFD in business as such, or acting as an employee of either, he would not have needed a firearm certificate – see paras 3.23 and 3.24 for the exceptions for firearms dealers and carriers from the requirement to hold a firearm certificate. It has also been observed that this case might have been decided differently had the issue of necessity been raised.

fact that a person did not know that what he possessed was a firearm was immaterial; the offence is an absolute one.[30]

3.20   Decided cases on this issue have introduced the concept of dual possession. In *Cotton & Treadwell* C had left two of his shotguns with T for safekeeping while C and T went on holiday together, and for later cleaning by T. The Court held that during the holiday C had 'proprietary possession' of the guns and T had 'custodial possession'.[31] Further, if you are aware that you have possession of a bag, even though you could not reasonably have known it contained a firearm, you are guilty.[32] This would be 'custodial possession'. In a drugs case you would at least have to believe that the bag contained *a* controlled drug, even if not the correct one. This anomaly has been pointed out to the courts who have made it clear that in relation to firearms the law will remain as it is for reasons of public policy, and this line of authorities will not be reopened,[33] so possession of a firearm (or component parts) without the correct certificate is an absolute offence.

3.21   It can be an offence in English law to engage in arms trafficking or a conspiracy to supply firearms where the guns themselves never come within this jurisdiction. Persons here involved in such activities are still exercising control over the items in question. A person with a holiday home abroad who keeps guns there is in possession of them under our law, although in that instance no offence is committed as the person is not in possession of them in this jurisdiction.

EXCEPTIONS FROM THE NEED TO HOLD A FIREARM CERTIFICATE

3.22   The specific cases in which a firearm certificate is not needed for a section 1 firearm are as follows.

---

[30]   *R v Hussain* [1981] 1 WLR 416; *The Times*, 28 November 1980. The weapon in question was an 8-inch metal tube with a striker pin activated by a spring, capable of firing .32″ cartridges.

[31]   *Hall v Cotton and Treadwell* [1986] 3 All ER 332. While the point at issue concerning possession was possession by T, who held no shotgun certificate, it is evident that the court was of the view that there was concurrent possession by C.

[32]   *R v Steele* [1993] Crim LR 298, CA, although if the court accepted you had no idea it was a firearm you might well be absolutely discharged. This principle was repeated in *Nasir Zahid v R* [2010] EWCA Crim 2158, 2010 WL 3807980.

[33]   *R v Vann & Davis* [1996] Crim LR 52, CA.

Firearms dealers

3.23   The purchase, hiring, accepting as a gift, borrowing or possessing, in the ordinary course of business, of a firearm by a person carrying on the business of a firearms dealer, and registered as such, or by an employee of such a person.[34] See Chapter 16 for further details.

Auctioneers, carriers and warehousemen

3.24   The possession,[35] in the ordinary course of business, of a firearm or ammunition by a person carrying on the business of an auctioneer,[36] carrier or warehouseman, or by an employee of such a person.[37]

3.25   The police and the Home Office do not consider this exception to cover the carriage or sale of prohibited weapons (despite the wording in section 9 of the FA 1968, and the fact that the relevant part of this Act is headed 'Special exemptions from section 1 to 5'!) on the basis that a 'certificate' can only be granted in respect of firearms within section 1, or for section 2 shotguns, and not for items within section 5. Some carriers are now granted authority by the Home Office to carry prohibited firearms and ammunition.

Slaughtering instruments[38]

3.26   This is defined as:

(a)   The possession by a licensed slaughterer[39] of a slaughtering instrument in any slaughterhouse or knacker's yard in which he is employed.[40]

---

[34]   FA 1968, ss 8(1), 57(4). As to firearms dealers and their registration, see Chapter 16. This exception applies notwithstanding that the firearm was in the possession of or bought or acquired by the dealer or his employee at a place which is not the dealer's place of business or where he is not registered as such (FA 1968, s 8(1A)).

[35]   Note that possession only is covered by this exemption, and not a purchase, hiring, accepting as a gift or borrowing.

[36]   Auctioneers require a police permit to cover the sale by auction of firearms. See Chapter 6 regarding police permits.

[37]   FA 1968, s 9(1). Failure to take reasonable precautions for the safe custody of a firearm by persons of these descriptions, or to report forthwith any loss or theft to the police, is an offence. The maximum punishment is 6 months' imprisonment, or an unlimited fine, or both (F(A)A 1988, s 14).

[38]   See more detail in para 2.20.

[39]   I.e. licensed under the Welfare of Animals (Slaughter or Killing) Regulations 1995 (SI 1995/731) or Slaughterhouses Act 1974, s 39 which was superseded by the 1995 Regulations.

[40]   FA 1968, s 10(1).

(b)   The possession[41] of slaughtering instruments[42] and ammunition for them for the purpose of storing them in safe custody at a slaughterhouse or knacker's yard by:

    (i)   the proprietor of that slaughterhouse or knacker's yard; or

    (ii) a person appointed by the proprietor to take charge of those slaughtering instruments and ammunition for the purpose of such storage.[43]

Ships and signalling apparatus

3.27   This is defined as:

(a)   The possession[44] of a firearm on board a ship,[45] or the possession of signalling apparatus on board an aircraft or at an aerodrome, as part of the equipment of the ship, aircraft or aerodrome.[46]

(b)   The removal of signalling apparatus, which is part of the equipment of an aircraft, from one aircraft to another at an aerodrome, or from or to an aircraft at an aerodrome to or from a place appointed for the storage of the apparatus in safe custody at that aerodrome; and the keeping of such apparatus at such a place.[47]

(c)   If a permit from a constable[48] is held for the purpose, the removal of a firearm from or to a ship or signalling apparatus from or to an aircraft or aerodrome to or from such a place and for such purpose as is given in the permit.[49]

---

[41]   Note that possession only is covered by this exemption. A free certificate will be issued for the purchase or acquisition of a slaughtering instrument and ammunition (FA 1968, s 32(3)(c)).

[42]   A slaughtering instrument is defined as a firearm which is specially designed or adapted for the instantaneous slaughter of animals or for the instantaneous stunning of animals with a view to slaughtering them (FA 1968, s 57(4)).

[43]   FA 1968, s 10(2).

[44]   Note that possession only is covered by this exemption, and not a purchase, hiring, accepting as a gift or borrowing.

[45]   The word 'ship' includes hovercraft (Hovercraft (Application of Enactments) Order 1972, Art 4, Sch 1, Part A).

[46]   FA 1968, s 13(1)(a).

[47]   FA 1968, s 13(1)(b).

[48]   As well as police constables, including special police constables, 'constable' includes others holding that office, e.g. harbour constables. The hallmark of a constable is his attestation as such before, usually, a magistrate.

[49]   FA 1968, s 13(1)(c).

Carrying firearms for others

3.28   The carrying of a firearm belonging to another person, who holds a firearm certificate, under instructions from, and for the use of, that person and for sporting purposes only.[50] If the person carrying the gun is under 18, the shooter must be over 18.

3.29   This covers gun bearers and the like when the certificate holder is shooting game. Although the Act does not specify this, the police would normally expect the certificate holder to be present, or at least nearby. The bearer is not permitted to use the guns.

Rifle clubs and muzzle-loading pistol clubs

3.30   The possession[51] by a member of a rifle club[52] or a muzzle-loading pistol club[53] approved by the Home Office of a rifle or a muzzle-loading pistol[54] and ammunition (as the case may be) when engaged as a member of the club in target shooting.[55] Such club approval may restrict the types of weapons to be used at the club, may be given subject to conditions, may at any time be varied or withdrawn, and shall endure for 6 years (unless withdrawn earlier) from its grant or renewal.[56]

3.31   A free firearm certificate will be given to a responsible officer of the club for the rifles and pistols used there by members for target shooting.[57] The Home Office publishes guidance for clubs seeking approval.[58] Constables,[59] and those

---

[50]   FA 1968, ss 11(1). The shooting of rats in a barn is not shooting for sporting purposes only (*Morton v Chaney* [1960] 3 All ER 632), although as Dr Barry Peachey, the wildlife expert, once observed of the judge who made this decision, 'His Lordship had obviously never tried it'! See also para 14.16 relating to young persons.

[51]   Note that possession only is covered.

[52]   A rifle club includes a miniature rifle club (F(A)A 1988, s 15(10)).

[53]   A muzzle-loading pistol club means a club where muzzle-loading pistols are used for target shooting (F(A)A 1988, s 15(12)).

[54]   A muzzle-loading pistol is defined as a pistol designed to be loaded at the muzzle end of the barrel or chamber with a loose charge and a separate ball (or other missile) (F(A)A 1988, s 15(11), (12)).

[55]   F(A)A 1988, s 15(1), (11).

[56]   F(A)A 1988, s 15(4), (5), (11).

[57]   The certificate may also be varied or renewed without charge, but these provisions may be limited by the terms of approval of the club (FA 1968, s 32(2), (2A).

[58]   F(A)A 1988, s 15(3), (11). For the most recent Home Office guidance on the criteria for the approval of clubs, see https://assets.publishing.service.gov.uk/government/uploads/system/uploads/attachment_data/file/533572/Clubs_Criteria_Leaflet_-_Final_.pdf.

[59]   As well as police constables, including special police constables, 'constable' includes others holding that office, e.g. harbour constables. The hallmark of a constable is his attestation as such before, usually, a magistrate.

defined in FA 1968 as 'civilian officers',[60] are given wide powers to inspect club premises and records to see whether the terms of an approval have been met.[61]

3.32   This exemption allows all full members of an approved club to have firearms and ammunition in their possession, not just at club premises, but also, for example, where a member of a club takes a firearm to another club, if they are 'engaged as a member of the club in connection with target shooting'.[62] This exemption applies not only to 'club guns' (i.e. those held by the club secretary on the club's firearm certificate) but to weapons owned by other members of the club or visitors. The possession of the firearms and ammunition must be connected in time to the target shooting, not necessarily 'on the day', but possession of ammunition a month after a cancelled shoot was too long for there to be a connection and the possession was not covered by this exemption.[63]

3.33   As one would expect, the police, who administer club approval on behalf of the Home Office, require approved clubs to be properly and democratically run by responsible persons. Note, however, that there is no requirement in law for the officers of a club to be certificate holders themselves, although if the club itself has a certificate this will usually be held by the secretary, who will have to meet all the usual criteria for grant of a firearm certificate. Details of the approval criteria are beyond the scope of this work, but are set out in the Home Office *Guide* and are available from all police firearms licensing departments.[64]

3.34   Approved clubs exist for the purpose of target shooting; no other shooting sport can be involved. Members of the public who wish to acquire firearms for target shooting will inevitably have to join a Home Office-approved club in order to demonstrate that they have a 'good reason' for each of the target weapons they wish to own. Unless a person is an existing member of another approved club, all clubs will require him to serve a probationary membership, usually 6 months, before granting him full membership and enabling him to apply for a firearm certificate. The person will have been required to demonstrate safe gun handling and an appropriate attitude to firearms generally. Clubs should, and do, refuse to make people full members if they are considered unsuitable. Sadly, there are

---

[60]   A civilian officer is, broadly speaking, a civilian employed by a police authority. The full definition is in FA 1968, s 57(4). This is designed to include firearms enquiry officers (FEOs), many of whom are retired police officers who have been re-employed as civilian staff.

[61]   F(A)A 1988, s 15(7), (8), (10), (11). Obstruction of these officers in performing their duties is an offence carrying a maximum punishment of a fine at level 3 on the standard scale (currently £1,000) (F(A)A 1988, s 15(9), (11)).

[62]   F(A)A 1988, s 15(1).

[63]   *R v Wilson (M)* [1989] Crim LR 901.

[64]   The best information is on the National Rifle Association (NRA) website at https://nra.org.uk/wp-content/uploads/2018/02/Club-Formation-Checklist.pdf.

well-known tragic examples where members of clubs have gone on to commit murder with licensed weapons. A contrasting example is Barry George, also known as Barry Bulsara, the gentleman who was eventually acquitted of murdering Jill Dando, who was turned down by the club he had attempted to join[65] after four visits, as he was not considered a suitable person to possess firearms.

3.35   There are a number of anomalies relating to the Home Office approval of clubs. There is, for example, no definition in law of a 'rifle', so can an approved club purchase for the use of its members a 'carbine' (which is also not defined, except to say that 'rifle includes carbine'[66])? An attempt by the Metropolitan Police to prosecute a club secretary for acquiring a 'long-barrelled pistol' on a club firearm certificate failed on this basis.[67] Perhaps partly as a result of that case and other issues which had arisen, Assistant Chief Constable Adrian Whiting of Dorset Police suggested in his report into the Cumbria shootings by Derrick Bird in 2010 that consideration should be given to allowing Home Office-approved clubs to be able to use all section 1 firearms.[68] This would have the advantage of clubs being approved for large capacity shotguns as well as long-barrelled pistols. Unfortunately, this sensible suggestion has not so far been accepted.

Practical shotgun

3.36   *Practical shotgun* or 'target' shotgun shooting, which involves the use of large magazine capacity 'section 1 shotguns' and/or solid slug (section 1) ammunition is *not* covered by the section 15 exemption. Such activities obviously do not use a 'rifle' or a 'muzzle-loading pistol' but are considered by the Home Office to be good reason for an applicant to have such a shotgun. It will generally be sufficient for the applicant to state that he has membership of the National Rifle Association (NRA), British Western Shooting Society (BWSS), United Kingdom Practical Shooting Association (UKPSA) or of a club affiliated to one of those organisations. This sport can include the use of solid slug ammunition in a section 2 shotgun.

3.37   The applicant will need to demonstrate that he has access to a suitable range if he wishes to possess solid slug ammunition and therefore will need to be

---

[65]   Kensington Rifle & Pistol Club, now merged with Northfields Shooting Club: www.ealingrange.org.uk/.

[66]   FA 1968, s 57(4).

[67]   *R v Michael Wells*, Kingston Crown Court, November 2010, unreported (HHJ Dodgson and a jury).

[68]   The report is available at: www.dorset.police.uk/Default.aspx?page=626. ACC Whiting was commissioned to write this report in his capacity as Chair of the Association of Chief Police Officers Firearms and Explosives Licensing Working Group (ACPO FELWG), although he has since retired from that post.

a member of an NRA-affiliated club if he wishes to use it on Ministry of Defence (MOD) ranges, or at a suitable private range. Those clubs which only practise practical or target shotgun cannot be Home Office 'approved', as they do not shoot either of the approved type of weapon. Members of a club can therefore only shoot their own gun; they cannot borrow a section 1 shotgun from the club or another member. Guests shooting at such a club are limited to using a 'normal' section 2 shotgun to complete the course of fire. That is permitted under the exemption in section 11A, see para 3.48 *et seq*, 'Authorised lending of firearms and shotguns on private premises'. These restrictions apply even if the club does have Home Office approval for rifle and muzzle-loading pistol shooting.

Cadet corps

3.38   This covers the following activities:

(a)   The possession[69] by members of a cadet corps approved by the Home Office[70] while engaged as corps members in, or in connection with, drill or target practice.
(b)   The possession[71] by such members of prohibited weapons or prohibited ammunition[72] when engaged in target practice on service premises.[73]
(c)   The possession[74] by persons providing instruction to such members while engaged as in (a) or (b) above.[75]

---

[69]   Note that possession only is covered, and not purchase, hiring, accepting as a gift or borrowing for which a certificate will have to be obtained by a responsible officer of the corps.

[70]   The Home Office have given a general approval to all 'recognised units' of the Combined Cadet Force, Sea Cadet Corps, Army Cadet Force and Air Training Corps.

[71]   As per fn 69.

[72]   For the meanings of 'prohibited weapons' and 'prohibited ammunition', see Chapter 2.

[73]   'Service premises' means any premises, including any ship or aircraft, used for any purpose of any of the naval, military or air forces of Her Majesty (F(A)A 1988, s 16A(3)). 'Premises' includes any land (FA 1968, s 57(4)), and 'land' includes land covered with water (Interpretation Act 1978 (IA 1978), s 5 and Sch 1).

[74]   As per fn 69.

[75]   FA 1968, s 54(4)–(6).

Persons supervised by members of the armed forces

3.39   The possession on service premises[76] of a firearm by a person under the supervision of a member of the armed forces,[77] but excluding a person engaged in providing security protection on those premises.[78]

Miniature rifle ranges and shooting galleries

3.40   There are two aspects to this exemption:

(a)   The purchase, hiring, accepting as a gift, borrowing or possessing of a miniature rifle[79] not exceeding .23″ calibre by a person conducting or carrying on a miniature rifle range (whether for a rifle club or otherwise) or a shooting gallery at which in either case no firearms are used other than non-dangerous air weapons[80] or miniature rifles not exceeding .23″ calibre.[81]

(b)   The use by any person at any rifle range or shooting gallery described in item (a) above of the miniature rifles there described and ammunition for them.[82]

3.41   Despite the wording, this is taken to mean .22″ rim-fire, and not, for example, .223″ centre-fire. A number of shooting clubs use the miniature rifle range exemption to permit any member of the public to try shooting, whether a club member or not. When conducted by responsible clubs, it is an excellent way of introducing people to shooting. This exemption was originally (it is in the Firearms Act 1920) intended to permit shooting galleries at fairgrounds and the like to operate. It is a matter of fact as to whether you are 'conducting or carrying on' such a rifle range and therefore benefit from the exemption. The National Small-bore Rifle Association and the Showman's Guild do issue certificates to those who operate such ranges, but they have no force of law. The only purpose of such certificates is for the operator to demonstrate to a dealer that they are exempt from the Act and do not need to produce a firearm certificate to purchase such firearms and ammunition. This is the only exemption in the Firearms Acts which permits the purchase and acquisition of firearms and ammunition without

---

[76]   As per fn 73.

[77]   'Armed forces' are defined as any of the naval, military or air forces of Her Majesty (F(A)A 1988, s 16A(3)).

[78]   F(A)A 1988, s 16A(1), (2).

[79]   The term 'miniature rifle' is not defined in the Firearms Acts. It includes non-dangerous air weapons (for which, see para 3.06 *et seq*, 'Air weapons') and rim-fire rifles up to .22″ may be used at the rifle range or shooting gallery without a firearm certificate.

[80]   For these weapons, see para 3.06 *et seq*, 'Air weapons'.

[81]   FA 1968, ss 11(4), 57(4).

[82]   FA 1968, s 11(4).

a certificate, where they can be possessed without a certificate, with no checks on the persons concerned and no requirements to keep the firearms and ammunition securely. We anticipate that Parliament may be asked to revisit this exemption in the near future. The exemption as it applies to the public does not present any danger to public safety; the exemption for those who operate such ranges and galleries is a potential loophole which is open to abuse.

3.42   Although any person is permitted to shoot, it would still be an offence if you were a prohibited person (see Chapter 5) or were under age (see Chapter 14).

Theatrical performances

3.43   The possession[83] by a person taking part in a theatrical performance or any rehearsal thereof, or in the production of a film, of a firearm during, and for the purpose of, that performance, rehearsal or production.[84] No live firing is permitted under this exemption, although the firing of blank ammunition is commonplace.

Athletics meetings

3.44   The possession[85] of a firearm by any person over 18 at an athletics meeting for the purpose of starting races at that meeting.[86]

Police permits

3.45   The possession,[87] in accordance with the terms of the permit, of a firearm by any person who holds a police permit.[88]

---

[83]   Note that possession only is covered by this exemption, and not a purchase, hiring, accepting as a gift or borrowing.

[84]   FA 1968, s 12(1). This exemption may be taken to apply equally to television productions and rehearsals.

[85]   Note that possession only is covered by this exemption, and not a purchase, hiring, accepting as a gift or borrowing.

[86]   FA 1968, s 11(2). Though clearly intended to permit the use of starting pistols, s 11(2) in fact allows the use of any firearm to start races.

[87]   Note that possession only is covered by this exemption, and not a purchase, hiring, accepting as a gift or borrowing.

[88]   FA 1968, s 7(1). As to police permits, see Chapter 6.

Military and police forces

3.46   The possession[89] by certain Crown servants,[90] by members of visiting military forces[91] and by police officers of a firearm in their capacities as such servants, members or officers. See Chapter 1 for more detail.

Museums

3.47   The possession, purchase, hiring, accepting as a gift or borrowing of firearms by a museum within the terms of a museum firearms licence.[92] Full details are contained in Chapter 17.

Authorised lending of firearms and shotguns on private premises

3.48   The previous provisions regarding the loaning of guns on private premises to non-certificate holders were found in two separate Acts of Parliament, section 11(5) of the FA 1968 in relation to the loaning of shotguns, and section 16(1) of the F(A)A 1988 for the loaning of rifles. However, both of those sections have been repealed and with effect from 2 May 2017 were replaced by a new section 11A of the FA 1968.[93] There had been some inconsistency between the two separate exemptions. Aside from that, the new consolidated provisions are intended to avoid the use of the word 'occupier' contained in both of the previous provisions, a term which occasionally caused difficulties of interpretation. Whether the new section 11A has simplified this exemption we leave to the reader to decide. We can only do it justice by setting it out in full:

11A Authorised lending and possession of firearms for hunting etc
(1)   A person ('the borrower') may, without holding a certificate under this Act, borrow a rifle or shotgun from another person on private premises ('the lender') and have the rifle or shotgun in his or her possession on those premises if—

    (a)   the four conditions set out in subsections (2) to (5) are met, and
    (b)   in the case of a rifle, the borrower is aged 17 or over.

---

[89]   Possession only is covered by this exemption. In some of these cases a purchase, hiring, accepting as a gift or borrowing may be done without a certificate; in other cases a free certificate will be given.

[90]   Principally, these will be members of the three armed forces. Others, such as customs officers, may be included.

[91]   FA 1968, s 54; the Visiting Forces and International Headquarters (Application of Law) Order 1999 (SI 1999/1736).

[92]   FA 1968, s 57(4); F(A)A 1988, ss 19, 25(1) and Sch, para 1(2).

[93]   P&CA 2017, s 130.

(2)   The first condition is that the borrowing and possession of the rifle or shotgun
       are for either or both of the following purposes—

       (a)   hunting animals or shooting game or vermin;
       (b)   shooting at artificial targets.

(3)   The second condition is that the lender—

       (a)   is aged 18 or over,
       (b)   holds a certificate under this Act in respect of the rifle or shotgun, and
       (c)   is either—

              (i)   a person who has a right to allow others to enter the premises for the
                     purposes of hunting animals or shooting game or vermin, or
              (ii)   a person who is authorised in writing by a person mentioned in sub-
                     paragraph (i) to lend the rifle or shotgun on the premises (whether
                     generally or to persons specified in the authorisation who include the
                     borrower).

(4)   The third condition is that the borrower's possession and use of the rifle or
       shotgun complies with any conditions as to those matters specified in the lender's
       certificate under this Act.
(5)   The fourth condition is that, during the period for which the rifle or shotgun is
       borrowed, the borrower is in the presence of the lender or—

       (a)   where a rifle is borrowed, a person who, although not the lender, is aged
              18 or over, holds a certificate under this Act in respect of that rifle and is a
              person described in subsection (3)(c)(i) or (ii);
       (b)   where a shotgun is borrowed, a person who, although not the lender, is
              aged 18 or over, holds a certificate under this Act in respect of that shotgun
              or another shotgun and is a person described in subsection (3)(c)(i) or (ii).

(6)   Where a rifle is borrowed on any premises in reliance on subsection (1), the
       borrower may, without holding a firearm certificate, purchase or acquire
       ammunition on the premises, and have the ammunition in his or her possession
       on those premises for the period for which the firearm is borrowed, if—

       (a)   the ammunition is for use with the firearm,
       (b)   the lender's firearm certificate authorises the lender to have in his or her
              possession during that period ammunition of a quantity not less than that
              purchased or acquired by, and in the possession of, the borrower, and
       (c)   the borrower's possession and use of the ammunition complies with any
              conditions as to those matters specified in the certificate.

3.49   Before making use of this exemption you should note and consider the
following points:

(a)   The loan can only be for the purposes of hunting or shooting game or vermin, or for shooting at artificial targets. The first purpose clearly covers deer stalking and hunting wild boar, game shooting of birds, rough shooting and control of all types of vermin. We will abbreviate these activities to 'hunting' for this discussion. In addition to hunting a gun can be lent to shoot at artificial targets. This includes clay pigeons, traditional paper targets and tin cans.

(b)   The lender must be lending a gun held on a firearm or shotgun certificate; guns held on a visitor's or police permit, or by a firearms dealer on an RFD certificate, cannot be lent under this exemption. The lender must also be over 18 and either be someone who has the right to give permission to enter the premises to hunt or have written permission from someone who does have that right.

(c)   Many readers will be aware that hunting rights on land are often reserved, rented out to a syndicate, for example. Section 11A(3)(c) allows only those who have or can give permission for hunting on the land to be the lender of the rifle or shotgun under this exemption. What about those who have permission to set up a clay trap on the land, but do not have permission to hunt? It would appear they cannot lend a gun to their friends. We are not sure that this is what Parliament intended. The previous exemptions for both rifles[94] and shotguns[95] did not specify any purpose for which the gun was being borrowed. It is unclear as to why these restrictions as to purpose have been imposed, or why the giving of permission is restricted to those who can give permission to shoot animals on the property. We can see no public safety or other benefit.

(d)   In the case of a rifle the borrower must be over 17 but note there is no age limit for a shotgun. The borrower must throughout his possession of the loaned gun be 'in the presence of the lender'. This repeats the previous version of this exemption and has generally been considered to mean within sight and earshot of the lender. It is not necessary to be standing next to him. The borrower may alternatively be in the presence of someone who is not the lender, provided that other person is someone who can give permission to shoot on that land, or who has written permission given to him. However, if the firearm being lent is a rifle, the other person present who is not the lender must also have that rifle on his certificate. It is possible to have a firearm on more than one certificate, but unusual. We wonder how often the lender of the rifle will not be present during the borrower's possession and use of it but someone else with the rifle on their certificate will be present?

---

[94]   FA(A)A 1988, s 16(1). Similar to the shotgun provision below, except that the borrower had to be over 17.

[95]   Section 11(5) of the FA 1968: 'a person may, without holding a shotgun certificate, borrow a shotgun from the occupier of private premises and use it on those premises in the occupier's presence'.

Where a shotgun is lent, the person present can be either the lender or any other person with a shotgun certificate who has the right to grant permission to shoot on that land. In all cases the lender and the person present must be over 18.

(e)   Where a rifle is borrowed in accordance with this exemption the borrower can purchase/be given ammunition for use in that rifle and lawfully be in possession of it on those premises for the period during which the rifle is borrowed. The amount acquired cannot exceed that permitted to be held by the lender's certificate. Although not expressly stated in the Act, the assumption seems to be that the ammunition will be acquired from the lender, since the borrower is restricted to purchasing or acquiring ammunition 'on the premises'. It is therefore odd to require the borrower to have no more than permitted by the lender's certificate. The borrower could only receive more than that amount from the lender if the lender had been in unlawful possession of an amount in excess of what he was authorised to possess. In any event, borrowers would be well advised to check their pockets and bags before they leave the premises, or they could find themselves in unlawful possession of section 1 ammunition. Ordinary shotgun ammunition is not referred to, as possession of such ammunition is uncontrolled.

(f)   In all cases the borrower must comply with any conditions on the certificate which relate to 'the possession and use' of the rifle or shotgun in question. As an example, a rifle conditioned only for target shooting cannot be used for deer stalking. Some territorial conditions may also be relevant here. There will be conditions requiring that firearms and section 1 ammunition be kept securely on all firearm and shotgun certificates. A breach of a condition on a certificate is a summary only offence, but the offence can only be committed by the certificate holder, the lender in this case. The borrower does not commit any offence because he is not subject to the conditions on the certificate. The lender might in some circumstances be guilty of causing or permitting such an offence.

(g)   There are some types of firearm that are not permitted to be borrowed under this exemption. These are the loan of a section 1 (large capacity) shotgun, because it is neither a 'shotgun' within the meaning of the Act,[96] nor, obviously, a rifle. This restriction means that those who take part in the sport of practical shotgun shooting cannot use this exemption, nor can they utilise the exemption for approved clubs as that is only for rifle and muzzle-loading pistol clubs. Membership of organisations such as the UKPSA[97] and other practical shooting clubs is accepted as a good reason to acquire a section 1 shotgun on a firearm certificate, but apparently there is no public safety benefit in allowing applicants to practise with such a firearm before they are

---

[96]   Sections 1(3)(a) and 57(4).

[97]   www.ukpsa.co.uk.

granted that authority. The UKPSA and other clubs run safety courses, both for beginners and for those who wish to take part in competitions, but prior to being granted a licence they cannot practise with any shotgun other than one with a magazine capacity of three rounds. This exemption also does not cover the loan of a muzzle-loading pistol. It probably covers a long-barrelled pistol, as it is a carbine, and 'rifle includes carbine'.[98]

Visitor's permits

3.50   For the possession[99] of firearms by a holder of a visitor's firearm permit,[100] see Chapter 7.

Firearms for export

3.51   The purchase of firearms for export purposes. The conditions under which this may be done are as follows:

(a)   the firearms must be bought from an RFD;[101] and
(b)   the buyer shall not have been in Great Britain[102] for more than 30 days[103] in the preceding 12 months; and
(c)   the firearms are to be bought for the purpose only of being exported from Great Britain without first coming into the buyer's possession.[104] This is an example of 'proprietary possession' as discussed in para 3.20.

As with section 1 firearms, there are numerous cases in which a firearm certificate is not needed for the handling of section 1 ammunition, namely any of the exceptions, as detailed in the preceding pages, where a certificate is not needed

---

[98]   FA 1968, s 57(4).

[99]   Note that possession only is covered by this exemption, and not a purchase, hiring, accepting as a gift or borrowing.

[100]   F(A)A 1988, s 17(1), (1A).

[101]   As to the registration of firearms dealers, see Chapter 16.

[102]   'Great Britain' means England, Wales and Scotland, and excludes the Channel Islands and the Isle of Man.

[103]   I.e. a continuous period of 30 days, or an accumulated period of 30 days composed of two or more shorter periods.

[104]   F(A)A 1988, s 18(1). The Act imposes certain duties on firearms dealers selling firearms under these provisions (s 18(2)–(4)), and these may be found in Chapter 16.

Further conditions are imposed in relation to firearms falling within Category B for the purposes of European Weapons Directive, Annex I (FA 1968, s 18(1A)–(6); Firearms Acts (Amendment) Regulations 1992, reg 8).

for a section 1 firearm.[105] A certificate is also unnecessary for firearms or ammunition for signalling apparatus which are part of the equipment of a ship or aircraft,[106] and for blank cartridges as they are not section 1 ammunition.

3.52   If your circumstances do not fall within any of the exceptions above, and you wish to have possession of one or more firearms, you need to obtain a firearm certificate.

HOW DO I GET A FIREARM CERTIFICATE?

3.53   In Great Britain all firearm and shotgun certificates are issued by the police. What follows is a general guide to obtaining a certificate, although as circumstances vary enormously, we have probably not covered every eventuality.

3.54   You will need to start by completing the application form, which is available on most local force websites, but the form is standardised, so you may find it easiest to go to www.gov.uk/government/publications/firearms-application-forms. Make sure you use the latest version. The application must be made to the chief officer of police for the police area in which you 'reside'.[107] For those with more than one address, it is advisable to apply from the address where you intend to store the guns, as this will be inspected to check your security. A fee is payable at the time of application,[108] which is refunded if you are refused.

3.55   The same application form (Form 201) is to be used to apply for a firearm or shotgun certificate or both. If you are applying for a firearm certificate your application must include declarations by two referees to the effect that your personal details given on the form are true. Referees no longer need to endorse any photos of you. Your application cannot be considered by the police until they

---

[105]   FA 1968, ss 7(1), 8(1), 9(1), 10, 11(1)–(4), 54, 57(4); F(A)A 1988, ss 15, 17(1), 18(1), 19 and Sch.

[106]   FA 1968, s 13(1)(a), (b).

[107]   FA 1968, s 26(1). An applicant cannot be said to reside at a property which he has let (*Burditt v Joslin* [1981] 3 All ER 203, *The Times*, 13 February 1981).

[108]   Currently it is £88 for a first application ('grant') for a firearm certificate and £79.50 for a shotgun certificate. For a renewal it is £62 for a firearm certificate and £49 for a shotgun certificate. If you apply for both certificates at the same time ('coterminous') it is £90, and £65 for the renewal of both, as long as it is done at the same time. You will also be charged £20 for a variation of a firearm certificate (except a 'like for like' variation which is free) and £4 for a replacement certificate.

have received references from the two referees.[109] If your application is solely for a shotgun certificate then only one referee is required.

3.56   To be qualified to act as a referee, a person must not be a member of your immediate family, a serving police officer, a police employee or an RFD,[110] and must be resident in Great Britain,[111] have known you personally for at least 2 years, and be of good character.[112] If you are applying for weapons for target shooting we would suggest you select as one of your referees an official (usually the secretary) of the Home Office-approved club of which you are a member, membership of such a club being essential in order to establish good reason for target shooting. There was a time when this was an absolute requirement, although that has now been dispensed with. Nonetheless, if your application includes details of your membership of a gun club, the police will make enquiries with that club as part of their assessment of you. Certainly, a positive reference from an official at your gun club is bound to assist your application.

3.57   Whoever you decide to put down as your referee(s), before doing so it would of course be sensible to seek their approval, and also enquire what they are likely to say when asked by the police their opinion of your suitability to possess firearms. You might have thought this is so obvious that it hardly needs saying. However, we have known of cases where the application has been thwarted by a referee being less than supportive or even downright negative. We can only wonder to what extent in those instances the applicant discussed it first with the referee.

3.58   It is very important when completing the forms to be as honest and accurate as possible. Read carefully the notes at pages 12 to 15 of the form and answer the questions as precisely as you can. This may seem obvious, but lying or giving inaccurate information, for example about your previous convictions, is a reason to refuse a certificate. As the explanatory notes on the application form make clear, you are expected to disclose *all* convictions, no matter how old or how minor the offence, and whether the conviction was in Great Britain or abroad.[113] A common mistake is to presume that this does not include motoring

---

[109] Firearms Rules 1998 (SI 1998/1941), r 4(2). A form is provided for this purpose (Firearms Rules 1998, Sch 1, Part III).

[110] An exception is that a referee can be an RFD where he is also the secretary of your target shooting club.

[111] 'Great Britain' means England, Wales and Scotland, and excludes the Channel Islands and the Isle of Man.

[112] Firearms Rules 1998, r 4(3). No referees are necessary for an application to vary a certificate.

[113] The Rehabilitation of Offenders Act 1974 does not apply to firearm and shotgun certificate applications; therefore all convictions must be disclosed even if they would be regarded as 'spent' for most other purposes.

offences. You are unlikely to be refused a certificate because you have a 10-year-old speeding conviction, or if you were cautioned for shoplifting when you were 15 (and you're now 45), but you might be if you fail to declare those convictions on the form! It is also a criminal offence to give false information in order to obtain a certificate.[114] The licensing system is rightly based on mutual trust, the police must be able to trust the certificate holder to co-operate with them and to be open and honest when making, or renewing, an application. It does not matter that an undeclared medical condition or conviction would not have resulted in the application being refused; it is the failure to disclose which is considered important.

Medical information

3.59   The application form requires you to provide details of your GP. If you are not registered with a GP in the UK, you will not be getting a certificate. The level of medical checks on gun owners has long been a contentious area, with concerns that there has been insufficient liaison between the police and the medical profession, and thus a failure on occasions, sometimes with terrible consequences, to identify those who may be mentally unstable or for other medical reasons present a danger to public safety through their possession of firearms or shotguns. The recent history of this issue is set out below, but at the time of writing no solution has been agreed which is acceptable to the police and the medical profession. The would-be certificate holder is left in the middle, sometimes with a request to pay large fees for a 'report'. In certain areas doctors have even resorted to telling the police that they 'must assume that there is something detrimental to the applicant' simply because the applicant has failed to pay the doctor's fee.

3.60   For some years now there have been questions on the application form regarding depression and other mental illness. However, the police would generally only contact your GP if a medical condition which might affect your suitability to safely possess firearms was disclosed by you, either on your form or in discussions with the police, or the police had other reasons for being concerned about your medical suitability. This approach was radically altered from 1 April 2016, when the Home Office implemented a new system of carrying out routine medical checks on every new applicant and every existing certificate holder applying for renewal of their certificate.

3.61   You are now asked to declare 'any relevant physical or mental health condition you have *ever* been diagnosed or treated for as this may affect your

---

[114]   FA 1968, ss 28A(7), 29(3), 51(1), (2) and Sch 6, Part I. The maximum punishment is 6 months' imprisonment or an unlimited fine, or both.

ability to safely possess and use a firearm (including a shotgun)'.[115] This is the list of relevant medical conditions which must be declared:

- Acute Stress Reaction or an acute reaction to the stress caused by a trauma.
- Suicidal thoughts or self-harm.
- Depression or anxiety.
- Dementia.
- Mania, bipolar disorder or a psychotic illness.
- A personality disorder.
- A neurological condition: for example, Multiple Sclerosis, Parkinson's or Huntington's diseases, or epilepsy.
- Alcohol or drug abuse.
- Any other mental or physical condition which might affect your safe possession of a firearm or shotgun.

This is a wide-ranging list, and you might wonder how some of these conditions would necessarily affect safe possession or use of a firearm. However, any of the specified conditions in that list must always be declared. If the applicant has any other mental or physical condition, it only needs to be declared if it 'might affect your safe possession of a firearm'. That is surely a subjective judgment on the part of the applicant, and interestingly that passage in the guidance notes which accompany the application form ends with the words 'if in doubt consult your GP'. So, if the applicant is unsure it then becomes a subjective judgment by the doctor. The onus is on the applicant or his GP, or both, to decide whether a condition not specified in the list is relevant. This is an important point as it is a failure to disclose *relevant* information that is an offence. Understandably, and correctly, the police are reluctant to enquire about medical conditions outside of those which are strictly relevant as they can be highly confidential.

3.62   The applicant is required to sign a consent giving his doctor permission for medical details to be disclosed to police, not merely for the purposes of assessing the application but for the life of the certificate. In a minority of cases, before deciding whether to grant the application the police will request a medical report where a relevant medical condition is disclosed, or if the police have other reasons to suspect any depression or mental illness or other problem. In such cases the *Guide* makes it clear that it is the applicant who must pay for such a report.[116] Where the police require a further medical report, either because the initial report obtained by the applicant does not contain sufficient detail, or after a certificate

---

[115] Question 10 and notes 4 and 5 on the 2017 version of Form 201.

[116] *Guide*, Appendix 11, Annexes A, B and C. This needs to be read in full if there is a medical issue of this sort.

has been granted or renewed, then it is the police who will be obliged to pay for that further report.

3.63   In all cases, as part of processing the application for grant or renewal, the police will ask every applicant's GP if the individual suffers from any relevant medical condition. Where the application is approved, and a certificate is issued, GPs will then be asked to place a code (referred to as the 'Firearm Reminder Code') on the patient's record to signify that the individual is a gun owner, with the expectation that the GP will inform the police if their patient's mental health deteriorates. The notes suggest that the applicant should pay the doctor for any initial response to the police enquiry, if the doctor chooses to charge.[117]

3.64   There has been widespread reluctance from some doctors to engage in this process, causing concerns amongst the police that they are not being provided with relevant information. Some police forces are now changing their approach and are asking the applicant to obtain a report in every case, providing a pro-forma letter to be handed to the doctor.[118] This policy is contrary to current Home Office advice. It is not possible at the time of writing to predict how this issue will be resolved. We can only advise that you check the up-to-date situation in your area.

3.65   Some GP surgeries have refused to take part in this scheme, either on the basis that they 'conscientiously object' to firearms ownership, or because any fee they can reasonably charge does not cover the work involved.

3.66   Home Office guidance which was published when the new scheme was implemented in April 2016 somewhat naively suggested that doctors were not expected to charge a fee for completing the standard form and returning it to the police. It is perhaps unsurprising that GPs began to resent this task as an increased burden on them. In September 2016 the British Medical Association (BMA) issued guidance to doctors actively encouraging them to decline to complete the police enquiry form on the basis that it is not part of the GP contract. The BMA have since updated their guidance more than once, most recently in February 2018.[119] This guidance now reminds doctors of their obligation to co-operate and engage in the process of firearms licensing when requested to do so. It also advises doctors if they have a conscientious objection to firearms, they should notify the

---

[117] Anecdotal evidence suggests that where a fee has been charged this has varied from £25 to £250 or more.

[118] We are currently aware of four police forces operating this policy. It was initially introduced by Kent and Merseyside Police, but has also very recently been adopted by Lincolnshire and Nottinghamshire Police.

[119] See the BMA website for current guidance, www.bma.org.uk/advice/employment/ethics/ethics-a-to-z/firearms.

patient of their objection in advance and refer the individual to another doctor. The BMA guidance continues to advise doctors that it is legitimate for them to charge their patient a fee for dealing with police enquiries on firearms licensing, but unhelpfully it still does not offer any guidelines as to what might be appropriate as the standard fees either for responding to the initial police enquiry or for providing a full medical report, where one is required.

3.67   It seems inevitable this situation will continue to evolve. In the meantime, the national shooting organisations continue to advise their members that they should politely decline to pay any fee requested by their GP for completing the standard medical enquiry form, particularly if the fee is only requested after the event. There had already been a significant increase in the application fees in 2015 and the shooting bodies have been proactive in resisting the gradual shift towards certificate holders being expected to routinely pay a fee to their doctor as a further increase by stealth in the cost of applying for a certificate.

3.68   The Home Office guidance is clear that 'the applicant or certificate holder should not be disadvantaged, nor the application delayed, by a GP's refusal to provide medical information'.[120] The police standard enquiry letter to GPs should therefore state that 'if the GP fails to respond within 21 days the police will draw the inference that the GP has no concerns'. You may wish to remind your local firearms licensing department of these points (as set out in Appendix 11 of the Home Office *Guide*) if they indicate that they cannot consider an application or renew the certificate until they receive a response from the individual's doctor. Contrary to the Home Office *Guide*, some forces have recently adopted a policy of refusing to issue a certificate until they do have a response from the doctor. As a number of doctors are refusing to co-operate with the scheme this leaves the applicant in a difficult position. We hope that this problem will be resolved in the near future, but we are not optimistic.

3.69   It might be thought that there are potential security implications in requiring information to be held outside of the police service about where firearms may be found. Whether any such danger created by this scheme is outweighed by the benefits to public safety remains to be seen. Curiously, the latest BMA guidance to doctors does not support the 'flagging' of patient records with an encoded firearms reminder, which arguably undermines one of the key objectives of this scheme. Further, will those who wish to retain their certificates not seek treatment – as they similarly do with conditions which may cause their doctor to contact the Driver and Vehicle Licensing Authority (DVLA) and so result in the loss of their driving licence – now they appreciate doctors are being asked to participate in this process?

---

[120]   See *Guide*, para 12.

3.70   For comments regarding the relevance of medical conditions and as evidence within the appeal process, please see Chapter 5.

DELAYS IN RENEWAL AND AUTOMATIC EXTENSION OF CERTIFICATES

3.71   An amendment to section 28, adding 28B, of the FA 1968[121] allows an existing firearm or shotgun certificate to be extended for up to 8 weeks past the original expiry date, during which period the police can decide to grant or refuse the renewal of that certificate. If granted, the 'extension period' counts as part of the 5 years of the new certificate, and section 28A is amended accordingly.

3.72   Given the delay with renewals which many certificate holders are now accustomed to experiencing, especially in certain police force areas, this is a welcome legal development. Hopefully, it will reduce the number of certificate holders who have diligently submitted their renewal applications a good 6 months or more before their current certificate expires, only to find they are still left in a position where they are obliged to press their local licensing department to issue them with a temporary permit, or alternatively lodge their guns with a dealer or fellow shooter, as their old certificate is about to run out with no sign of the new one.

3.73   This change in the law was introduced by the P&CA 2017. It came into force from 17 April 2018 and applies to all renewal applications submitted after that date. Having said that, it should be noted that the extension is only available to those who submit their renewal application at least 8 weeks before their current certificate expires, and where the police are unable to decide the application before the certificate expires. Provided your renewal application is submitted sufficiently early, the extension is automatic, and so the police cannot refuse or deny you the extension period. However, if your renewal is submitted with less than 8 weeks to run before your certificate expires, you cannot benefit from the automatic extension. This development should therefore not be viewed as a reason to submit your renewal application any less early than you would have done previously.

3.74   The obvious advantage of this provision for automatic extensions is that it should reduce the level of demand on overstretched police licensing departments for temporary permits, and so free them up to get on with actually processing renewals. The automatic extension period cannot be further extended beyond the maximum period of 8 weeks. So if it is fast approaching 8 weeks past the expiry

---

[121]   P&CA 2017, s 131.

of your old certificate, and you have not been assured your new certificate is on its way, then you will need to ask the police to issue you with a temporary permit, as you did in the past.

3.75   Bearing in mind that you will only benefit from the automatic extension if you submitted your renewal application at least 8 weeks before your old certificate expired, you may be wondering what paperwork you will need to show your local gun dealer or shooting ground to satisfy them that you did in fact submit your renewal early enough to be entitled to the extension period.

3.76   The answer lies in the National Firearms Licensing Management System (NFLMS), which is the national police database where records are held of all shotgun and firearm certificate holders. In April 2018 when this law came into force the Home Office circulated guidance[122] indicating that the NFLMS computer system had been updated to enable police forces to issue a standard letter confirming that your certificate has been automatically extended. Once your old certificate has expired it would therefore be sensible to carry that letter with you so that you can present it if required. If your certificate is rapidly approaching its expiry date and you have not had any news from your licensing officer as to the progress of your renewal, it is time to press them to issue you with such a letter.

3.77   Assuming your renewal is subsequently granted, any extension period used will count as part of the 5-year term of your new certificate, and so, as the police have done in the past where there have been delays with renewals, your new certificate will be backdated to start from the date your old one expired.

'GOOD REASON' FOR REQUIRING FIREARMS[123]

3.78   You must include on the application form details of the firearms and ammunition in your possession (if it is a renewal) and of those you wish to acquire[124] and your reasons for acquiring each of those other firearms. The reasons given must be applicable to each firearm that you wish to possess. The number of firearms to be covered by the certificate will be limited by the reasons for which they are required. Genuine collectors of firearms and ammunition, including those

---

[122]   See Home Office Circular 014/2018, www.gov.uk/government/publications/circular-0142018-limited-extension-of-validity-of-firearm-and-shotgun-certificates/circular-0142018-firearms-limited-extension-of-validity-of-firearm-and-shotgun-certificates.

[123]   This topic is also dealt with further in Chapter 5 when dealing with the question of appeals.

[124]   Firearms Rules 1998, Sch 1, Part I.

capable of use, will be regarded by the police as having a good reason for their possession.[125]

3.79   It is very important to state the 'good reason' for requiring each firearm as fully as possible; it is a common ground for refusal where insufficient detail has been given. For example, a certificate for a sporting rifle, or one for vermin control, would not be granted unless you could show that you have, or are likely to have, some opportunity of using it for those purposes. You will be expected to provide evidence that you have permission to shoot over land where quarry suitable for the particular weapon is present. Unless the land is already known to police as suitable for shooting over they will want to check that it will be safe. They keep records of land and if necessary make enquiries with other forces to check that this is so. In addition to demonstrating good reason in principle, the firearms you intend to acquire must be suitable for the stated purpose in terms of power and range. This can sometimes be a matter of opinion, and while most forces take a reasonable approach to such questions, be prepared to argue your point of view, particularly if your application is out of the ordinary. For shooting deer there are additional requirements; see Chapter 12.

3.80   As already stated, for target shooting you will need to be a full member of a club and you will need to demonstrate access to ranges suitable for the use of the firearm(s) you are applying for; most ranges have muzzle velocity limits. There are several other more specialist examples of good reason to possess firearms, such as the humane killing of animals, or for a 'trophy of war', but in each case, you will need to establish that good reason.

ASSESSMENT OF THE APPLICATION

3.81   The initial enquiries will be conducted by a Firearms Enquiry Officer (FEO) who will check your background and the information you have given, and will contact your referees to verify what they say about you, and that they are who they say they are. You will be visited by the FEO to inspect your security arrangements and to see your home circumstances. When those checks are completed your file will be passed to the Firearms Licensing Manager who will review it and decide whether your application should be granted in whole, or perhaps in part if you have applied for a number of weapons, or refused. Do not be surprised to find that everyone you deal with is in fact a civilian, although they may well once have been serving police officers who have now retired.

---

[125]   As to antique firearms and firearms of historic interest, see para 1.53 *et seq*.

3.82   This process of assessing the application applies equally on a renewal as it does on a first application, albeit the enquiries made on renewal may not be quite as thorough as when the original application was considered. Do bear in mind that the requirement to demonstrate good reason for each firearm is ongoing and therefore, even if the police previously granted authority to acquire or possess a particular firearm, they may not be prepared to renew that authority if they are no longer satisfied you have a good reason to possess it. This may arise where the police form the view you have used the firearm in question only very infrequently.

WHEN SHOULD A FIREARM CERTIFICATE BE GRANTED – THE TEST

3.83   The police *must* grant a certificate when they are satisfied that the applicant:

(a)   is fit to be entrusted with a section 1 firearm. Reasons for revocation of a certificate are defined as 'the holder is of intemperate habits or unsound mind, or is otherwise unfitted to be entrusted with a firearm'.[126] Clearly the police would not grant a certificate in the first place if they felt the applicant came within this description; and

(b)   has not been prohibited by the FA 1968 from possessing a section 1 firearm. This arises when he has been given certain punishments by the courts;[127] and

(c)   has a good reason for having possession of or acquiring the firearms and ammunition which are the subject of the application; and

(d)   can, in all the circumstances, be permitted to have the firearm and ammunition in his possession without danger to public safety or to the peace.[128]

Note that this test is slightly different to the test to be applied for a shotgun certificate – see Chapter 4.

3.84   As can been seen, there are a number of criteria which must be met, and there are a number of decided cases on the test. These are considered in more detail in Chapter 5.

3.85   Note that the criterion in (d) above, that the certificate will not be granted if 'your possession of firearms would be a danger to the public safety or the peace', is by far the most common objection raised as a reason to refuse or revoke

---

[126]   FA 1968, s 30A(2)(a).

[127]   See para 5.60 *et seq*, 'Prohibited persons – applications to remove a prohibition under section 21'.

[128]   FA 1968, s 27(1).

a certificate. This criterion is considered in detail in paras 4.10 *et seq* and para 5.39 as it is the principal reason to refuse or revoke a shotgun certificate. The phrase has the same meaning whether applied to a firearm or shotgun certificate, or to the registration of a firearms dealer.

3.86   If the police refuse your application for a certificate, or they subsequently revoke it, they will have to justify their decision to a Crown Court if you choose to appeal.

CONDITIONS IMPOSED UPON FIREARM CERTIFICATES

3.87   The certificate will be issued subject to a number of conditions.[129] Five will be imposed in all cases, and others[130] may be added by the police. The five 'statutory' conditions are as follows:

(a)   The holder must, on receipt of the certificate, sign it in ink with his usual signature.

(b)   The holder must, as soon as is reasonably practicable,[131] but within 7 days, inform the chief officer of police by whom the certificate was granted of the theft, loss or destruction in Great Britain[132] of the certificate. (There is also a requirement to report a loss or destruction outside Great Britain within 14 days[133] by means of registered post, or the nearest local equivalent.)

(c)   Any change in the permanent address of the certificate holder shall be notified without undue delay to the chief officer of police by whom the certificate was granted.

(d)   The firearms and ammunition to which the certificate relates must at all times (except in the circumstances described in (e) below) be stored securely so as to prevent, so far as is reasonably practicable, access to them by unauthorised persons.

(e)   Where a firearm or ammunition to which the certificate relates:

---

[129]   Failure to comply with a condition is an offence for which the maximum punishment on summary conviction is 6 months' imprisonment, or an unlimited fine, or both (FA 1968, ss 1(2), 51(1), (2) and Sch 6, Part I).

[130]   E.g. that the firearms and ammunition shall only be used for certain purposes or on certain land.

[131]   'As soon as reasonably practicable, but' was added by the Firearms (Amendment) Rules 2018 (SI 2018/1042), effective from 16 October 2018.

[132]   'Great Britain' means England, Wales and Scotland, and excludes the Channel Islands and the Isle of Man.

[133]   FA(A) 1997, s 35(3).

(i)   is in use;[134] or

(ii) the certificate holder has the firearm with him for the purpose of cleaning, repairing or testing, or for some other purpose connected with its use, transfer[135] or sale; or

(iii) is in transit to or from a place in connection with its use for any of the purposes at (ii) above,

reasonable precautions must be taken for the safe custody of the firearm or ammunition.[136]

For further details of these security requirements, see Chapter 8.

3.88   Any of the conditions, except those five just mentioned, may be varied by the police at any time, and they may require you to send them the certificate for alteration within 21 days.[137] You may yourself apply to the police for it to be altered.[138] You should, for example, do this if the quantity or description of the firearms in your possession varies during the lifetime of a certificate, or if you want to hold or buy more ammunition than is authorised by the certificate.

3.89   It appears that there is no right of appeal against the conditions attached to a firearm certificate by the police.[139] As the police are a public body and are required to act reasonably, the imposition of a totally unreasonable condition could, however, still be subject to challenge in the High Court; see Chapter 5.

3.90   If you apply for a firearm certificate for a rifle or muzzle-loading pistol[140] (not being a prohibited weapon[141]) and the police are satisfied that your only

---

[134] In a case decided under the earlier Firearms (Dangerous Air Weapons) Rules 1969 (SI 1969/47), which referred to 'actual use', it was held that live ammunition concealed in the back of an unattended car for about half an hour was not in actual use nor kept in a secure place with a view to preventing access to it by unauthorised persons (*Marsh v Chief Constable of Avon & Somerset, The Independent*, 8 May 1987, DC).

[135] 'Transfer' is defined to include let on hire, give, lend and part with possession (FA 1968, s 57(4)).

[136] Firearms Rules 1998, r 3(4). Further conditions can be imposed in the case of specialised weapons and ammunition, such as humane killers, shot pistols and starting pistols, restricting their use to their special purposes (Firearms Rules 1998, r 3(5)).

[137] FA 1968, s 29(1).

[138] FA 1968, s 29(2). The usual application form is used for this purpose (Firearms Rules 1998, r 3(1) and Sch 1, Part I).

[139] This is the view of the Home Office which they say has been supported by the courts, but this has been disputed. No express right of appeal regarding conditions has been given by the Firearms Acts.

[140] A muzzle-loading pistol is defined as a pistol designed to be loaded at the muzzle end of the barrel or chamber with a loose charge and a separate ball (or other missile) (F(A)A 1988, s 15(11), (12)).

[141] For the meaning of 'prohibited weapon', see Chapter 2.

reason for having it is for target shooting, the certificate will be given (or renewed) subject to the following conditions, in addition to any others:

(a)   it is to be used only for target shooting; and
(b)   you must be a member of an approved rifle club or muzzle-loading pistol club[142] (as the case may be) named in the certificate.[143]

There are many other conditions which are routinely added to certificates, for example to allow the possession of a rifle for target shooting, or a condition as to when solid slug ammunition for a shotgun may be used, etc. A firearm certificate is a legal document that allows possession of firearms and ammunition. If you do not abide by the conditions you will be committing a criminal offence. It is therefore important to check your certificate and any conditions attached to it upon receipt to ensure it allows you to do what you require; if not, go back to the police. We also recommend that you keep an up-to-date copy of your certificate separate from the original. It can be extremely useful if you should lose your certificate, or even if it is taken by or submitted to the police for any reason.

3.91   As a certificate is a legal document, the construction of a certificate in a criminal trial is a matter for the judge, not the jury.[144] Keep in mind however that it would, for example, still be a question of fact for the jury as to whether a particular gun was covered by the certificate, as construed by the judge.

WHAT ELSE SHOULD I KNOW ABOUT FIREARM CERTIFICATES?

3.92   When granted, the certificate will specify particulars of the firearms already possessed and of those authorised by the certificate to be acquired,[145] and will give authority for the possession and acquisition of stated amounts of ammunition. On later purchases of firearms or ammunition, the details are to be

---

[142]   A muzzle-loading pistol club means a club where muzzle-loading pistols are used for target shooting (F(A)A 1988, s 15(12)).

[143]   F(A)A 1997, s 44. For approval of clubs, see para 3.30 *et seq*, 'Rifle clubs and muzzle-loading pistol clubs'.

[144]   *R v Paul* [1999] Crim LR 79, CA.

[145]   FA 1968, s 27(2); F(A)A 1988, s 9; Firearms Rules 1998, r 3(6), Sch 1, Part II. The exchange by a person with a firearms dealer of one firearm for another, even though similar, is not covered by that person's certificate unless it has been previously varied by the police to authorise the acquisition of the second firearm (*Wilson v Coombe* [1989] 1 WLR 78; *Law Society Gazette*, 26 October 1988, p 44).

entered in the certificate by the seller. A photograph of the holder of the certificate will be affixed to it.

3.93   The certificate will last for 5 years, unless previously revoked by the police[146] or cancelled by the court,[147] and may be renewed every 5 years[148] by completing a further application form.[149]

3.94   Arrangements may be made for your firearm certificate and shotgun certificate to be coterminous,[150] i.e. falling due for renewal on the same date even if they were originally granted on different dates. In the long run this will obviously save time for both you and the police.

3.95   In addition to the fees payable for the grant and renewal of firearm certificates, there is a fee payable for a variation to a certificate. In some circumstances there is no fee, for example in relation to a trophy of war. The police will be able to advise you.

3.96   If you wish to change a firearm in your possession for a similar one, say in the same calibre, it is necessary to obtain a 'one for one' variation. You cannot simply dispose of one firearm and replace it, because each 'acquisition' requires a fresh authority. There is no charge for this type of variation.

3.97   Until we leave the EU the holder of a firearm (or shotgun) certificate in the UK is entitled to also have issued to them free of charge a European Firearms Pass. For further details see Chapter 7. Having a firearm certificate does not excuse you from obtaining a game licence when, according to the law, such a licence is necessary.[151]

---

[146] As to revocation, and appeal against it, see Chapter 5.

[147] The court has power to cancel a certificate on conviction in relation to most firearms offences (although not those relating to air weapons) or for any other offence for which a term of imprisonment was imposed. This also applies where a person is bound over to keep the peace. The court also has a discretion to order forfeiture and destruction of any firearms possessed by the offender (FA 1968, s 52).

[148] The 5-year period applies to certificates granted or renewed after 1 January 1995 (FA 1968, s 28A(1); Firearms (Period of Certificate) Order 1994 (SI 1994/2614); Firearms (Amendment) Rules 1994 (SI 1994/3022) (revoked)). The period may be further revised by order of the Home Office (FA 1968, s 28A(3)).

[149] FA 1968, s 28A(1); Firearms Rules 1998, r 3(1) and Sch 1, Part I. The rules which govern the grant or refusal of the first certificate (see above) also apply on a renewal (FA 1968, s 28A(2)).

[150] F(A)A 1988, s 11.

[151] FA 1968, s 58(5). As to game licences, see Chapter 10.

3.98   When carrying firearms or ammunition you must produce your certificate to a constable, if asked to do so.[152] If you fail to do so, or fail to permit the constable to read the certificate, or fail to show him that you are entitled to hold the firearm or ammunition without a certificate, the constable may seize and detain the firearm or ammunition and may require you to give him at once your name and address.[153] Similar provisions apply to the production of a visitor's European Firearms Pass.[154]Although this is the law, in the current climate there is a good chance that rather than simply being required to give your name and address, you will also be arrested on suspicion of unlawful possession of a firearm and/or ammunition. So make sure you carry your certificate, or at least a good copy of it, with you. The police should accept a good copy from people behaving lawfully with firearms. The Countryside Alliance recommend that you carry a copy in circumstances where there is a risk the original could be lost. All police control rooms can check the NFLMS and so a claim by a legitimate certificate holder that he has a valid certificate, and that the guns in question are covered by it, can be resolved quickly without undue inconvenience to the holder.

3.99   If you should be unwise enough to make a statement which is false in any material particular for the purpose of obtaining a certificate, or having it renewed or varied, whether for yourself or somebody else, you will be liable to prosecution.[155] Not surprisingly, it is also an offence[156] if, with a view to purchasing or acquiring, or procuring the repair, test or proof of, a section 1 firearm or ammunition, you produce a false firearm certificate or such a certificate in which any false entry has been made, or impersonate a person to whom such a certificate has been granted or knowingly or recklessly make a statement false in any material particular.[157]

---

[152]   FA 1968, s 48(1). As well as police constables, including special police constables, 'constable' includes others holding that office, e.g. harbour constables. The hallmark of a constable is his attestation as such before, usually, a magistrate.

[153]   FA 1968, s 48(2). If you refuse to give your name and address, or give them incorrectly, you will be liable upon summary conviction to a maximum fine at level 3 on the standard scale (currently £1,000) (FA 1968, s 48(3), 51(1), (2) and Sch 6, Part I). Furthermore, you may be arrested without warrant if you make such a refusal, or if the constable suspects you of giving a false name or address or of 'intending to abscond' (FA 1968, s 50(3)).

[154]   FA 1968, s 48(1A), (2), (3).

[155]   FA 1968, s 28A(7), 29(3), 51(1), (2) and Sch 6, Part 1. The maximum punishment is 6 months' imprisonment or an unlimited fine.

[156]   The maximum punishment on summary conviction is imprisonment for 6 months or an unlimited fine, or both; or, on indictment, 5 years' imprisonment, or an unlimited fine, or both (FA 1968, s 3(5), 51(1), (2) and Sch 6, Part I).

[157]   FA 1968, s 3(5).

SECTION 1 AMMUNITION

3.100 You will be limited in quantity as to the amount of section 1 ammunition you can purchase and possess in each calibre. Bear in mind that for each calibre you will be given one limit as to the maximum quantity authorised to be possessed at any one time, and a second somewhat lower limit as to the maximum quantity authorised to be purchased or acquired at any one time. These limits will be clearly set out on your certificate. The limits set should be reasonable for your proposed use and to allow you to take advantage of the opportunity, within reasonable limits, to be able to 'bulk purchase'. If you feel the limits imposed are inadequate for your purposes, and can justify that to your licensing department, you can apply for a variation of your certificate to increase your authorised limits.

3.101 It is important to stay within your limits in each calibre as you are committing the criminal offence of unlawful possession if you exceed it. As stated elsewhere, bear in mind that the limit includes not only complete rounds of ammunition, but in the case of expanding ammunition, where it is 'ammunition designed to be used with a pistol', the bullet heads as well. Re-loaders beware!

TRANSFER, DEACTIVATION AND LOSS OR DESTRUCTION OF SECTION 1 FIREARMS AND AMMUNITION

3.102 The FA 1968 imposed a number of restrictions on the handling of these types of firearms and ammunition, as follows:

(a) You must not[158] sell or transfer[159] to any other person in the UK[160] these firearms and ammunition except in the following cases:

(i) when 'the other person' is an RFD;

---

[158] FA 1968, s 3(2). The maximum punishment on summary conviction is imprisonment for 6 months or an unlimited fine, or both; or, on indictment, 5 years' imprisonment, or an unlimited fine, or both (FA 1968, s 51(1), (2), Sch 6, Part I).

[159] 'Transfer' is defined to include let on hire, give, lend and part with possession (FA 1968, s 57(4)). The case of *Hall v Cotton and Treadwell* [1986] 3 All ER 332 confirms that the leaving of a firearm with another person for safekeeping and cleaning is caught by this definition.

[160] 'United Kingdom' means England, Wales, Scotland and Northern Ireland, and excludes the Channel Islands and the Isle of Man.

(ii) when 'the other person' produces a firearm certificate authorising him to buy or acquire[161] the firearm[162] or ammunition, or shows that he is entitled[163] to buy or acquire them without holding such a certificate;[164]

(iii) a person may part with the possession of a firearm or ammunition, otherwise than in pursuance of a contract for sale or hire or by way of gift or loan, to another person who shows that he is entitled to have possession of them without holding a firearm certificate;[165]

(iv) when a firearm or ammunition is delivered by a carrier or warehouseman, or by an employee of either, in the ordinary course of his business or employment as such.[166]

(b) You must not[167] by way of trade or business, unless you are an RFD, manufacture, sell, transfer,[168] repair, test, prove, expose for sale or transfer, or possess for sale, transfer, repair, test or proof, any section 1 firearms or ammunition.

(c) You must not sell or transfer any firearm or ammunition to any person whom you know, or have reasonable ground for believing, to be drunk or of unsound mind,[169] or to have been sentenced to certain punishments[170] by the courts.[171]

---

[161] 'Acquire' is defined to mean hire, accept as a gift or borrow (FA 1968, s 57(4); F(A)A 1988, s 25(1)).

[162] A firearm certificate does not authorise the purchase or acquisition of a firearm bought or borrowed by way of exchanging it with another firearm unless the certificate specifically authorised that purchase or acquisition (*Wilson v Coombe* [1989] 1 WLR 78; *Law Society Gazette*, 26 October 1988, p 44).

[163] For the cases where a person would be so entitled, see para 3.22 *et seq*, 'Exceptions from the need to hold a firearm certificate'.

[164] FA 1968, s 3(2).

[165] FA 1968, s 3(2), 8(2)(a).

[166] FA 1968, s 3(2), 9(4).

[167] FA 1968, s 3(1). The maximum summary punishment is 6 months' imprisonment or an unlimited fine, or both. On indictment, the maximum is 5 years' imprisonment, or an unlimited fine, or both (FA 1968, s 51(1), (2) and Sch 6, Part I).

[168] 'Transfer' is defined to include let on hire, give, lend and part with possession (FA 1968, s 57(4)).

[169] FA 1968, s 25. The maximum punishment on summary conviction is 3 months' imprisonment, or a fine at level 3 on the standard scale (currently £1,000), or both (FA 1968, s 51(1), (2) and Sch 6, Part I).

[170] This is a reference to prohibited persons, for which see para 5.60 *et seq*, 'Prohibited persons – applications to remove a prohibition under section 21'.

[171] FA 1968, s 21(1), (3), (5). The maximum summary punishment is 6 months' imprisonment or an unlimited fine, or both. On indictment, the maximum is 3 years' imprisonment, or an unlimited fine, or both (FA 1968, s 51(1), (2) and Sch 6, Part I). This includes air weapons.

In addition to the foregoing restrictions, the F(A)A 1997 added further provisions[172] about some of the dealings with section 1 firearms and ammunition which are discussed above. As will be seen from the next paragraph, the most significant is the requirement that where one or both parties to the transfer of section 1 firearms or ammunition is the holder of a firearm certificate, all such transfers must now take place on a face-to-face basis.[173]

3.103 If, in Great Britain,[174] you sell, let on hire, lend or give a section 1 firearm or section 1 ammunition to another person who is neither an RFD[175] nor a person who is entitled to buy or acquire the firearm or ammunition without holding a firearm certificate[176] or a visitor's firearm permit:[177]

(a) the transferee must produce to you the certificate or permit which entitles him to buy or acquire the firearm or ammunition;

(b) you must comply with any instructions in the certificate or permit produced; and

(c) you must hand the firearm or ammunition to the transferee who must receive it in person.[178]

3.104 The F(A)A 1997 also imposed greater obligations to give notice to the police of certain transactions involving section 1 firearms than had previously existed. In each of the following circumstances you will need to give notice to the chief police officer who granted your certificate or permit:

(a) If you sell, let on hire, lend or give any section 1 firearm for which you hold a firearm certificate or a visitor's permit. If you are the transferee in such a transaction and hold such a certificate or permit relating to the firearm, the same requirements about giving notice will apply.[179]

---

[172] These provisions replace and extend those formerly contained in FA 1968, s 42.

[173] 'Dealer to dealer' transactions need not be face to face.

[174] 'Great Britain' means England, Wales and Scotland, and excludes the Channel Islands and the Isle of Man.

[175] As to the registration of firearms dealers, see Chapter 16.

[176] For persons who are so entitled, see para 3.22 *et seq*, 'Exceptions from the need to hold a firearm certificate'.

[177] See Chapter 7 for provisions about these permits.

[178] F(A)A 1997, s 32(1)(a), (2). Failure to comply with these requirements is an offence with a maximum punishment on summary conviction of 6 months' imprisonment or an unlimited fine, or both; or, on indictment, 5 years' imprisonment or an unlimited fine, or both (F(A)A 1997, ss 32(3), 36(a)).

[179] F(A)A 1997, s 33(1)–(3) contains the provisions for such transactions within Great Britain and F(A)A 1997, s 35(1), (5),(6) the corresponding provisions for such transactions outside Great Britain. Note, however, that where the sale or other transaction takes place outside Great Britain, notice must be given in relation to 'any firearm' and is not confined solely to section 1 firearms.

(b)   If you deactivate,[180] destroy or lose (by theft or otherwise) a firearm to which a firearm certificate or a visitor's permit relates, and you were the last certificate or permit holder in possession of it.[181]

(c)   When section 1 ammunition is lost (by theft or otherwise), and that ammunition is covered by a firearm certificate or a visitor's permit, and you were the last certificate or permit holder in possession of it.[182]

All such notices must give a description of the firearm (including any identification number) or ammunition, and state the nature of the transaction, or otherwise 'state the nature of the event', i.e. deactivation, destruction or loss. Where it is a transfer, the notice must in addition include the name and address of the other party to the transaction. In relation to the lending of section 1 firearms, do not allow yourself to get caught out by the exemption from the need to notify the transfer of a shotgun lasting less than 72 hours. That exemption relates solely to shotguns, and the loan of a section 1 firearm must always be notified to the police, however short the period of the loan.

3.105   The time limit for giving notice, and the method by which that notice should be sent, is determined by whether the transfer or other event took place within or outside Great Britain. If the transfer or other event occurred within Great Britain then notice must be given within 7 days, the notice to be sent by registered post or recorded delivery service. Where the transfer or other event took place outside Great Britain, the notice must be given within 14 days by registered post or recorded delivery service, or if sent from outside the UK,[183] must be sent by such means as most closely correspond to registered post or recorded delivery service.

3.106   In all such circumstances, it is an offence if you fail without reasonable excuse to give notice of the transfer or other event within the requisite timescale and by the specified method.[184] That said, while notification of any transfer should be sent by registered post or recorded delivery service, in the modern age of electronic communications police forces have for some time now accepted

---

[180]   A firearm is said to be deactivated if it would, by virtue of F(A)A 1988, s 8 (for which, see Chapter 1), be presumed to be rendered incapable of discharging any shot, bullet or other missile (F(A)A 1997, s 34(5)).

[181]   F(A)A 1997, s 34(1), (3) contains the provisions for such events within Great Britain and F(A)A 1997, s 35(3)(a)–(6) the corresponding provisions for such events outside Great Britain.

[182]   F(A)A 1997, ss 34(2), (3) contains the provisions for such events within Great Britain and F(A)A 1997, s 35(3)(b)–(6) the corresponding provisions for such events outside Great Britain.

[183]   'United Kingdom' means England, Wales, Scotland and Northern Ireland, and excludes the Channel Islands and the Isle of Man.

[184]   In all such cases the maximum punishment on summary conviction is 6 months' imprisonment or an unlimited fine, or both; or, on indictment, 5 years' imprisonment or an unlimited fine, or both (F(A)A 1997, s 36(a)).

notification by email. This practice was given legal approval by the Firearms (Electronic Communications) Order 2011,[185] which permits certificate holders and firearms dealers to notify the police of transactions and other matters by email.[186] We would recommend that you always request a reply to confirm receipt of your email, and that you print and retain copies of such emailed notifications, at least until such time as you receive a reply from the police.

3.107 A notification regarding a transfer is only required where there is in fact a transfer. Giving a gun to an RFD to hold on a 'sale or return' or conditional sale basis is not a transfer.[187] The *Guide* is silent on the position where a gun is given to a dealer for testing, repair or storage but universal practice is that no notification is required in those circumstances either as it is not a transfer. The only reference in the Act to an RFD 'testing repairing or proving a firearm' is in section 8(2)(b) where an exemption is provided from the need for the person to whom the gun is returned to produce a certificate, thereby the RFD avoiding an offence under section 3(2).

3.108 There are special restrictions on the handling of section 1 firearms and ammunition by young people under 17; these are considered in Chapter 14. Further regulations are contained in the FA 1968 about the holding of firearms and ammunition by persons given certain punishments by the courts ('prohibition').[188] For details of the criminal use of firearms, such as using firearms to endanger life, to injure property, to resist or prevent arrest[189] or with intent to commit an indictable offence,[190] possessing firearms with intent to cause belief that unlawful violence will be used,[191] and various others, see Chapter 15. There is also an offence of taking in pawn firearms and ammunition.[192]

---

[185] SI 2011/713.

[186] Emailed notifications must be sent to the email address published for this purpose by the police in your area. Check with them first what address you should use. This order also permits the police to send notices by email to certificate holders and firearms dealers, subject to you first having given your consent.

[187] *Guide*, para 5.19: 'A firearm or shotgun placed with a registered firearms dealer or auctioneer for sale or return is not regarded as a transfer'.

[188] FA 1968, s 21. See Chapter 5 for the process of applying to court for the removal of such a prohibition.

[189] FA 1968, ss 16, 17.

[190] FA 1968, s 18.

[191] FA 1968, s 16A.

[192] FA 1968, s 3(6).

WORK ON SECTION 1 FIREARMS AND AMMUNITION

3.109 You will commit an offence[193] if you undertake the repair, test or proof of a section 1 firearm or ammunition for any other person in the UK[194] unless:

(a) 'the other person' is an RFD;[195] or
(b) 'the other person' produces, or causes to be produced, a firearm certificate authorising him to have possession of the firearm or ammunition, or shows that he is entitled[196] to have possession of it without holding such a certificate.

You must not repair, prove or test any firearm or ammunition for any person whom you know, or have reasonable ground for believing, to be drunk or of unsound mind,[197] or to have been sentenced to certain punishments[198] by the courts.[199]

3.110 None of this prevents you from working on your own guns, subject to notifying the police if you change the status of a firearm, as already indicated.

---

[193] The maximum punishment on summary conviction is imprisonment for 6 months or an unlimited fine, or both; or, on indictment, 5 years' imprisonment, or an unlimited fine, or both (FA 1968, ss 3(3), 51(1), (2) and Sch 6, Part I).

[194] 'United Kingdom' means England, Wales, Scotland and Northern Ireland, and excludes the Channel Islands and the Isle of Man.

[195] You would then be acting as their servant in accordance with s 8 of the Act. As to the registration of firearms dealers, see Chapter 16.

[196] For the cases where a person would be so entitled, see para 3.22 *et seq*, 'Exceptions from the need to hold a firearm certificate'.

[197] FA 1968, s 25. The maximum punishment on summary conviction is 3 months' imprisonment, or a fine at level 3 on the standard scale (currently £1,000), or both (FA 1968, s 51(1), (2) and Sch 6, Part I).

[198] This is a reference to prohibited persons, see para 5.60 *et seq*, 'Prohibited persons – applications to remove a prohibition under section 21'.

[199] FA 1968, s 21(5). This includes air weapons. The maximum summary punishment is 6 months' imprisonment or an unlimited fine, or both. On indictment, the maximum is 3 years' imprisonment, or an unlimited fine, or both (FA 1968, s 51(1), (2) and Sch 6, Part I).

3.111 Unless you are an RFD,[200] you must not convert into a firearm anything which, though having the appearance of being a firearm,[201] is so constructed as to be incapable of discharging any missile through any barrel.[202]

3.112 It is an offence to shorten the barrel of a section 1 firearm which is a smooth-bore gun to a length of less than 24 inches[203] unless the barrel has a bore exceeding 2 inches (but an RFD[204] may do so for the sole purpose of replacing a defective part of it so as to produce a barrel not less than 24 inches long).[205]

---

[200] As to the registration of firearms dealers, see Chapter 16.

[201] For imitation firearms, see Chapter 9.

[202] FA 1968, s 4(3). The maximum punishment on summary conviction is imprisonment for 6 months or an unlimited fine, or both; or, on indictment, 7 years' imprisonment, or an unlimited fine, or both (FA 1968, s 51(1), (2) and Sch 6, Part I). For a procedure for certifying that a firearm is incapable in this way, see para 1.30 *et seq*, 'Deactivated firearms'.

[203] Measurement is from the muzzle to the point at which the charge is exploded (FA 1968, s 57(6)(a)).

[204] As to the registration of firearms dealers, see Chapter 16.

[205] F(A)A 1988, s 6. The maximum punishments for this offence are: on summary conviction, 6 months' imprisonment, or an unlimited fine, or both; on indictment, 5 years' imprisonment, or an unlimited fine, or both (F(A)A 1988, s 6(1)).

Chapter 4

Shotguns and their Ammunition

DEFINITION OF 'SHOTGUN'

4.01   The F(A)A 1988, substituting a new definition of 'shotgun' for that formerly supplied by the FA 1968, defines that term to mean:

A smooth-bore gun (not being an air gun)[1] which—

(a)   has a barrel not less than 24 inches long[2] and does not have any barrel with a bore exceeding 2 inches in diameter; and
(b)   either has no magazine or has a non-detachable magazine incapable of holding more than two cartridges; and
(c)   is not a revolver gun.[3]

As to paragraph (b) above, a gun which has been adapted to have a non-detachable magazine will not fall within the definition unless the conditions concerning approved marks, which are detailed in para 3.04, items (a) and (b), are fulfilled.[4]

4.02   In short summary a 'shotgun' is a smooth-bored gun, either single- or double-barrelled, with barrels at least 24 inches long. It may be pump-action or self-loading (but not a revolver), but if so it must have a magazine capacity limited to two shots. This is in addition to the round in the chamber. If such a gun has a greater magazine capacity it falls within section 1 and must be held on a firearm certificate. If it has a barrel less than 24 inches it is in section 1. If it were to have a large capacity magazine *and* a barrel shorter than 24 inches, then it becomes a

---

[1]   The term 'air gun' is not defined by the Firearms Acts.

[2]   This length is measured from the muzzle to the point at which the charge is exploded on firing (FA 1968, s 57(6)(a); F(A)A 1988, s 25(1)).

[3]   FA 1968, s 1(3)(a); F(A)A 1988, s 2(1), (2). 'Revolver gun' means a gun containing a series of chambers which revolve when the gun is fired (FA 1968, s 57(2B); F(A)A 1988, s 25(2)).

[4]   FA 1968, ss 1(3A), 58(1); F(A)A 1988, s 2(1), (3).

The Firearms Law Handbook

prohibited weapon.[5] If a gun falls within the ordinary definition of a shotgun then it is described as a 'section 2 shotgun' and can be held on a shotgun certificate.

4.03 The definition of 'shotgun ammunition' is only provided by the Firearms Acts by exemption. As we have seen at para 3.12, ordinary shotgun ammunition[6] is excluded from the kinds of ammunition which are classified as section 1 ammunition and therefore does not require separate certification.

WHEN DO I NEED A SHOTGUN CERTIFICATE?

4.04 Shotgun certificates were introduced in 1968 to counter the increasing use of shotguns for criminal purposes. Briefly, the intention was to control the use of shotguns by means of certificates similarly to, but less strictly than, the ways in which rifles and handguns had been controlled by firearm certificates for many years. Shotgun ammunition is not, however, controlled by certificates, although production of a certificate is required to purchase shotgun ammunition.

4.05 You will commit an offence[7] if you have in your possession[8] or purchase or acquire[9] a shotgun without holding a shotgun certificate,[10] but a certificate is not needed for the possession of component parts of a shotgun, nor in the following cases:[11]

(a) If you use a shotgun at a time and place approved for shooting at artificial targets by the chief officer of police for the area in which that place is situated.[12]

(b) If you hold a firearm certificate issued in Northern Ireland which authorises you to possess a shotgun.[13]

---

[5] This is if it is a pump-action or semi-automatic gun. Large capacity lever action or bolt-action shotguns remain in s 1.

[6] It must have more than five shot, none of which are larger than .36 of an inch, FA 1968, s 1(4)(a), see para 3.12.

[7] The maximum punishment on summary conviction is imprisonment for 6 months, or an unlimited fine, or both or, on indictment, 5 years' imprisonment or an unlimited fine, or both (FA 1968, ss 2(1), 51(1), (2) and Sch 6, Part I).

[8] For some guidance on the meaning of 'possession', see para 3.13 *et seq*, 'When do I need a firearm certificate?'.

[9] 'Acquire' is defined to mean hire, accept as a gift or borrow (FA 1968, s 57(4)).

[10] FA 1968, s 2(1).

[11] See also paras 1.53 and 1.67 for two general exceptions to the need for a shotgun certificate.

[12] FA 1968, s 11(6). It is important to note that the exception only operates while a gun is being used in this way at the approved time and place and will not cover the possession of a gun immediately before or after such a use.

[13] FA 1968, s 15.

(c)   If you borrow a shotgun from the occupier of private premises[14] and use it on those premises in the presence[15] of a person with permission to shoot.[16]

(d)   If you are able to bring your case within any one of the exceptions applying to firearm certificates which are at para 3.22 *et seq*, 'Exceptions from the need to hold a firearm certificate'. In the case of the exception regarding the person for whom a shotgun is carried, that person will require a shotgun certificate instead of a firearm certificate. See para 3.28 *et seq* for details.

(e)   If you hold a visitor's shotgun permit.[17]

HOW DO I GET A SHOTGUN CERTIFICATE?

4.06   Firearms Rules regulating applications for shotgun certificates came into force on 1 September 1998. For general observations about making applications for a firearm certificate, which apply equally to applications for a shotgun certificate, see para 3.53 *et seq*, 'How do I get a firearm certificate?'.

4.07   Your reasons for having the gun are not required to be given on your application. This appears to be a strange omission since, as mentioned below, the absence of a good reason will entitle the police to refuse the certificate. Despite this omission, satisfactory reasons will be needed by the police. That said, the threshold to demonstrate good reason for having a shotgun certificate is generally somewhat lower than the corresponding requirement to demonstrate good reason for having a firearm certificate.

4.08   The certificate will list particulars of the shotguns to be covered by it and provide for entries to be made when a gun is transferred (including the identification numbers if known).[18]

---

14   The term 'private premises' is not defined in the Firearms Acts, though the word 'premises' includes any land (FA 1968, s 57(4)), and 'land' includes land covered with water (IA 1978, s 5 and Sch 1). Contrasting the term with 'public place', discussed in Chapter 15, it is suggested that it means any land, water or buildings other than those to which the public are admitted with or without payment.

15   It remains for the courts to decide how near to you the occupier must be when you are using a gun. Meanwhile, it is suggested that if the occupier is at your side or perhaps in the same shoot as yourself the condition is fulfilled, but not otherwise. Further, 'occupier' ought to include the occupier's agents, such as a gamekeeper.

16   See para 3.48 *et seq*, 'Authorised lending of firearms and shotguns on private premises' for full details.

17   FA 1968, ss 7(1), 8(1), 9(1), 11(1), (2), 12(1), 13(1), 54, 57(4); F(A)A 1988, ss 16(1), 17(1), 18(1), 19, 25(1). As to visitors' shotgun permits, see Chapter 7.

18   FA 1968, s 28(2A); Firearms Rules 1998, r 5(6) and Sch 2, Part II.

4.09   Except in the cases mentioned in para 4.20, where the police cannot issue a certificate, a certificate will be issued to you if the police are satisfied that you can be permitted to possess a shotgun without danger to the public safety or to the peace.[19]

'DANGER TO PUBLIC SAFETY OR THE PEACE'

4.10   This test applies to shotgun certificates and to registration as a firearms dealer, where in both cases it is the major consideration with regards to public safety, and applies to firearm certificates as well, although with those there is an additional test of being 'unfitted to be entrusted with a firearm'.

4.11   This criterion has been judicially considered on a number of occasions. In a 1974 case it was held that it was right to refuse a certificate if there was a danger of the gun being misused in such a way that good order is disturbed, and poaching with the gun was cited as an example of that, but in 1978 a court decided that it was wrong to refuse a certificate on the grounds of a previous poaching conviction.[20]

4.12   In the leading case of *Ackers and Others v Taylor*[21] (a case regarding some poachers) Ashworth J established the following principles on the second part of the test in section 30A(2)(b) of the FA 1968:

(a)   When the chief constable exercises his discretion in considering the revocation of a firearms or shotgun certificate he is involved in a branch of preventative justice as part of his discretionary powers over the maintenance of order and the preservation of the peace (410–411).

(b)   The chief officer of police 'should consider whether there is a danger that the gun may be misused in such a way that good order is disturbed or that there is a risk of that happening' (410 H).

(c)   'Danger to the public peace may be expressed as involving disturbance to good order' (411 B).

(d)   The danger to the peace must arise out of the possession or use or misuse of the shotgun, which the chief officer of police must consider' (410 E–F).

(e)   It is wrong to limit the discretion of the chief officer of police to the possibility of the misuse of the firearm/shotgun in the circumstances of violence (410 F–G).

---

[19]   FA 1968, s 28(1); F(A)A 1988, s 3(1).

[20]   *R v Wakefield Crown Court, ex parte Oldfield* [1978] Crim LR 164.

[21]   *Ackers and Others v Taylor* [1974] 1 WLR 405, page references are to this report; [1974] 1 All ER 771.

In *Spencer-Stewart v Chief Constable of Kent*,[22] Bingham LJ agreed that 'preventative justice' in *Ackers* did not mean waiting until a firearm or shotgun was misused but gauging the likelihood of 'misbehaviour with a shotgun [or firearm]' by examining other behaviour (such as drink driving or drunkenness generally) and acting accordingly. This was because 'if there were evidence of a man who was given to gross bouts of drunkenness, there might very well be room for the conclusion that he was not a safe man to be entrusted with a shotgun'. *Spencer-Stewart* was in fact a case regarding an applicant who had more than one conviction for handling stolen goods. He may have been dishonest, but where was the evidence to suggest he would be a danger with a shotgun? The previous convictions did not provide a basis for that belief.

4.13   In *Chief Constable of Essex v Germain*,[23] Stuart-Smith LJ held that the Chief Constable is entitled to take account of 'irresponsible and uncontrolled' behaviour generally when assessing whether an appellant had the necessary 'self-control and proper discipline and restraint' to be permitted to possess a shotgun (in that case the certificate holder had three convictions for drink driving in a period of 5 years).

4.14   From these decisions in the cases discussed in the preceding paragraphs, and one other court decision in 1980,[24] clearer guidance in general terms emerged, which may be summarised as follows:

(a)   It is not necessary, in order to justify a refusal or revocation, for there to be a possibility of dangerous misuse.[25]

(b)   The police must give individual consideration to each case.[26]

(c)   It is right for the police to take account of the applicant's irresponsibility in other activities,[27] but if he has committed offences which do not involve the slightest risk or likelihood of the use of a shotgun, there are no grounds for refusal.[28]

---

[22]   [1989] Cr App R 307, [1989] COD 372.

[23]   [1991] 156 JP 109, [1991] 4 Admin LR 237, [1991] COD 385.

[24]   *Luke v Little* 1980 SLT (Sh Ct) 138, a case in which the applicant had been convicted three times for drunken driving.

[25]   *R v Wakefield Crown Court, ex parte Oldfield* [1978] Crim LR 164.

[26]   *R v Wakefield Crown Court, ex parte Oldfield* [1978] Crim LR 164.

[27]   *Luke v Little* 1980 SLT (Sh Ct) 138, a case in which the applicant had been convicted three times for drunken driving.

[28]   *Spencer-Stewart v Chief Constable of Kent* [1989] Cr App R 307, [1989] COD 372.

The application of these principles is perhaps most neatly demonstrated in a more recent judgment of the High Court. In the appeal of *Shepherd*,[29] the certificate holder had two unlicensed pistols and ammunition at his home address. He had been unable to bring himself to part with his handguns when the 1997 ban came in and had hidden them at home. Burton J concluded that he was therefore 'unfitted' to be granted a firearm certificate. He went on:

> 13.   Likewise, in relation to a shotgun the chief officer of police must be satisfied that the holder cannot be permitted to possess a shotgun without 'danger to the public safety or to the peace'. Quite apart from reference to Ackers, it seems to me that there was no evidence in this case that there was any risk either to public safety or to the peace from the facts found in relation to Mr Shepherd. He is not suggested to have any propensity towards anger or violence. He is not suggested to be at risk, as it was put in the Spencer-Stewart case, of misusing the guns, and the items that were found without a licence at his home address were all concealed, some of them very well concealed, according to paragraphs 3 and 8 of the case stated.
> 14.   In those circumstances, it appears to me that there was no evidence upon which the conclusion could be reached that there was a risk of 'danger to the public safety or to the peace' by virtue of the facts found against the appellant. Therefore, I uphold the revocation of the firearms certificate within section 30A(2)(a) but I discharge the revocation of the shotgun certificate under section 30C(1).

4.15   This is an important clarification of the law and analysis of the test which the police considering applications and revocations, and the courts hearing licensing appeals should keep well in mind. A number of licensing departments seem to equate previous convictions of any sort as indicating that a person is 'unsuitable' to hold a certificate. That is not the test; the test is 'would that person's possession of firearms represent a danger to public safety?' A deputy chief constable recently expressed the view to one of the authors that 'anyone on the sex offenders register should not hold a firearm or shotgun certificate'. Whatever one might think about some sex offences and offenders, that bare assertion has no basis in law. How does that necessarily demonstrate danger with a gun? A refusal to grant or a revocation of a certificate is not some additional form of punishment for a criminal offence or other perceived bad behaviour. The courts impose an appropriate sentence, and if it fulfils the criteria, the person concerned becomes prohibited from possessing firearms,[30] either for 5 years, or for life. It is not for the licensing system to add to that regime laid down by Parliament.

---

[29]   *Shepherd v Chief Constable of Devon & Cornwall* [2002] EWHC 1653 (Admin), [2002] LLR 745.

[30]   This generally arises when you have been sentenced by a court to various punishments other than a fine. For full details, see para 5.60 *et seq*, 'Prohibited persons – applications to remove a prohibition under section 21'. In addition, if you are under 18, you are prohibited from possessing a shotgun in many cases; for details, see Chapter 14.

4.16   All of these authorities were recently summarised in the case of *R (Mason) v Crown Court at Winchester*,[31] except the case of *Shepherd* to which they do not seem to have been referred. Paragraphs [27] to [34] of *Mason* are a useful summary of the tests to be applied and the case gives some guidance on appeals procedure; see further Chapter 5.

4.17   We could summarise the position by posing this question: Looking at the evidence objectively, does it demonstrate that the person in question lacks self-control or proper responsibility, or are there likely to be circumstances arising where a firearm could be misused by him?

4.18   The word 'likely' is included in the question because the police or the court must be satisfied that there is a real risk of danger. It cannot be a theoretical or fanciful risk, or no one would have a certificate. There will always be some risk associated with firearms, for obvious reasons.

4.19   Further analysis of cases where these issues have arisen are considered in Chapter 5.

4.20   The cases in which the police cannot issue a shotgun certificate are if:

(a)   they have reason to believe that you are prohibited by FA 1968 from possessing a shotgun; or

(b)   they are satisfied that you do not have a good reason for possessing, purchasing or acquiring[32] a shotgun.[33]

You will be regarded, in particular,[34] as having a good reason if the gun is intended to be used for sporting or competition purposes or for shooting vermin. An application is not to be refused by virtue of item (b) merely because you intend neither to use the gun yourself nor to lend it for anyone else to use.[35]

4.21   Special provision is made about good reasons for youngsters under 18.[36] Although in a different terminology, this duplicates the provision made in relation to firearm certificates.

---

[31]   [2018] EWHC 1182 (Admin), [2018] 1 WLR 3850.

[32]   'Acquire' is defined to mean hire, accept as a gift or borrow (FA 1968, s 57(4)).

[33]   FA 1968, s 28(1A); F(A)A 1988, s 3(1).

[34]   The use of the words 'in particular' indicates that the purposes mentioned are to be accepted as good reasons, and that other purposes may also be accepted.

[35]   FA 1968, s 28(1B); F(A)A 1988, s 3(1). Work that one out! Presumably this would apply where the gun is an heirloom or has some other sentimental value.

[36]   FA 1968, s 28(1C). For the general rules applying to youngsters, see Chapter 14.

4.22 Arrangements may be made for shotgun certificates and firearm certificates to be coterminous;[37] see para 3.54, fn 108 and para 3.94.

WHAT ELSE SHOULD I KNOW ABOUT SHOTGUN CERTIFICATES?

4.23 A fundamental difference between a shotgun certificate and a firearm certificate is that once granted a shotgun certificate authorises acquisition and possession of an unlimited number of shotguns, the only requirement being that their acquisition is notified to police in the approved manner.[38] Note the comment at para 4.24. No notification or entry on the certificate is required, however, if the loan or hire is for 72 hours or less.[39] The seller should enter the gun onto the buyer's certificate if it is a 'private' sale.

THE POSSESSION OFFENCE IN RELATION TO SHOTGUNS

4.24 Because a shotgun certificate permits possession of an unlimited number of shotguns, someone who holds a shotgun certificate can lawfully have any shotgun in his possession. This may seem an obvious point, but it needs to be made, as it is not uncommon for police to charge a shotgun certificate holder with unlawful possession where a particular gun has not been entered upon his certificate. The certificate holder, and/or the seller, may have committed offences in failing to notify the police of the sale or acquisition of the gun, but the certificate holder will not be in unlawful possession.

4.25 Shotgun certificates will be issued subject to six conditions. Unlike firearm certificates, the police may not add further conditions.[40] The six conditions are:

(a) the conditions listed in items (a) to (e) in para 3.87, 'Conditions imposed upon firearm certificates' except that conditions (d) and (e) apply solely to the shotguns themselves and cannot be applied to shotgun ammunition;

---

[37] F(A)A 1988, s 11. See para 3.92 *et seq*, 'What else should I know about firearm certificates?' for further information.

[38] Usually by recorded delivery and within 7 days of the transaction. F(A)A 1997, s 33.

[39] F(A)A 1997, s 32. All transfers of firearms and shotguns must be in person. See para 3.102 *et seq* for further details.

[40] FA 1968, s 28(2)(a).

(b)   that, where a shotgun disguised as another object is possessed, purchased or acquired[41] for the purpose only of a collection, it shall be used for that purpose only.[42]

Failure to comply with any condition is an offence.[43]

4.26   A shotgun certificate will give the descriptions of the shotguns to which it relates (including, if known, the identification numbers of the guns), the makers' names and the gauge or calibre of the guns. A photograph of the holder will be affixed to it. The certificate will also provide for entries to be made in it recording details of any sale or other transfer of a shotgun to the certificate holder.[44]

4.27   The certificate will last for 5 years,[45] unless previously revoked by the police or cancelled by the court,[46] and may be renewed every 5 years for the same period by completing another application form.[47] A renewal may be refused for the same reasons as the grant of the original certificate may be refused.[48]

4.28   Fees are payable for the grant and renewal of a certificate, and a lower fee is charged for the replacement of a certificate which has been lost or destroyed.[49]

---

[41]   'Acquire' is defined to mean hire, accept as a gift or borrow (FA 1968, s 57(4)).

[42]   Firearms Rules 1998, r 5(4), (5).

[43]   The maximum punishment on summary conviction is imprisonment for 6 months, or an unlimited fine, or both (FA 1968, ss 2(2), 51(1), (2) and Sch 6, Part I).

[44]   FA 1968, s 28(2A); F(A)A 1988, s 3(2); Firearms Rules 1998, r 5(6) and Sch 2, Part II. For the requirements imposed on a transferor of a shotgun to a certificate holder, see para 3.102 *et seq*, 'Transfer, deactivation and loss or destruction of section 1 firearms and ammunition'.

[45]   The 5-year period applies to certificates granted or renewed after 1 January 1995. Formerly, the period was 3 years (FA 1968, ss 26(3), (3A), (3B), 28A(1)); Firearms (Period of Certificate) Order 1994; Firearms (Amendment) Rules 1994. The period may be further revised by Home Office order (FA 1968, s 28A(3)).

[46]   See para 3.92 *et seq*, 'What else should I know about firearm certificates?' for the circumstances in which a certificate can be cancelled by a court.

[47]   FA 1968, s 28A(1); Firearms Rules 1998, r 5(1) and Sch 2, Part I. The same form is used for original applications and for renewals. In the latter case, the application is to be accompanied by the certificate to be renewed, if it is available.

[48]   FA 1968, s 28(1), (1A).

[49]   FA 1968, s 32(1), as amended by the Firearms (Variation of Fees) Order 2015 (SI 2015/611). Currently it is £79.50 for a first application ('grant') for a shotgun certificate and for a renewal it is £49. If you apply for a firearm certificate at the same time ('coterminous certificates') it is £90 for the grant of both, and £65 for the renewal.

4.29   The police may revoke your shotgun certificate if they are satisfied that you are prohibited by FA 1968 from possessing your gun[50] or that you cannot be permitted to possess it without danger to the public safety or to the peace.[51] You may appeal to the Crown Court against a revocation.[52]

4.30   The rules which are applicable in the case of firearm certificates to cancellations, appeals,[53] surrenders on revocation or cancellation, false statements to obtain certificates, production of false certificates and impersonation, and production of certificates to the police apply equally to shotgun certificates.[54]

TRANSFER, DEACTIVATION AND LOSS OR DESTRUCTION OF SHOTGUNS AND THEIR AMMUNITION

4.31   Many of the restrictions on transferring section 1 firearms and their ammunition, which were considered at para 3.102 *et seq* apply, some with modifications, to the transfer of shotguns and their ammunition. These restrictions and modifications are as follows:

(a)   The sale or other transfer of firearms generally, but this does not apply to shotgun ammunition. The certificate required to be produced in the case of shotguns is a shotgun certificate.[55]

(b)   The sale, transfer and other dealings with firearms and ammunition by way of trade or business, but this does not apply to shotgun ammunition.[56] It does, however, apply to component parts of shotguns and accessories for diminishing their noise or flash.[57]

---

[50]   This generally arises when you have been sentenced by a court to various punishments other than a fine. For full details, see para 5.60 *et seq*, 'Prohibited persons – applications to remove a prohibition under section 21'. In addition, if you are under 18, you are prohibited from possessing a shotgun in many cases; for details, see paras 14.21 to 14.23.

[51]   FA 1968, s 30C(1). For a discussion about this danger, see para 4.06 *et seq*, 'How do I get a shotgun certificate?'. Strangely, the police are given no power to revoke if you cease to have a good reason for having the shotgun, despite it being grounds for refusing the certificate in the first instance. Also, a firearm certificate may be revoked on this basis: see Chapter 5

[52]   FA 1968, ss 30C(2), 44. For further details about appeals, see Chapter 5.

[53]   Except that there can be no variation by the police of a shotgun certificate and thus no question of an appeal against such a variation arising.

[54]   FA 1968, ss 3(5), 28A(6), (7), 30C(2), 30D(1), 44(1), 48, 52, 58(5); F(A)A 1988, s 12. As to these rules, see Chapters 3 and 5.

[55]   FA 1968, s 3(2). See para 3.102 *et seq* for details.

[56]   FA 1968, s 3(1). See para 3.102 (b) *et seq* for details.

[57]   FA 1968, ss 3(1), 57(4).

(c) The sale or other transfer of firearms and ammunition to persons who are drunk or of unsound mind.[58]

(d) The sale or transfer of firearms or ammunition to, or the repair, testing or proof for, persons prohibited from possessing firearms or ammunition.[59]

(e) In addition to the exceptions noted above, it is also permissible to return to a person a shotgun which another person has lawfully undertaken to repair, test or prove for that person.[60]

4.32 As with section 1 firearms and their ammunition, the F(A)A 1997 has added provisions requiring notice to be given to the police about some kinds of transfer of shotguns and about their deactivation, loss or destruction. These provisions[61] are very similar to those relating to firearms at para 3.104 *et seq* and are not repeated in full here. It is sufficient, for the purpose of applying those provisions to shotguns, to make the following adjustments:

(a) for references to lending, substitute references to lending for more than 72 hours;

(b) for references to firearms, substitute references to shotguns;

(c) for references to firearm certificates, substitute references to shotgun certificates;

(d) for references to visitors' firearm permits, substitute references to visitors' shotgun permits.[62]

SHOTGUN AMMUNITION

4.33 In relation to the possession and storage of shotgun ammunition, there are a couple of important distinctions as compared with section 1 ammunition. Firstly, there is no obligation to store shotgun ammunition securely in the way that there is with section 1 ammunition, although it is still recommended that reasonable precautions are taken.[63] Secondly, while it is illegal to possess section 1 ammunition without holding a firearm certificate, there is no corresponding requirement to have a shotgun certificate in order to possess shotgun ammunition. However, restrictions do apply to the sale and purchase of

---

[58] FA 1968, s 25. See point (c) in the list at para 3.102 for details.

[59] FA 1968, s 21(5).

[60] FA 1968, s 8(2)(b).

[61] These provisions replace and extend those formerly contained in F(A)A 1988, s 4.

[62] F(A)A 1997, ss 32–35. Failure to comply with the requirements about notices relating to shotguns is an offence with a maximum punishment on summary conviction of 6 months' imprisonment, or an unlimited fine, or both (F(A)A 1997, s 36(b)).

[63] For further guidance on storage, see Chapter 8 on security of firearms.

ammunition which is not section 1 ammunition[64] *and* which is capable of being used in a shotgun *or* in a smooth-bore gun to which that section applies.[65]

4.34   You will commit an offence[66] if you sell any such ammunition to a person in the UK[67] who is neither an RFD[68] nor a person who sells it by way of trade or business, unless that other person:

(a)   produces a firearm or shotgun certificate which authorises him to possess a shotgun or a smooth-bore gun to which section 1 applies; or

(b)   shows that he is entitled[69] to possess such a gun without holding such a certificate; or

(c)   produces such a certificate which authorises another person to possess such a gun, together with that person's written authority to buy the ammunition on his behalf.[70]

There are special restrictions on the handling of shotguns and their ammunition by young people under the age of 18; these are considered in Chapter 14.

4.35   Note that transferring shotgun ammunition by way of gift is not controlled.

WORK ON SHOTGUNS AND THEIR AMMUNITION

4.36   All of the restrictions about carrying out work on section 1 firearms and their ammunition, which were considered at para 3.109 *et seq*, 'Work on section 1 firearms and ammunition', apply to shotguns and their ammunition, but with one exception and one modification:

(a)   The restrictions on shortening shotgun barrels where the gun comes within section 1 do not apply, but for similar restrictions on shotguns which are not section 1 firearms, see below.

---

[64]   See para 3.12 for what constitutes section 1 ammunition.

[65]   For smooth-bore guns within this description, see para 4.01 *et seq*.

[66]   The offence is punishable on summary conviction by a maximum of 6 months' imprisonment, or an unlimited fine, or both (F(A)A 1988, s 5(3)).

[67]   'United Kingdom' means England, Wales, Scotland and Northern Ireland, and excludes the Channel Islands and the Isle of Man.

[68]   As to the registration of firearms dealers, see Chapter 16.

[69]   For the cases where he would be so entitled, see para 3.22 *et seq*, 'Exceptions from the need to hold a firearm certificate'.

[70]   F(A)A 1988, s 5(1), (2).

(b)   In the case of a shotgun being loaned in accordance with section 11A, the certificate to be produced will be a shotgun certificate.[71]

It is an offence[72] to shorten the barrel of a shotgun to a length of less than 24 inches;[73] but an RFD[74] may do so for the sole purpose of replacing a defective part of the barrel so as to produce a barrel of not less than that length.[75]

PURCHASES IN THE EUROPEAN COMMUNITY

4.37   Regulations made to implement the European Weapons Directive contain detailed provisions about buying shotguns and their ammunition in other Member States of the European Community.[76] The holder of a firearm or shotgun certificate in the UK is entitled to also have issued to him a European Firearms Pass. For further details, see Chapter 7.

---

[71]   FA 1968, ss 3(1), (3), 4(3), 25.

[72]   The maximum punishment on summary conviction is imprisonment for 6 months, or an unlimited fine, or both; or, on indictment, 7 years' imprisonment, or an unlimited fine, or both (FA 1968, s 4(1), 51(1), (2) and Sch 6, Part I).

[73]   This length is measured from the muzzle to the point at which the charge is exploded on firing (FA 1968, s 57(6)(a); F(A)A 1988, s 25(1)).

[74]   As to the registration of firearms dealers, see Chapter 16.

[75]   FA 1968, s 4(1), (2).

[76]   Details of the provisions may be found in the Firearms Acts (Amendment) Regulations 1992, regs 5 and 9, which inserted ss 18A, 32A, 32B and 32C into the FA 1968.

Chapter 5

Refusal, Revocation and Appeal

5.01   This chapter deals with both firearm and shotgun certificates as, following the F(A)A 1988, the criteria for obtaining a certificate are very similar, save that the 'good reason' for requiring shotguns is less onerous than that for firearms. Firearms law is the same across Great Britain (but not Northern Ireland) and what is said here will generally apply to Scotland as it does to England and Wales. Scottish readers and lawyers may wish to consider the judgment in a Scottish case[1] to be aware of some differences in the procedure relating to appeals north of the border. The appeal process also covers the certificate of registration as a firearms dealer (RFD). Where there are differences, they are identified, but in general the following applies to both types of certificate and an RFD.

REFUSAL AND REVOCATION

5.02   The police are entitled to refuse to grant or renew, or to revoke, your certificate in the following five instances:

(a)   If they have reason to believe that you are of intemperate habits or unsound mind or are otherwise unfitted to be entrusted with a firearm.[2]

(b)   If they have reason to believe that you can no longer be permitted to have the firearm or ammunition to which the certificate relates in your possession without danger to the public safety or to the peace.[3]

(c)   If they are satisfied that you are prohibited by the FA 1968 from possessing a section 1 firearm.[4]

---

[1]   *Luke v Little* 1980 SLT 138, Sheriff Kermack.

[2]   FA 1968, s 30A(1), (2)(a).

[3]   FA 1968, ss 30A(1), (2)(b), and 34(2) for RFDs. For a commentary on the meaning of 'danger to the public safety or to the peace', see para 5.39 and in detail at para 4.10 *et seq*.

[4]   FA 1968, s 30A(1), (3). This arises if you have been given certain punishments by the courts; see para 5.60 *et seq*, 'Prohibited persons – applications to remove a prohibition under section 21'. For the definition of a section 1 firearm, see paras 1.05 and 3.01 *et seq*.

(d)   If they are satisfied that you do not have, or no longer have, a good reason[5] for possessing, or for buying or acquiring,[6] the firearm or ammunition which you are authorised by the certificate to possess, purchase or acquire.[7]

(e)   If you fail to comply with a notice from the police requiring you to deliver the certificate to them for variation of its conditions.[8]

With regard to shotgun certificates, and also dealers, the only statutory criteria for refusal or revocation are grounds (b) and (c) in the above list. In relation to an RFD, the police can further refuse to register, or de-register you, if they are satisfied that you will not engage in business to 'a substantial extent' or 'as an essential part of another trade business or profession'.[9] The registration of firearms dealers, and refusal thereof, is considered in more detail in Chapter 16.

5.03   The FA 1968 now provides for the partial revocation of firearm certificates. The police may partially revoke your certificate if satisfied that you no longer have a good reason for possessing, buying or acquiring[10] the firearm or ammunition to which the partial revocation relates.[11]

5.04   If your certificate is revoked for any of the reasons given in grounds (a) to (d) above, the police may by written notice require you to surrender to them forthwith the certificate and any firearms and ammunition in your possession by virtue of it.[12] Failure to do so is an offence.[13]

5.05   Where your firearm certificate is partially revoked, the police notice will require the surrender of the certificate alone (so it can be varied), and failure to

---

[5]   As a ground for revocation, this only applies to firearm certificates and bizarrely not to shotgun certificates, despite the requirement to demonstrate good reason to acquire a shotgun certificate in the first place. For a commentary about 'good reason', see para 3.78 *et seq*. This applies to firearms, but see the comments as to 'good reason' in relation to shotguns at para 4.20 *et seq* and para 4.29, fn 52.

[6]   'Acquire' is defined to mean hire, accept as a gift or borrow (FA 1968, s 57(4); F(A)A 1988, s 25(1)).

[7]   FA 1968, s 30A (1), (4).

[8]   FA 1968, s 30A(1), (5). For such a notice, see further para 3.87 *et seq*, 'Conditions imposed upon firearm certificates'.

[9]   FA 1968, s 34(1A).

[10]   'Acquire' is defined to mean hire, accept as a gift or borrow (FA 1968, s 57(4), F(A)A 1988, s 25(1)).

[11]   FA 1968, s 30B(1), (2).

[12]   F(A)A 1988, s 12(1); FA 1968, s 30D(5).

[13]   The maximum punishment on summary conviction is 3 months' imprisonment, or a fine at level 4 on the standard scale (currently £2,500), or both (F(A)A 1988, s 12(2)).

do so within 21 days from the date of the notice is an offence.[14] If you appeal against partial revocation, the requirement to surrender your firearm certificate is suspended, unless the appeal is abandoned or dismissed, when the 21-day period will instead run from the date of such abandonment or dismissal.[15]

5.06   There is also a right of appeal where the police refuse to grant a variation of your firearm certificate for which you have applied,[16] i.e. to acquire additional firearm(s) and/or calibres/quantities of ammunition. This will usually arise where the police are not satisfied you have demonstrated good reason for the additional firearm(s)/ammunition you wish to acquire.

5.07   However, it should be noted that there is no provision in the Firearms Acts to appeal against a decision of the police to impose or vary conditions on a firearm certificate, nor against the police refusal of an application to vary or remove firearm certificate conditions. By contrast, the law does provide RFDs with a right of appeal against the imposition or variation of conditions on their certificate, or the refusal of the police to grant the dealer's application for removal or variation of any such conditions.[17]

5.08   Further, where any firearm certificate is revoked because of the failure of the holder to comply with a 21-day notice requiring him to surrender his certificate for the conditions to be amended, there is no right of appeal against such revocation. Consequently, if the police notify you that they require you to surrender your firearm certificate for the purpose of amending the conditions, you would be well advised to comply, irrespective of your view on the reasonableness or otherwise of the additional or varied conditions to be imposed. While it would of course be open to you to reapply following such a revocation, and to appeal if your application were refused, the police could then rely on your failure to co-operate with the licensing authority by not complying with the notice to surrender, and indeed that this amounts to a criminal offence, even if they did not actually prosecute you for it.

5.09   In relation to those police decisions which are not susceptible to appeal in the Crown Court, it would be possible to challenge them by way of 'judicial review' if it were totally unreasonable, for example, to have imposed such a condition in the circumstances. However, judicial review in the High Court is

---

[14]   FA 1968, s 30D (1)–(3), (5). In a case of partial revocation, the police will amend the certificate and return it to you. The maximum punishment on summary conviction is a fine at level 3 on the standard scale (currently £1,000) (FA 1968, s 51(1), (2), Sch 6, Part I).

[15]   FA 1968, s 30D(4).

[16]   FA 1968, s 29(2).

[17]   FA 1968, s 36(3).

usually a far more costly process of litigation, and is therefore best avoided if at all possible.

5.10   Whatever the reasons for the refusal or revocation, the police 'must give reasons for their decision'.[18] It is expected this will normally be in writing as part of the revocation notice and this letter is an important document which you should keep. Firearms licensing departments should always have the possibility of an appeal in mind and set out clearly in the letter the precise grounds on which they are refusing or revoking, not merely by reciting one or more of the statutory criteria, but with specific reference to the particular circumstances of the individual case. A failure to do so may be the subject of criticism by the court and may give rise to costs implications. The letter should advise you as to your right of appeal and will usually indicate the relevant Crown Court.

5.11   The police are also required to notify you in writing when varying a condition of a firearm certificate, and when requiring you to surrender a firearm certificate or shotgun certificate, or firearms and ammunition where your certificate has been revoked by them or cancelled by order of the court. The same applies to notices served on an RFD notifying an intention to remove from the register or requiring the dealer to surrender his certificate of registration.[19] You are well advised to keep all such correspondence from the police.

5.12   In most cases the police are not keen on seizing the weapons themselves (unless they think they are exhibits in a serious criminal allegation) and are usually content to allow your firearms and ammunition to be held by an RFD or another certificate holder nominated by you if that is possible. If you successfully appeal against the revocation, your certificate(s) will be returned to you, along with any firearms and ammunition held by the police. If the appeal is dismissed, the court has the power to make an order for their disposal, but this is unheard of in our experience. If no appeal is made, or an appeal is abandoned, the firearms and ammunition will be disposed of in such a manner as may be agreed between you and the police. In default of agreement, the police may decide on the method of disposal; but their decision must be notified to you and may itself be appealed against to the Crown Court. The court may either dismiss your appeal[20] or make its own order for disposal.[21]

---

[18]   See *Guide*, paras 10.39 and 10.73 re firearm certificates and also 11.50 re shotgun certificates, which is similarly worded.

[19]   For all these notices see variously FA 1968, ss 29(1), 30A, 52(2)(b), 38(6) and 38(8).

[20]   In which case the police decision on disposal stands.

[21]   FA 1968, s 44; F(A)A 1988, s 12(3)–(5). You should consult a solicitor if you are considering an appeal of either kind.

5.13   If you are unfortunate enough to be convicted of certain offences or be given certain punishments[22] by a court, the court may cancel your firearm certificate or shotgun certificate and registration as a dealer and order any firearm or ammunition found in your possession[23] to be forfeited or disposed of. You must then, under threat of a further penalty,[24] surrender the certificate to the police within 21 days from the date of a notice from them to that effect. Firearms and ammunition so forfeited may be seized and detained by the police who can, if the court so orders, destroy or otherwise dispose of them.[25]

THE PROCESS OF APPEAL

5.14   Within 21 days from receiving the decision of the police to revoke, you may appeal to your local Crown Court (or the Sheriff in Scotland). Note that this 21-day time limit within which to appeal commences from the date you actually received the police letter notifying you of the revocation or other decision, and not from the date printed on the letter, which can sometimes be days or even weeks earlier. If you intend to appeal, you must give notice in writing to the police and the Crown Court, briefly setting out your reasons for challenging the police decision, and we would advise you to notify them as soon as possible. However, in practice most police forces do not attempt to enforce this time limit strictly; if a certificate holder is 'out of time' in lodging an appeal, all he would need to do is make a fresh application and, when that is refused, appeal again. This would be

---

[22]   The offences are any under FA 1968 or the F(A)A 1988 and F(A)A 1997, except an offence under FA 1968, s 22(3), or offences relating specifically to air weapons. The punishments are, briefly: imprisonment; detention in a young offender institution; detention in a detention centre or in a young offender institution in Scotland; an order to enter into a recognisance to keep the peace or to be of good behaviour, a condition of which is that the offender shall not possess, use or carry a firearm; and probation with a requirement that the offender shall not possess, use or carry a firearm (FA 1968, s 52(1); F(A)A 1988, s 25(5); F(A)A 1997, s 50(4)).

[23]   The time of this finding is not specified. It is suggested that this must be at, or very shortly after, the commission of the offence for which one of the punishments in fn 22 has been given.

[24]   The maximum fine on summary conviction is at level 3 on the standard scale (currently £1,000) (FA 1968, s 51(1), (2) and Sch 6, Part I).

[25]   FA 1968, s 52(2)–(4). The statements in this paragraph are qualified in the following cases:

   (a) In the case of air weapon offences and in the case of the offence of giving a shotgun or ammunition to a person under 15 (see Chapter 14), the court's power to order forfeiture or disposal extends to guns and ammunition in respect of which the offence was committed as well as to those found in the convicted person's possession.

   (b) In the case of air weapon offences, in the case of illegal possession of a shotgun by a person under 15, and in the case of any shotgun or ammunition in respect of which the offence of giving them to a person under 15 is committed, there is no power given to the police by the Act (though they may otherwise have it) to seize and detain either kind of gun or, subsequently, on the court's order, to destroy or otherwise dispose of them (FA 1968, ss 51(3), 52(2)–(4), 57(3), 58(4) and Sch 6, Part I, and Part II, paras 7–9).

a waste of everybody's time! Firearms licensing appeals are sometimes referred to as 'section 44 appeals' since that is the relevant section of the FA 1968. If you have any dealings with the Crown Court about your appeal you will probably need to make this clear, or they will think you are appealing a criminal conviction or sentence from a magistrates' court, which is a quite different procedure.

5.15   When hearing the appeal the court may consider any evidence or other matter, whether or not it was available when the police decision to revoke was made.[26] An appeal to the Crown Court in England and Wales is heard by a judge[27] sitting together with two magistrates, and to the Sheriff in Scotland.[28] They sit to exercise an administrative function left over from Quarter Sessions. When you notify the police and the court that you intend to appeal, the police should then provide you with the evidence they have as to why they have refused or revoked your certificate. If this has not been done by the time the matter comes before the court for a preliminary hearing the court may well order the police to serve their evidence within a given time. The court does not always require the appellant (the certificate holder) to serve his evidence in advance, but it is good practice and it is preferable that the court have an opportunity to consider the evidence from both sides in writing before the hearing. See *Mason*, referred to at para 5.23 *et seq*.

A SECTION 44 APPEAL IS 'ON THE MERITS'

5.16   Under section 44, these are civil proceedings and the Crown Court is sitting in its appellate jurisdiction. The burden of proof is on the respondent to satisfy the court that on the balance of probability the decision to revoke was and remains 'correct' (section 44(2)). The appeal shall be determined on the merits, by way of a rehearing, not a review, and the Crown Court must place itself in the position of the chief officer and make a fresh decision, applying its own discretion, based upon the evidence currently presented to the Crown Court, including any relevant new material adduced during the appeal hearing. The court does not have to give any weight to the fact that the chief officer refused or revoked the certificate if this court feels that it is not appropriate to do so. This was confirmed in *Chief Constable of Norfolk v Edwards*,[29] where Brooke LJ, giving the judgment

---

[26]   FA 1968, s 44(1), (3), Sch 5, Part I, para 2.

[27]   It was said in a recent case that it was 'unfair' to expect Recorders to hear firearms licensing appeals, they should only be heard by full-time circuit judges except with the consent of the presiding judge: *The Chief Constable of the Essex Police v Donald Campbell* [2012] EWHC 2331(Admin), [2012] LLR 835. It is doubtful that a failure to abide by this advice renders the appeal invalid, but any objection to a Recorder hearing the matter ought to be raised at the outset of the hearing.

[28]   See FA 1968, Sch 5, Part II for the provisions relating to appeal.

[29]   *Chief Constable of Norfolk v Edwards* [1997] EWCA Admin 294, DC.

of the Divisional Court quoted with approval the speech of Lord Atkin in *Evans v Bartlam*:[30]

> I wish to state my conviction that where there is a discretionary jurisdiction given to the Court or a judge the judge in Chambers is in no way fettered by the previous exercise of the Master's discretion. His own discretion is intended by the rules to determine the parties' rights: and he is entitled to exercise it as though the matter came before him for the first time. He will, of course, give the weight it deserves to the previous decision of the Master: but he is in no way bound by it.

Brooke LJ went on to observe:

> In my judgment exactly the same principle applies to a judgment of the Crown Court in the exercise of its discretion on an appeal from a decision by a Chief Constable in the exercise of his discretion under the Firearms Act. The Crown Court is of course bound to give appropriate weight to the decision of the Chief Constable and to pay serious attention to the reasons that he has given, but in the last resort the decision is that of the Crown Court and not that of the Chief Constable.

5.17   Further confirmation, if it were needed, that this is the position, and that there is no onus on the appellant in any way to demonstrate that the original decision taken by the respondent was incorrect, is provided by the amendments to section 44 of the FA 1968 set out in section 41(2) and (3) of the F(A)A 1997:

(2)   An appeal shall be determined on the merits (and not by way of review).

(3)   The court or sheriff hearing an appeal may consider any evidence or other matter, whether or not it was available when the decision of the chief officer was taken.

This amendment puts this issue beyond question. This court will hear different evidence and see different material to that considered by the chief officer. It follows that the court must make its decision on the material presented to it in this hearing. Parliament clearly intended the court to see the material before the chief officer, but not necessarily attach any weight to his decision.

5.18   It is not unknown for counsel representing the respondent to argue that the fact that the chief officer of police has already refused or revoked the certificate can be taken in to account in the respondent's favour. That may be a principle which applies in some other types of licensing appeals, but not in relation to firearms.

---

[30]   *Evans v Bartlam* [1937] AC 473.

THESE ARE *INTER PARTES* PROCEEDINGS

5.19   Unlike the criminal cases which are the usual work of the Crown Court, appeals under section 44 of the Act are administrative cases between the parties. Either side can withdraw their case at any stage. This is implicit in the wording of paragraph 4 of Schedule 5 to the FA 1968 which set out the procedure for such appeals and permits the appellant to withdraw the appeal up to 2 days before the hearing of the matter is listed.

5.20   The chief constable may be presented with further evidence or information which alters his view about whether there is any longer a danger to public safety, whether the applicant now has a good reason for a particular firearm, and so on. Similarly, an appellant might withdraw his appeal in the light of new information.

5.21   We have known some licensing departments to say: 'We have revoked the certificate now and we can't reverse the decision'. The department may not wish to change their mind, but we see no legal basis for the assertion that they cannot go back on their earlier decision. After all, the police are the licensing authority and so, provided they act within the law and exercise reasonable judgment, they are entitled to change their mind. Negotiations between the parties can sometimes prove fruitful and avoid unnecessary court hearings and costs on both sides. If the police are persuaded to reverse their earlier revocation or refusal decision, they will sometimes require a new application form to be completed before reinstating or granting the applicant's certificates, particularly if there has been a change in the applicant's personal circumstances, the form itself, or a new requirement, such as notification of the applicant's GP.

DIRECTIONS/DOCUMENTS FOR THE APPEAL

5.22   There were no specific rules or regulations governing the progression and preparation of firearms appeals, and there were wide variations in approach by different Crown Courts. Some were very keen on holding an early mention hearing soon after notice of appeal has been lodged and then setting a timetable of directions. Other courts simply issue a date for the full hearing of the appeal without any consultation or directions. In any event, early disclosure of the police evidence will enable a realistic assessment and advice as to the prospects of success with the appeal, and likewise disclosure of the evidence in support of the appeal can lead to the police's legal advisors giving them realistic advice, and sometimes objections to the appeal being withdrawn. Consequently, an exchange of evidence some time in advance of the final hearing is usually beneficial to both sides.

5.23   In a recent case the Divisional Court has helpfully given some guidance on how the Crown Court should now deal with firearms appeals, which it is hoped may bring greater consistency of approach. Jeremy Baker J, giving the judgment of the court in *Mason*,[31] reiterated the overriding requirement for fairness, stating (paragraph [45] of the judgment):

> However, whether it be the chief constable acting in an administrative capacity or the Crown Court in its appellate capacity, the rules of natural justice will apply, such that adherence to these is an essential pre-requisite to the lawfulness of any such decision. Albeit, the extent of the procedural requirements which will be necessary for fairness to be achieved will depend upon the nature of the decision and the context in which it is being considered. Moreover, the nature of the decision being taken by the Crown Court may well engage the requirements of Article 6(1) ECHR.

5.24   The court went on to set out the procedure which should be followed in such appeal hearings, including that the respondent (i.e. the police) call their evidence and make submissions first, followed by the appellant (the individual bringing the appeal). With regards to the pre-hearing stage the court recommended as follows (with some comments and additions from the authors in square brackets):

i.   Service by the respondent upon the appellant and the Crown Court of a bundle containing the evidence and material which is relied upon to support the original decision within 28 days of the service of the appellant's notice of appeal;

ii.   Service by the appellant upon the respondent and the Crown Court of a bundle containing the evidence and material which is relied upon to support the appeal within 21 days of the service of the respondent's bundle;
      [These time limits for service will normally be sufficient, but might need to be varied by agreement between the parties and the court as appropriate in more complex cases.]

iii. The parties to serve upon the Crown Court a joint time estimate to be agreed between the parties, or in the absence of agreement, individual time estimates together with an explanation for the same, within 7 days of service of the appellant's bundle;
      [The court will also need to be provided with dates to avoid for all the witnesses it is intended to call live at the hearing so the court can fix a suitable date.]

iv.   Skeleton arguments together with copies of any authorities relied upon to be exchanged and served upon the Crown Court at least 7 days before the hearing of the appeal;
      [A skeleton argument is a document summarising the legal arguments and precedents to be raised by that party at the hearing. It is unlikely the court would expect a skeleton argument from an appellant who is conducting his own appeal without legal representation. It would be more helpful to have the respondent's skeleton argument served before that for the appellant, following which both

[31]   *R (Mason) v Crown Court at Winchester* [2018] EWHC 1182 (Admin).

should be served on the court. This will allow the appellant to deal with what is said by the respondents; after all, the burden of satisfying the court is on the respondents.]

v.   The Crown Court to provide copies of the parties' bundles, skeleton arguments and authorities to the members of the court at least 24 hours prior to the hearing of the appeal.
[We fully support this suggestion, but in our experience the justices (i.e. magistrates) asked to sit on such cases never see the bundles until they arrive at court for the hearing. If this can be done, then good.]

vi.   At the hearing of the appeal, unless for good reason the court directs otherwise, the evidence for the respondent is to be followed by the evidence for the appellant, and thereafter submissions made in the same order.

The court then concluded by saying:

57.   In the event that a procedure in line with the above requirements is adopted, then not only will this lead to these appeals being efficiently dealt with at the Crown Court but will also provide a structure that assists in complying with the court's duties to provide a fair and carefully scrutinised hearing of these appeals.

5.25   The judgment in *Mason* is a helpful review of the authorities governing these appeals and we recommend that anyone intending to conduct such an appeal should consider the judgment in full. Apart from emphasising the requirement for fairness and the procedure to be adopted, the judgment highlights the following issues:

- At paragraph [23] onwards the court deals succinctly with the principal statutory provisions which apply in firearms licensing appeals under section 44 of the Act.
- Paragraphs [26] to [32] deal with the principal decided cases of the higher courts which have interpreted the provisions of the Firearms Acts.
- Paragraph [33] restates the decision in *Kavanagh*[32] that the Crown Court (and the appellant) are entitled to see the material on which the chief constable based his decision. If the police have information upon which the decision was based which they do not wish to share with the appellant and the court, this may put them in a difficult position. The passage quoted from Lord Denning's judgment in *Kavanagh* also reiterates that hearsay evidence is permitted. Jeremy Baker J summarised this at paragraph [47] of the judgment in *Mason*:

---

[32]   *Kavanagh v Chief Constable of Devon and Cornwall* [1974] 2 WLR 762.

This material will not be circumscribed by strict rules of evidence. Provided the chief constable, and likewise the court, gives due allowance to the fact that hearsay evidence and other material may attract less weight, it may be taken into account if it is logically probative and relevant to the decision under consideration.

▪ Hearsay evidence can be called by the appellant as well as the respondent.

5.26   The judgment goes on to state:

48.   Thereafter, as was pointed out by Denning MR in Kavanagh, at the hearing of the appeal the individual must be given the opportunity of correcting or contradicting this material. Although this does not mean that the individual has to be given the chance to cross-examine the witnesses providing the underlying evidence, it does require that the individual is given the opportunity of providing contradictory or explanatory evidence. In this regard, I accept Mr Onslow's [counsel for Mason] submission that this is a particularly important aspect of the appellate procedure, as it may be the first time that the individual will have had the opportunity of being heard in person by the decision maker, initially the chief constable (albeit usually on the recommendation of the chief officer based on the reports of others), and certainly by the court.

This is an important point. The police make a 'paper-based decision'. Only in rare cases will they have interviewed an applicant or certificate holder before the refusal or revocation or been given any explanation from him. The appeal hearing is therefore the first time the appellant will be able to put forward his version of events.

5.27   An important point in relation to those directions is this: the respondents will be in possession of the material which has satisfied them that the certificate should be refused or revoked. Only they know what that is, even if the refusal or revocation letter has summarised it. It is therefore important that this material is fully disclosed before the appellant can be expected to give a considered response. Hopefully, *Mason* should see an end of police solicitors suggesting 'a mutual exchange of bundles'.

5.28   In a proportion of cases a well set out respondent's bundle may lead to the appellant abandoning his appeal at a relatively early stage. In the recent past, there have been attempts to invite the court to order that the appellant serves his bundle of evidence first and then the respondents will consider that material and serve their bundle at a later stage, in a timetable to be set by the court. The decision in *Mason* should again put an end to such requests.

5.29   An attempt was made at Reading Crown Court in March 2016[33] for an appellant to serve his evidence first. Apart from the issues already considered, HHJ Dugdale highlighted another potential problem:

> what lies behind the revocation [in this case] is potential criminal activity and therefore the proceedings, which are civil, become quasi criminal in nature rather than civil. It is then fair and proper that the Appellant knows the evidence on which the revocation is based so he can answer it, otherwise his answers [evidence] may place him in jeopardy elsewhere [i.e. through self-incrimination].

That observation will apply to nearly all firearms licensing appeals as most relate to quasi-criminal allegations of some sort. Not only is an appellant entitled to know what the police objections are, more importantly (as HHJ Dugdale appreciated), the evidence upon which those objections are based may, or may not, be open to challenge and an appellant is entitled to decide how, and if, he should answer it.

5.30   Jeremy Baker J in *Mason* did not consider the position of an appellant in person, or one with limited means. However, the Crown Court is easily capable of dealing with such situations.

5.31   Setting a timetable of directions can often be dealt with by the court on an administrative basis, and so negate the need for a mention hearing, thereby limiting costs for both parties, although a mention hearing can sometimes be a useful opportunity to gauge to what extent there is any scope for negotiation/reconsideration and to bring some pressure to bear, particularly if one side is dragging their heels about serving their case.

5.32   Since licensing appeals are not governed by either the Civil Procedure Rules or the Criminal Procedure Rules (except as to costs, see para 5.55 *et seq*), there is no particular sanction available if either party fails to comply with the directions previously made by the court, save for the fact that the court may well take it into account when determining at the conclusion of the case what is the appropriate award of costs to make.

5.33   At times when the Crown Court is busy with criminal work most judges will list a number of criminal 'mentions' before the appeal hearing. Whether your appeal hearing is a single day or longer, this can substantially add to the costs, which are not recoverable, particularly if you are the appellant.

---

[33]   The case of *Gurpeet Bhangra v Chief Constable of Thames Valley Police*, 16 March 2016, unreported.

EVIDENCE

5.34 It is important to bear in mind that that there are effectively no rules of evidence in this type of hearing.[34] Obviously the court must follow the rules of natural justice and, where it is relevant, must apply the Human Rights Act 1998, but 'hearsay', for example, is permissible. It should also be noted that the hearing is not concerned with whether the police were correct or not in their decision; the question for the court is are *they* satisfied, on the evidence *now* available, that the appellant can be granted his certificate. In almost all cases the court will be concerned with grounds (a) and (b) of the statutory criteria set out in para 5.02, i.e. are they 'satisfied' that you are of intemperate habits or unsound mind or are otherwise unfitted to be entrusted with a firearm,[35] or are they 'satisfied' that you can no longer be permitted to have the firearm or ammunition to which the certificate relates in your possession without danger to the public safety or to the peace.[36] The only other reason to refuse or revoke which often comes before the courts is the question as to whether a certificate holder (or applicant) has shown a good reason for requiring a particular firearm. Again the court would have to be 'satisfied' on the appellant's evidence that he did have a good reason. Clearly, if a certificate is refused or revoked because the holder is prohibited under the Act, it is difficult to imagine any basis of appeal! We put 'satisfied' in inverted commas because this is a slightly different test to that usually found in the courts. We would suggest that it equates to 'satisfied on the balance of probabilities'. The court can refuse the appeal, or grant it, in whole or in part.

THE HEARING

5.35 At the hearing the barrister representing the police (the 'respondents' as they will formally be referred to in court) will open the case (explain what it is about) to the court and will then call the evidence that the police rely on in objecting to you having your certificate. This evidence will either be 'live' by having the witnesses in the witness box, or by tendering written statements. The appellant is entitled to request the attendance of those witnesses whose evidence is not accepted so they can be cross-examined. The court may also wish to ask questions of the witnesses. The respondents might decline to call a particular witness that has been requested, but they do so at their peril. If there is reasonable evidence given on oath which contradicts an absent witness whose statement has

---

[34] *Kavanagh v Chief Constable Devon & Cornwall* [1974] 1 QB 624. See the judgment of Lord Denning.

[35] FA 1968, s 30A(1), (2)(a).

[36] FA 1968, s 30A(1), (2)(b). For a commentary on the meaning of 'danger to the public safety or to the peace', see further para 5.39 and also para 4.10 *et seq*.

been read, the court might well accept the live evidence. This applies to evidence from both sides.

5.36   In most cases one of the witnesses the police will rely upon will be the person who made the decision to refuse or revoke. The practice varies amongst different forces and this can be anyone from a sergeant or inspector, or a firearms licensing manager (usually a civilian employee), up to a deputy chief constable. Whoever it is, that person will probably list the various factors which he took into account in reaching his decision. If you are the appellant you will want to give careful consideration to the reasons given. For example:

(a)   Are the facts on which the objections are based correct? If not they will need to be challenged by cross-examining the witnesses who state those facts.
(b)   Even if the facts are accepted, has the person making the decision to refuse/revoke taken an unreasonable view of the facts, or reached decisions which are not justified on the facts? Bear in mind, however, as stated above, it is for the court to reach their own decision on the facts and the case; it does not matter if the police and their decision maker got it wrong. There may be many reasons for this; the police may not have seen an important witness give evidence (as the court will) or they may not have had evidence from a witness that the appellant has called to court.
(c)   Is there now other evidence available to the court (which was not considered by the police) which puts the whole matter in a different light? One important piece of evidence which the police rarely consider is what the appellant has to say about the matter. Further there may be witnesses who come to court to give evidence on behalf of the appellant of whom the police were not aware, or who they chose not to take a statement from.

5.37   It follows from the above that careful thought should be given to the evidence which can be called on behalf of an appellant when considering an appeal. In addition to any witnesses who deal with the facts of any alleged incident which gave rise to the revocation, for example, consider whether there are character witnesses who can speak of the good behaviour of the appellant or testify to his suitability and safe handling of firearms.

THE ISSUES TO BE CONSIDERED BY THE COURTS

5.38   What are the courts (and the police in the first instance) looking for when considering whether they are satisfied that a person can be permitted to possess firearms within the framework of the law? This book cannot cover every issue that will arise in these appeals, but a large majority of these cases will cover the following topics.

Danger to public safety or the peace

5.39   This is the single most important test to be applied by the police, and subsequently by the court when considering an appeal. The phrase is used in each section of the Firearms Acts which deals with the refusal to grant, or revocation of, a firearm or shotgun certificate, or the registration of a firearms dealer. This issue is considered in detail, with commentary from the leading cases, at para 4.10 *et seq*. The question of danger to public safety and the other considerations set out at para 5.40 *et seq* are usually interlinked. Careful consideration needs to be given in each case as to whether a given piece of evidence itself is a ground for refusal (e.g. unsound mind) or whether it simply demonstrates a danger to public safety.

Fitness to be entrusted with a firearm

5.40   The issue of fitness to be entrusted with a firearm[37] is closely linked with the other criterion of whether the appellant can be permitted to possess firearms or shotguns without danger to public safety or the peace, the same facts often being relied on, not always appropriately, to justify concerns about both issues. 'Fitness' is only a test for a firearm certificate, not for a shotgun certificate or an RFD. Not surprisingly you are considered to be 'unfit' if you are prohibited under section 21 of the Act because you have received a sentence of imprisonment of more than a certain length. Depending on the offence of which you were convicted you may still be considered unfit even if the prohibition were no longer to be in force. See para 5.60 *et seq*, 'Prohibited persons – applications to remove a prohibition under section 21' for the circumstances where such a prohibition applies and when you may be able to ask a court for it to be lifted.

5.41   The police will also consider any other previous convictions carefully before granting a certificate, whether they gave rise to a prohibition or not. The Rehabilitation of Offenders Act 1974 does not apply in firearms licensing and the assessment of applications, you must therefore disclose all convictions, however minor and however old. Having said that, common sense ought to prevail, and usually does. A woman in her 40s who now leads an industrious life will not be prevented from having a firearm certificate because of a shoplifting conviction when she was 15.[38] Conversely, someone with a conviction for armed robbery is unlikely to be granted a certificate, however old the conviction. These examples are fairly obvious, but the courts have reached decisions which are perhaps sometimes less so.

---

[37]   Used in ss 27(1)(a) and 30A(2)(a) concerning grant and revocation, respectively.

[38]   *Spencer-Stewart v Ch Con Kent* [1989] Cr App R 307 – handling stolen goods conviction not likely to suggest a shotgun certificate should be revoked on the basis of future danger involving firearms.

5.42   A woman of good character was refused a certificate because her husband had two ancient drugs convictions, but perhaps more importantly was believed to still associate with drug users.[39] *Dabek* is often cited as authority for the proposition that those who associate with undesirables should be refused a certificate. That may well be reasonable in some cases, but as always the devil can be in the detail. It is clear from the judgment of Farquharson LJ in *Dabek* that the concern was that 'drug users' visited the family home, and this was a time, in 1988, when it was not a requirement to keep a shotgun locked up. It was not possible to condition a shotgun certificate to make that a requirement, although Mrs Dabek had offered to keep the gun and ammunition under lock and key. Therefore the real concern of the chief constable in that case was a potentially insecure shotgun in a home which 'undesirables' might visit. That was the risk to public safety that was being addressed, not the simple fact of associating with the wrong people. Another example where certificates have been revoked is where it comes to police attention that the son of a perfectly law-abiding certificate holder is a member of a violent 'street gang'. If the boy lives at home, police may have concerns about potential access to firearms. This is a difficult example as no blame can be attached to the father.

Intemperate habits

5.43   Drug use or excessive alcohol abuse may be considered intemperate habits and be a reason for refusal. Bear in mind the police have the right to consult your doctor. A recurring theme in these cases is those who have been convicted of drinking and driving, particularly more than once.[40] A revocation on the basis of one conviction has been upheld, and may be justified particularly if you have a bad attitude to the offence.[41] In most cases, however, the police will be looking for a pattern of behaviour which demonstrates loss of temper or control, or other irresponsibility. Those who have volatile relationships, particularly where there are repeated allegations of domestic violence, even if they have not resulted in convictions, will find this is put forward as an objection. The usual concern is the availability of firearms in the home when a person might lose his temper. This will also apply to applicants who display prejudicial attitudes of a racist, anti-religious or homophobic nature, particularly when often expressed and in violent terms. It is increasingly common for police to assess applicants and certificate holders on the basis of their 'posts' on social media. Displaying extremist views or a lack of acceptance of the firearms licensing regime in the UK have been relied

---

[39]   *Dabek v Ch Con Devon & Cornwall* (1991) 155 JP 55.

[40]   *Ch Con Essex v Germain* (1992) 156 JP 109. It demonstrates irresponsibility with a dangerous item, a bit like a gun. See also *Luke v Little* 1980 SLT (Sh Ct) 138.

[41]   *Lubbock v Chief Constable, Lothian and Borders Police*, Jedburgh Sheriff Court, 18 June 2001, unreported.

on in recent times as reasons why the person is unsuitable, or as a basis for suggesting that he is unlikely to co-operate with the licensing department.

Unsound mind

5.44   This may also seem obvious as an objection, but it does not only cover those who are mentally ill in the sense that when affected by their illness they present a danger to the public. In recent years police forces have refused certificates to those who have in the past suffered from depression of any form. Given some of the recent tragedies involving firearms, a conservative approach to this issue on the part of the police and the courts is perhaps not entirely surprising. Concerns include suicidal thoughts and tendencies as well as danger to others. If the applicant's GP is willing to confirm such problems are no longer present, this will help. In some cases it may be necessary to instruct a consultant psychiatrist to prepare a report confirming that the applicant is perfectly well and in the expert's professional opinion can safely be entrusted with firearms.[42]

Breach of security conditions

5.45   The security of firearms and ammunition is dealt with in Chapter 8. Breaches of these rules, particularly where such a breach has led to the loss or theft of firearms or ammunition in circumstances where the certificate holder had not taken reasonable precautions for their safekeeping. is almost certain to result in the revocation of your certificate. Do not leave items subject to certification in your car! The precautions have to be reasonable in the circumstances; see Chapter 8 for further details regarding the security of firearms and ammunition.

5.46   It will be understood that the above four issues, although dealt with separately, can all be examples of where there could be a danger 'to the public safety or to the peace', to use the words of the Act,[43] if the circumstances were found to be proved.

Lack of co-operation with the licensing authority

5.47   Those who hold certificates, and those who apply for them, are expected to co-operate with the police, not only in providing the necessary information for the original application and any renewal or variation, but also on an on-going basis. A failure to co-operate may form the basis of a revocation decision or refusal to renew, or at least support other reasons. Maintaining good communication with your licensing department is therefore well advised. This

---

[42]   See *Guide*, para 12.29.

[43]   FA 1968, s 27(1)(c).

includes notifying transfers and acquisitions of weapons on a timely basis, and similarly notifying any change of address without delay. At the extreme end of the spectrum, making threatening and abusive phone calls to your licensing enquiry officer is a very good way to get your ticket pulled, as is refusing to allow him to inspect your weapons or security arrangements. The certificate holder may feel there are good reasons for such obstructive behaviour, but it is best avoided. If a certificate holder has genuine reasons for not keeping appointments or not responding to correspondence and messages, or has a legitimate complaint about the actions of the licensing department, these should be explained clearly and calmly, if necessary to the relevant force professional standards department. This can also be a sensitive area and you may wish to involve a lawyer at an early stage if you have serious concerns.

Social media

5.48   Posts on social media are not themselves a ground in the Firearms Acts to object to the grant of a certificate, or a basis for revocation, but in recent times we have come across 'the curse of social media' in circumstances where certificates have been refused or revoked based on posts they have put up or 'liked'. On the basis of such activity it has variously been suggested that they are 'unfitted' to possess firearms, have intemperate habits, are a danger to public safety, will not co-operate with the licensing department, are risking the security of their firearms and even occasionally that their posts display signs of mental illness. Some examples are:

- posting or liking on Facebook the view that firearms licensing in Britain is pointless/stupid and we should have the American approach where guns should be carried for self-defence;
- 'The police are stupid and don't understand the law';
- expressing views about the law relating to firearms which either are incorrect or do not accord with accepted views on the subject;
- expressions of support for serious violence, particularly against minorities, or in particular circumstances – 'I don't see what's wrong with shooting burglars', for example, etc;
- expressing or supporting strong racist or sexist views;
- being 'friends' on social media with persons who have serious convictions or who themselves post material which would be a cause for concern;
- photographs and videos of 'inappropriate' shooting and circumstances;
- posts which suggest drug use or excessive alcohol intake;
- information which identifies you as a certificate holder with details of your location;
- inflammatory or derogatory remarks about your partner where there are allegations of domestic abuse.

5.49   No one, the police and the courts included, would wish to restrict free speech, and very often what is said on social media has to be taken 'with a large pinch of salt', but unfortunately it can be all too easy to give the wrong impression. The reality is that such posts are handing an argument to the police to take your licence away from you, and the court might well agree with the concerns voiced by the police. The risk with social media is giving the impression that a person is not 'normal' or 'stable' or does not accept that the 'rules' apply to him.

Lack of good reason

5.50   This really only applies to firearm certificates; as to good reasons for having shotguns, see the comments at para 4.20 *et seq* and para 4.29, fn 52. 'Good reason' applies to each firearm you require, and to each type of ammunition. The application form will ask you to state your reasons for requiring each weapon you wish to have and there is a space to give a brief reason, for example, 'vermin control' or 'target shooting'. In most cases this will be self-evident to the police as being good reasons because of other information they will already have; details of land over which you have permission to shoot vermin, or your shooting club, to keep with the above examples. Where they do not have such supporting information, they will probably ask for further details. This is likely to be covered when the enquiry officer comes to inspect your security arrangements. At the end of the day the issue of good reason is a question of fact in the particular circumstances of the applicant and it is difficult to set any hard and fast rules, or to cover all the likely examples of a 'good reason'. Your local enquiry officer may well rely on Chapter 13 of the *Guide* in determining whether you have established good reason for a particular gun and, in unusual cases, you would be well advised to consult it yourself before discussing the matter with the police.

5.51   Some general principles should be borne in mind:

(a)   When considering 'good reason' the police should look firstly 'from the standpoint of the applicant, rather than from that of a possible objector'.[44] However, simply wishing to own a particular gun for its own sake is not sufficient; it is the reasons for which you want to use it that are important.

(b)   Good reason is not limited to 'need'. It is for the individual to decide what type of weapon he wishes to use for a particular purpose and as long as the gun is a reasonable choice for that purpose the certificate should be granted. The police cannot say to the applicant 'you don't need that gun for that use', that is not the test; the test is 'do you have a good reason for that gun?'. If so, you should have it.

---

[44]   *Anderson v Neilans* 1940 SLT (Sh Ct) 13 and *Joy v Ch Co Dumfries & Galloway* 1966 SLT (Sh Ct) 93 are cited as authority for this proposition in the *Guide*, para 10.40.

(c)   Since good reason relates to the use of the gun, the police will want to be
      satisfied that you will not only have the opportunity to use it, but are likely
      do so. A failure to demonstrate potential regular use may result in refusal.
      At renewal the police may look at the amount of ammunition purchased in
      the previous period to ensure that all of the guns on the certificate have been
      used. If guns are for target shooting, the club secretary is required to notify
      the police of any member who has not shot at least once during each year.

(d)   Good reason has to be demonstrated for each weapon on your certificate.
      This can lead to questions from the police if you have two or more weapons
      which are similar to each other. For example, 'Why do you need three .22"
      rifles?'. There can be many answers to questions such as this; 'I am a keen
      target shooting competitor and I need one or more spare guns in case of a
      malfunction', or 'I prefer a lighter gun at that shoot as there is always a lot
      of walking'. Guns may have different capabilities or work better in different
      conditions, and so on.

There will always be cases where the police and the shooter will not agree as to
whether there is a good reason, which may end up in court as the subject of an
appeal. To avoid time and expense it is advisable to give the police as much
information as you can, together with any supporting documentation, when you
make the application.

5.52   The most common subject areas for appeals relating to good reason are the
following:

(a)   'Duplicate guns' as mentioned in point (d) above. In practice, the more often
      you actually go out shooting the more likely the police are to accept multiple
      ownership of similar guns.

(b)   'Land'. With most hunting, rough shooting and vermin destruction, the
      police will want to be satisfied that you have the opportunity to shoot over
      land on which it is safe to use that particular type of firearm. You will be
      expected to provide written evidence that you have permission to shoot on
      some suitable land, although this does not limit you to that property, subject
      to any conditions on your certificate. The police should keep records of land
      over which shooting is conducted in their area and which is considered to be
      safe and suitable. If the land you nominate is not within their knowledge
      they may well wish to obtain further information from the landowner (or his
      agent) or inspect it themselves. If the police do inspect it they may ask the
      applicant to be present to demonstrate their knowledge of any particular
      dangers or difficulties that may be present. The presence of occupied
      buildings, public footpaths and the like on or near the land will be taken into
      account. Depending on the circumstances, they may restrict shooting on
      given land to particular calibres, or, for example, only shooting from a high

seat, or precluding shooting when the ground is frozen. The responsibility for shooting safely rests with the shooter in all cases, and causing accidents to, or complaints from, members of the public is likely to lead to revocation! The police will also wish to be satisfied that the type of animal you wish to hunt or exterminate is present on the land in some numbers, or causes a particular problem there.

(c) 'Quarry'. A detailed analysis of the types of firearms and ammunition which are most suitable to kill a particular species of animal would result in a book larger than this one, and will not be attempted here. The Home Office have issued guidance[45] as to what they consider to be appropriate calibres for given quarry. This is guidance, not law, and if the applicant feels that a different calibre or type of weapon would be more suitable, they should argue it. No doubt the police will need some convincing, and evidence from an experienced gamekeeper, for example, who agrees with you might well be helpful. In some cases the law does prescribe the minimum calibre to be used, such as .243″ on most deer[46] and restrictions on some other wildlife[47] control.

(d) 'Overseas use'. The law allows the acquisition of rifles for use abroad, in particular for 'big game' in larger calibres than would be considered suitable for any animal found in the UK. The police will want to be satisfied that you will make trips abroad for such purposes, although these trips may not be very frequent for obvious reasons. In some cases you may also be permitted to use the same large calibre rifle for some types of deer, or wild boar in Great Britain. It should be noted that it is not possible to permit possession of expanding ammunition solely for use abroad because of the wording of the exemption in section 5A(4)(b)(ii) – 'concerned with the management of any estate' has been held to mean 'any estate in Great Britain',[48] and therefore it is not a good reason to have the ammunition in this country. You will normally be permitted to possess a small amount of non-expanding ammunition to zero the rifle.

(e) 'Target shooting'. As already stated, you are required to be a member of a target shooting club, whether it is for rifle or muzzle-loading pistol, as appropriate.[49] Approved clubs only cover rifles and muzzle-loading pistols at present, which can cause some anomalies. Current police policy is that an individual can have a long-barrelled pistol for target shooting, but a club cannot, as clubs cannot be approved for this type of weapon. If that is correct, how does the individual show 'good reason' for the long-barrelled

---

[45] See *Guide*, Chapter 13.

[46] The Deer Acts, see further Chapter 12.

[47] Wildlife & Countryside Act 1981, see Chapter 12.

[48] *Lacey v Com Met Police* [2001] LLR 495.

[49] F(A)A 1997, s 44.

pistol?[50] In all cases the police will wish to ensure that you have the opportunity to use a range which has a range safety certificate that covers the type of weapon you wish to use.

(f)   'Practical shotgun'. A large magazine capacity semi-automatic or pump-action shotgun is classified under section 1 of the Act. These can be used for practical shotgun, usually shooting at steel plates from different positions. This activity is not covered by 'approved clubs' but is nonetheless a discipline recognised by the police. The police usually require such weapons to be used either on a range with a safety certificate, or on a course of fire supervised by a qualified member of the UKPSA.

(g)   'Collectors'. Creating a collection of either firearms or ammunition is considered to be a good reason for the purposes of the Act. Collections of firearms are sometimes subject to a condition that they are not to be fired, and in any event you may not be permitted to possess ammunition for the guns in the collection. The good reason is being a '*bona fide* collector' and so the police will probably wish to see evidence of membership of a relevant collector's society, or perhaps of a long-standing academic interest in the subject.

5.53   Other examples of 'good reason' to possess firearms will relate to slaughtering instruments, trophies of war, controlling races, theatrical use, signalling apparatus and many others. Those who fall into these specialist categories are likely to be aware of their particular requirements and will be able to satisfy the good reason test. Pistols for humane dispatch, as permitted under the F(A)A 1997,[51] have caused some debate in recent years. The Home Office[52] suggest that such pistols should be in .32" calibre and should be restricted to two shots. This calibre is considered by most users to be totally unsuitable for use on larger animals, including large deer and wild boar; indeed it might result in an 'inhumane' dispatch. Further the limitation of two shots can also render the weapon inadequate, particularly when dealing with more than one animal. There is no guidance as to how the pistol ought to be restricted. Parliament chose to say 'pistol' and not, for example, 'revolver' or 'self-loading pistol'. It is relatively easy to restrict a revolver to two shots by blocking up all but two of the chambers in the cylinder, but with a magazine-fed gun the usual method is to limit the magazine to two shots. It could be argued that this creates a three-shot gun (as you could put one in the chamber as well), but for health and safety reasons most deer stalkers, for example, would not consider it appropriate to go stalking carrying a pistol with a round in the chamber. In any event, if it is a condition of your certificate that you have a two-shot pistol for this purpose, you commit the offence of breaching your licence conditions if you load it with more than two

---

[50]   See para 3.30 *et seq*, 'Rifle clubs and muzzle-loading pistol clubs', for further information.

[51]   Section 3, and see also the comments regarding humane dispatch in para 2.20, point (c).

[52]   *Guide*, para 13.38.

shots. If you can show good reason for needing a larger calibre, or an unrestricted gun, you should be granted one. There have been several successful appeals on this subject.[53]

5.54   With all of the above issues (not just good reason) it is good practice for the police to ask for further information if they have doubts. You should ask for any concerns that have been expressed to be put in writing (email is sufficient) so that you can deal with them. Ask for time to obtain further information if it is necessary, before they make a final decision. This would be important if you wished to get evidence from a doctor, for example.

THE COSTS OF APPEAL

5.55   Legal aid is not available for any type of firearms licensing appeal to the Crown Court or the Sheriff's Court, and even if the appellant wins, he is unlikely to recover his costs from the police as the police are 'only performing a public function'.[54] Costs in appeals, including firearms appeals, to the Crown Court are now governed by Part 45 of the Criminal Procedure Rules 2015 (CPR), in particular rule 45.6.[55] This gives the court a wide discretion to award costs and makes no reference to the principle that 'the police are only serving a public function'. It is therefore arguable that this principle no longer applies, having been superseded by the CPR, and the court should simply order costs as they think appropriate. In addition to the normal costs of a hearing – 'costs in cause' as lawyers say – the Rules also cover wasted costs of every sort; see rule 45.8. In both cases costs can be awarded on the application of the party who incurred the costs, or on the court's own initiative.

5.56   If the principle in *Newton & Goodman* still applies, to recover costs the appellant would have to show that the police either wasted costs or acted in a wholly improper manner in coming to the original decision which is the subject of the appeal. In relation to applications for removal of a prohibition, there are no

---

[53]   E.g. *Toufexis v Commissioner of Metropolitan Police*, Wood Green Crown Court, April 2010, and *Snell v Chief Constable of Dorset*, Bournemouth Crown Court, November 2017, both unreported. In both of those cases the court accepted that there was a need either for an unrestricted revolver, or a .45″ ACP pistol with a magazine restricted to two rounds.

[54]   *Chief Constable of Derbyshire v Newton & Goodman* [2001] LLR 127 and other cases cited therein.

[55]   This is not in doubt following the decision of Hickinbottom J in *R (Hucklebridge Engineering Ltd) v Chichester Crown Court and The Chief Constable of Sussex* [2015] EWHC 3216 (Admin). It is important to study the Rules and comply with the various requirements. *Chief Constable of Derbyshire v Newton & Goodman* [2001] LLR 127 and other cases cited therein.

circumstances in which you can ever expect to recover your costs, as it is your criminal conviction that led to you being prohibited in the first place.

5.57   Most of the national shooting organisations have member insurance schemes, some of which may cover the legal expenses of an appeal against revocation or refusal by the police. However, joining such an organisation after a problem has already arisen with your certificate will not enable you to benefit from their legal expenses policy. So do ensure that you do not allow your membership to lapse, as you never know when you might find yourself needing to make a claim on the policy. Further, the scope of cover varies and, even if it is available, do bear in mind the insurers will have quite strict criteria as to the circumstances in which they will agree to fund the legal costs of a licensing appeal. It is usually an absolute requirement that any potential claim for legal costs cover must be notified to the insurers before commencing proceedings, so do not wait until you have won your appeal to contact the insurers as they may then refuse to pay out your legal costs. In any event, readers who are minded to appeal would be well advised to contact the General Secretary of their respective organisation before proceeding. The major shooting organisations[56] are usually able to give sensible preliminary advice on such matters to their members. Failing funding being available by way of insurance the shooter has to either fund personally the legal costs of his appeal, or represent himself.

5.58   A final warning on costs: readers should be mindful that if you proceed with an appeal and are unsuccessful, not only will you end up having to bear your own legal costs, but there is also a distinct possibility you may be ordered to pay a substantial contribution towards the police's legal costs in defending your appeal.

5.59   Nonetheless, in most cases it would be advisable to at least consult a specialist lawyer. Sometimes early intervention from a solicitor or direct access barrister can lead to the issue being resolved with the police by negotiation and without going to the full extent and cost of a contested appeal hearing.

---

[56]   Such as the Sportsman's Association of Great Britain & Northern Ireland, the Clay Pigeon Shooting Association, the Country Land and Business Association, the NRA, the National Small-bore Rifle Association, the British Association for Shooting and Conservation (BASC), the Gun Trade Association (GTA), the British Deer Society, the National Gamekeepers' Organisation, the UKPSA, the Shooters' Rights Association, the Muzzle Loaders Association of Great Britain, the Countryside Alliance, the Saint Hubert Club of Great Britain, The Sealed Knot and several others of which the reader may be a member. Nearly all of these organisations have websites and all make a positive contribution to the many types of shooting sports pursued in Great Britain.

PROHIBITED PERSONS – APPLICATIONS TO REMOVE A PROHIBITION UNDER SECTION 21

5.60   As already mentioned, it is not possible for the police to grant a certificate to a person who is prohibited under the Act from possessing firearms. Persons are automatically prohibited under the Act[57] from 'possessing' firearms for life if they receive a sentence of imprisonment of 3 years or more, and the prohibition is for 5 years from the date of release from prison if the sentence is between 3 months and 3 years. The 'date of release' can become more complicated in relation to sentences such as detention and training orders and the wording of the Act, as amended, needs to be studied in such cases.

5.61   The prohibition applies to all forms of custodial sentence, including partly suspended sentences. From July 2014, the prohibition provisions were extended to also include wholly suspended sentences of 3 months or more.[58] In those cases the prohibition takes effect 2 days after the suspended sentence is passed, allowing a holder the opportunity to dispose of anything he should not now have. Where a person held firearms on certificate on the day the Act came into force in 2014, their possession was not unlawful by virtue of the new provision while the certificate remained in force. A prohibition does not apply to any type of community order. The prohibition arises whenever there is a sentence of the requisite length, whatever the criminal offence for which the sentence was imposed, and not merely in those cases where the offence relates to firearms.

5.62   When released from custody, the prisoner should be asked to sign an acknowledgement of this restriction on release, if it applies to him. However, there does not appear to be any system in place to notify those who receive suspended sentences that they have now become a prohibited person. The prohibition does not depend on the acknowledgement having been signed, but simply on the length of the sentence imposed. It is possible, therefore, that a person was not asked to sign such an acknowledgement, or has genuinely forgotten the warning from 25 years ago and is unaware that he is subject to the prohibition. That would be no defence, but might be considerable mitigation of any penalty. We have never succeeded in obtaining a copy of the acknowledgement from the Prison Service; it would seem to be impossible, even in cases where the prisoner was released relatively recently.

5.63   For the purposes of these prohibition rules, 'possessing' is taken to mean in the widest sense of that word, i.e. not just owning or storing firearms at home,

---

[57]   FA 1968, s 21.

[58]   Anti-social Behaviour, Crime and Policing Act 2014, s 110(1). The period of prohibition will be 5 years in all cases.

nor indeed is it restricted to actual use of a firearm. Merely handling a firearm briefly while subject to a prohibition will place the person in breach of their prohibition, and is a serious criminal offence which usually results in a custodial sentence of some length. It would include controlling the ownership of a firearm 'at arm's length'. This may seem a remote possibility until a prohibited person acts as the administrator for a deceased person's estate which includes an air rifle. The only exception to these rules is that it does not prevent a person possessing firearms outside the jurisdiction of the British courts.

5.64   It is also important to understand that this prohibition applies to all firearms, not just those subject to licensing. For example, a person subject to a prohibition will commit an offence by having in his possession a standard air weapon, or blank ammunition, neither of which normally require a licence, but are still 'firearms' and 'ammunition' in law. Further, since July 2014 the antique exemption does not apply to prohibited persons, so that person cannot possess an antique firearm either.[59]

5.65   A person who is subject to a prohibition may apply to the Crown Court (Sheriff in Scotland) for the area where he resides to have that prohibition removed, and if the application is granted the prohibition shall no longer apply to that person.[60] This type of application is heard by a Crown Court judge and justices. The court will want to see evidence that the applicant is now a reformed character who has 'gone straight' and led an industrious life in the intervening years. There will normally have been a number of years gone by since release from prison, or since the suspended sentence was imposed, during which no further offences have been committed. If possession of firearms is now required for work or the like, the application is perhaps more likely to be granted than if a person wished to shoot purely for sport, although this is certainly not a rule of law. The factors outlined at para 5.40 *et seq* regarding 'fitness to possess firearms' are also likely to be relevant here. We are not aware of any decisions of the higher courts regarding the approach that should be taken by the court to applications under section 21(6) or how the court should exercise its discretion in deciding such applications. The Act simply says 'a person prohibited may apply...; and if the application is granted that prohibition shall not then apply to him'.

5.66   In practice, the application process is similar to that followed in any other firearms appeal; notice must be given to the court and the police, and the police may attend the hearing of the application to make any representations to the court they consider relevant. In appropriate cases the police may indicate that they have no representations to make and will not be attending the hearing. The hearing

---

[59]   Anti-social Behaviour, Crime and Policing Act 2014, s 110(2).

[60]   FA 1968, s 21(6) and Sch 3.

must be at least 21 days after the service of the Notice of Application; the procedure is set out in Schedule 3 to the FA 1968.

5.67   It should be borne in mind that even if the application to remove the prohibition is successful, this merely puts the individual in the same position as any other member of the public who does not hold a certificate. It does not automatically follow that any subsequent application that person makes for a firearm or shotgun certificate will be granted. As in any other case, the police will still retain the discretion to refuse the application if it is considered there are grounds to do so.

5.68   There are no circumstances where an applicant can recover the costs of an application to lift a prohibition – Schedule 3, paragraph 4 to the FA 1968. The applicant can give notice that he abandons the application up to 2 days prior to the hearing, but the court can still order the applicant to pay the chief officer's reasonable costs up to the point the application is abandoned.

Chapter 6

Police Permits

6.01   Visitors' permits are covered in Chapter 7.

6.02   A *police permit* allows the holder to have in his possession[1] firearms and ammunition without holding a firearm certificate or a shotgun certificate.[2] Another form of police permit allows an auctioneer to sell by auction, expose for sale by auction and have in his possession for sale by auction firearms and ammunition without holding a certificate of either kind.[3]

6.03   Permits are obtainable from the chief officer of police for the police area where the applicant resides or, as the case may be, for the area where the auction is to be held.[4]

6.04   A general permit will only be granted in special cases where it may not be necessary or desirable to issue a firearm certificate or a shotgun certificate and, in general, the duration of the permit will be short. A permit will, for example, be appropriate to authorise possession of firearms or ammunition by a person who has been refused a certificate, or has had it revoked, until he is able to dispose of them; or by a relative or executor of a deceased person or a receiver of a bankrupt's estate when firearms or ammunition form part of the property of the deceased person or bankrupt.

6.05   One circumstance where it is sometimes appropriate to request a permit is where an applicant for renewal of his firearm or shotgun certificate has put in his

---

[1]   A purchase or other form of acquisition cannot be covered by a permit.

[2]   FA 1968, s 7(1). For these two kinds of certificate, see Chapters 3 and 4, respectively.

[3]   FA 1968, s 9(2). See also para 3.24 for the possession of firearms and ammunition by auctioneers and their employees. A third form of permit (prescribed by the Firearms Rules 1989 (SI 1989/854) (now revoked), r 9(3) and Sch 4, Part V) is available for handling firearms and signalling apparatus in connection with ships and aircraft; see, further, para 3.27. Forms for each kind of permit are prescribed by the Firearms Rules 1998, r 9 and Sch 4.

[4]   FA 1968, ss 7(1), 9(2). An applicant cannot be said to reside at a property which he has let (*Burditt v Joslin* [1981] 3 All ER 203, *The Times*, 13 February 1981).

application in good time, but there has been a delay by the police in issuing the certificate. As we have seen, in these circumstances the continued possession of firearms or ammunition past the expiry date of the certificate is a criminal offence. It should be said that if the delay in issuing the new certificate was entirely that of the police, and there were no other problems regarding the application, it would probably amount to an 'abuse of the process of the court' for the police to prosecute in these circumstances. What they should concentrate their efforts on is sending you the certificate! However, to remain within the law the applicant should ask the police for a permit to cover his firearms (and shotguns) and ammunition until the certificates can be reissued. In practice such a request is likely to result in the certificate being sent to you without further delay.[5] See also para 3.71 *et seq*, 'Delays in renewal and automatic extension of certificates'. This allows a certificate to be extended for up to 8 weeks, if you put in the renewal application in good time.

6.06   There are two general forms of permit and two special forms for auctioneers, in each case one being for shotguns and the other for section 1 firearms and their ammunition. The latter, like a firearm certificate, gives full particulars of each firearm or type of ammunition; a shotgun permit describes each shotgun in the same way as a shotgun certificate.[6] All permits are likely to be issued subject to some or all of the following conditions:[7]

(a)   The person to whom the permit is granted shall inform the chief officer of police at once of the name and address of any person, except an RFD,[8] purchasing or acquiring any of the firearms or ammunition listed in the permit.
(b)   Reasonable precautions shall be taken to ensure the safe custody of the firearms and ammunition, and any loss or theft shall be reported at once to the chief officer of police.
(c)   The permit shall be returned to the chief officer of police on or before the date on which it expires.

---

[5]   The *Guide* makes it clear that the police should not use permits routinely to deal with delays in the reissue of certificates.

[6]   Firearms Rules 1998, r 9(1), (2) and Sch 4. Neither the FA 1968 nor the Firearms Rules 1998 stipulate the duration of a permit, thus leaving that aspect to the police to decide in the light of the circumstances. A new permit can be sought on expiry. No forms of application for permits are prescribed, though police forms are available.

[7]   The Firearms Rules (Dangerous Air Weapons) 1969 (now revoked) prescribed the conditions to which permits would be subject. The 1998 Rules do not do so but allow for unspecified conditions to be imposed. The three conditions listed in the text are recommended in the *Guide*. There is evidently no bar to further conditions being added. Additionally, permits will bear a footnote requesting holders to report the loss of the permit to the local police at once.

[8]   As to the registration of firearms dealers, see Chapter 16.

You should consult your local police firearms licensing department if you feel that the circumstances of your case call for the issue of a permit. No fee is payable, and there is no right of appeal against refusal by the police to grant a permit or against any of its conditions.

6.07   The use of a firearm or ammunition by a permit holder otherwise than in accordance with the terms and conditions of his permit will be an offence.[9] An offence is also committed if you knowingly or recklessly make a statement which is false in any material particular for the purpose of procuring, whether for yourself or for another person, the grant of a permit.[10]

---

[9]   FA 1968, ss 1(1), 2(1), 3(1)(b), 7(1), 9(2).

[10]   FA 1968, s 7(2), 9(3), 13(2). The maximum punishments upon summary conviction are 6 months' imprisonment, or an unlimited fine, or both (FA 1968, s 51(1), (2) and Sch 6, Part I).

Chapter 7

Exports and Imports of Firearms: Visitors' Permits and European Firearms Passes

EXPORT AND IMPORT

Export

7.01   In 2006 the United Nations (UN) passed a resolution to establish an Arms Trade Treaty (ATT). This led to the Treaty coming into force in 2014; 153 countries voted in favour, three voted against and 23 abstained, so a large proportion of the world is covered, and even those that voted against, such as the United States, have similar controls in place. The purpose of the Treaty is to control the international trade in conventional weapons; the objectives being to prevent arms 'crossing existing arms embargoes', being used for human rights abuses or in terrorism. It is not intended to control arms within a sovereign state. To achieve these objectives all member states of the UN are expected to track exports of arms to ensure they do not 'end up in the wrong hands'. Any country which is a member of the UN is expected to 'track' the movement of a firearm when it is exported and record the 'end user'; such information is supposed to be retained for 20 years.

7.02   It would not be possible in this book to discuss the details of the requirements under the ATT; suffice it to say, the UK is a signatory. This means that in every case where an individual or company wishes to export a gun from the UK an export licence will be required. Currently this does not apply to an individual who is taking a firearm to another EU country as part of his 'personal effects' and has a European Firearms Pass for the gun in question. Keep in mind that the country to which you move might well require an import licence for firearms and you are likely to need to obtain the relevant certification or comply with local notification requirements, as appropriate. This requirement for export paperwork already applies to other EU countries, and will obviously continue to do so after we leave the EU.

7.03   A certificate holder in Britain who moves abroad permanently will need to notify the police who issued the certificate when he moves. The police will then cancel the certificate. This is not necessary if a person continues to maintain a property here and intends to carry on using his guns when in this country, but expect the police to look carefully at the question as to whether you still 'reside' at your British address. If you do reside here, and spend a few months here every year, it should not be a problem.

7.04   To state the obvious: the rules as to what is allowed, or not allowed, in respect of the possession of firearms, and the reasons for which they can be possessed, are different in every country, so it is advisable to check before you leave. In light of the requirements of the ATT, it is also worth checking in advance whether the country to which you are moving will subsequently require an export licence before you can leave again with your guns.

Import

7.05   It is possible to import firearms and shotguns into this country if you have either a shotgun certificate, or a firearm certificate with a relevant 'space' to acquire that type of firearm. This is confirmed in the 'Notes' section on both types of certificate which requests Border Force to notify such importations to the police force which issued the certificate. If the country from which the gun has come correctly applies the rules set out in the ATT, they will also notify the UK authorities that it is coming here.

The UK Export Control Order 2008

7.06   This provision further controls dealing in firearms and associated goods. To take one entirely hypothetical example, making a phone call to someone in South Africa asking them to arrange a transfer of firearms to Colombia – if done without the necessary authorities and paperwork – is an offence here punishable by up to 10 years in prison. This will be the case even though you have never been to South Africa, and never touched the guns in question. This is known as 'brokering'. As with all issues relating to the movement of firearms between countries, it is best to get expert advice if this is a real issue. The 2008 Order has been amended to conform to EU Directive (EU) 2017/853. These amendments came into force on 14 September 2018 and revise the items controlled by the Order.[1]

---

[1]   The guidance notes can be found at: www.gov.uk/government/publications/notice-to-exporters-201822-export-control-order-2008-amended-and-firearms-export-guidance-note-published/firearms-guidance.

SEIZURE OF GOODS BROUGHT INTO THE UNITED KINGDOM

7.07   For guidance on what to do if items are seized by Border Force on entry into the UK and a Notice of Seizure is issued, see para 9.13 *et seq*, 'Realistic imitation firearms'. It is important to seek specialist advice straight away if goods have been seized. There are strict time limits which, if not adhered to, will result in the forfeiture and destruction of the goods.

VISITORS' PERMITS

7.08   The provision of the Firearms Acts allows the grant by the police to visitors to this country of permits for those kinds of firearms for which a firearm or shotgun certificate would otherwise be required.

7.09   A *visitor's firearm permit* will permit the possession of section 1 firearms[2] and the possession, purchase or acquisition[3] of such ammunition for firearms as is specified in the permit. A *visitor's shotgun permit* will permit the possession, purchase or acquisition of shotguns but, unless one of a number of conditions is met, a permit authorising the purchase or acquisition of shotguns with a magazine will not be granted.[4]

7.10   Applications for both kinds of permit may be made on behalf of a visitor by a person (called 'the sponsor') resident[5] in Great Britain[6] to his local chief officer of police.[7] The police may[8] grant a permit if satisfied that:

(a)   the person named in the application is visiting or intending to visit Great Britain; and

---

[2]   For the definitions of 'section 1 firearms' and 'ammunition', see respectively para 3.01 *et seq* and para 3.12.

[3]   'Acquire' is defined to mean hire, accept as a gift or borrow (FA 1968, s 57(4), F(A)A 1988, s 25(1)).

[4]   F(A)A 1988, s 17(1), (1A); Firearms Rules 1998, r 8(2), (3) and Sch 3, Parts II and III. For the definition of 'shotguns', see para 4.01 *et seq*.

[5]   FA 1968, s 26(1). An applicant cannot be said to reside at a property which he has let (*Burditt v Joslin* [1981] 3 All ER 203, *The Times*, 13 February 1981).

[6]   'Great Britain' means England, Wales and Scotland, and excludes the Channel Islands and the Isle of Man.

[7]   Firearms Rules 1998, r 8.

[8]   The police are not required to grant a permit even if satisfied on the matters at items (a) and (b) in the text; nor if there is no bar to a grant under the provisions in the following paragraph. There is no right of appeal against refusal to issue a permit.

(b)   the person has a good reason[9] for possessing, purchasing or acquiring the firearms or ammunition for which the application is made while visiting Great Britain.[10]

But a permit will be refused if the police have reason to believe:

(a)   that the person's possession of the weapons or ammunition in question would represent a danger to the public safety or to the peace;[11] or
(b)   that the person is prohibited by the FA 1968 from possessing those weapons or ammunition.[12]

A permit will also be refused unless:

(a)   the applicant can produce a valid European Firearms Pass relating to the firearm; or
(b)   the applicant can prove that the visitor is not entitled to be issued with such a pass; or
(c)   the applicant can show that the visitor requires the permit exclusively as a collector of firearms or is a body concerned in the cultural or historical aspects of weapons.[13]

You will note that obtaining a visitor's permit if you reside in another EU country could be more onerous than if you come from elsewhere. If the applicant does hold a European Firearms Pass the original needs to be sent to the police so it can be endorsed appropriately. You would be well advised to send all applications for visitors' permits to the sponsor's local police at least 2 months before the proposed trip.

7.11   We expect that this distinction between EU and non-EU visitors will disappear once the UK leaves the EU and all visitors will need to obtain a permit in the same way as non-EU citizens do now.

7.12   A permit will be in force for the period stated in it, which cannot exceed one year.[14]

---

[9]   For some considerations which may be relevant to 'good reason', see para 3.78 *et seq* and para 5.01 *et seq*.

[10]   F(A)A 1988, s 17(2).

[11]   For an analysis of this criterion, see paras 4.10 *et seq* and para 5.39.

[12]   F(A)A 1988, s 17(3).

[13]   F(A)A 1988, s 17(3A).

[14]   F(A)A 1988, s 17(6).

7.13   Home Office rules[15] prescribe the form of permits, and conditions may be applied to them. A permit will specify the number and description of firearms to which it relates (including identification numbers if known) and the quantities of ammunition to be purchased, acquired and held at any one time.[16] Conditions may be varied by written notice from the police to the permit holder; but no shotgun permit can have a condition imposed, initially or on variation, which restricts the premises where the shotgun or guns may be used.[17]

7.14   A single application may be made for the grant of a permit of either kind for a maximum of 20 permits for the visitors named in the application (this is called a 'group application'). The application must satisfy the police that the visitors' purpose in possessing the weapons in question while visiting Great Britain[18] is:

(a)   using them for sporting purposes on the same private premises[19] during the same period;[20] or

(b)   participating in the same competition or other event or the same series of competitions or other events.[21]

A fee of £12 is payable on the grant of a visitor's permit. In the case of a group application, when six or more permits are granted the fee will be £60 for all the permits.[22]

---

[15]   See the Firearms Rules 1998, r 8 and Sch 3.

[16]   F(A)A 1988, s 17(4).

[17]   F(A)A 1988, s 17(5). Apart from this provision, the police are free to impose such conditions as they think fit. The *Guide* recommends conditions similar to those imposed on police permits (see Chapter 6); others, relevant to the occasions or locations of use, may be added.

[18]   'Great Britain' means England, Wales and Scotland, and excludes the Channel Islands and the Isle of Man.

[19]   The term 'private premises' is not defined in the Firearms Acts, though the word 'premises' includes any land (FA 1968, s 57(4); F(A)A 1988, s 25(1)), and 'land' includes land covered with water (IA 1978, s 5 and Sch 1). Contrasting the term with 'public place', discussed in para 15.58, it is suggested that it means any land, water or buildings other than those to which the public are admitted with or without payment.

[20]   E.g. for a game shoot.

[21]   F(A)A 1988, s 17(7). The provisions mentioned earlier concerning refusal of permits, their validity and duration and the form of permits will apply to group applications and permits issued under them.

[22]   F(A)A 1988, s 17(8). It follows that, when five or fewer permits are granted, the fee will be £12 for each. These fees may be varied, or abolished altogether, by order made by the Home Office (FA 1968, s 43; F(A)A 1988, s 17(9)).

7.15 You will commit an offence if you knowingly or recklessly make a statement which is false in any material particular for the purpose of obtaining a permit, or if you fail to comply with any condition in a permit.[23]

7.16 There is no right of appeal against a refusal by the police to grant a visitor's permit or against any conditions placed on the permit.

7.17 It should be noted that the British authorities have 'derogated' from the European Firearms Pass scheme. This means that visitors from another EU country have to produce a European Firearms Pass for any firearms or ammunition to be brought in to this jurisdiction, but they are still required to obtain a visitor's permit before arrival. Conversely holders of a UK-issued European Firearms Pass do not need to obtain the equivalent of a visitor's permit to take firearms to any EU state within the Schengen zone.

EUROPEAN FIREARMS PASS

7.18 The current rules are set out below, but this may not remain the case when Britain leaves the EU. Both the UK Government and the EU authorities are understood to wish to retain this system as part of any deal as the European Firearms Pass system and the Europe-wide registration of arms are considered to be an important part of overall security measures across the continent. At present this provides widespread control of civilian firearms with a database which is accessible by authorities in all EU countries. Even some countries which are not within the EU will currently accept a European Firearms Pass as authority to possess in that country, Serbia, for example. If a deal is not reached when we leave the EU the UK Government have said they will not support the continuation of the European Firearms Pass scheme, even assuming Brussels would be willing to do so.

7.19 At present the holder of a firearm (or shotgun) certificate in Great Britain is entitled to have issued to them, free of charge, a European Firearms Pass, sometimes referred to as a 'European Weapons Pass'. This pass can have included upon it any or all of the weapons which are included on the holder's firearm or shotgun certificate. This enables the holder to take his weapons with him to other EU countries. This system follows the EU Directive on control of the acquisition and possession of firearms,[24] and the police cannot refuse to issue a European Firearms Pass to a certificate holder. All weapons are broadly categorised in

---

[23] The maximum punishment on summary conviction is 6 months' imprisonment, or an unlimited fine, or both (F(A)A 1988, s 17(10)).

[24] European Weapons Directive, as amended by Directive 2008/51/EC and Directive (EU) 2017/853.

accordance with European rules and some categories are restricted in some countries. In general terms, the four categories are as follows:[25]

(A) Military missiles and fully automatic firearms. Firearms disguised as other objects. Explosive, armour piercing, etc ammunition.
(B) All pistols and other small firearms with a barrel of less than 30 cm or an overall length of 60 cm, except for single-shot .22″ pistols over 28 cm. All semi-automatic rifles and smooth-bore guns which have a magazine plus chamber capacity of more than three rounds, or a detachable magazine, which includes guns that can be readily converted to fit this category. Smooth-bore guns with a barrel length of less than 24 inches. Repeating (pump-action, lever action and bolt action) smooth-bore guns and smooth-bore revolver guns with a barrel less than 24 inches.
(C) Repeating (as above) and other manually operated and single-shot rifles. Repeating and other manually loaded smooth-bore guns with a barrel over 24 inches. Semi-automatic rifles and smooth-bore guns which have a total capacity of three shots or less, do not have a detachable magazine, and if a smooth-bore gun have a barrel at least 24 inches long. Weapons in Category C must not 'resemble' fully automatic weapons.
(D) Any shotgun without a magazine, i.e. one round per barrel.

7.20 A European Firearms Pass also entitles the holder to carry suitable ammunition for the weapons in question. A European Firearms Pass does not permit the purchase of weapons in other EU countries, but it will certainly be accepted as evidence of the holder's good standing in most countries and will probably enable him to purchase ammunition if he wishes, although given the number of countries now in the EU it is beyond the scope of this work to give precise details for all countries.

7.21 The European Firearms Pass contains space in the fifth section for Member States to indicate prior authorisation to carry specified firearms to their country. Some countries will require this and others will not, and those who intend to travel need to check before doing so. This is, however, subject to this caveat: prior authorisation is not *in principle* required for firearms in categories C and D to be carried with a view to engaging in hunting, and it is not required for firearms in categories B, C and D when the purpose of the trip is to take part in target shooting. This is subject to the holder being in possession of a European Firearms Pass *and* being able to establish the reasons for his trip. When travelling in Europe it is therefore wise to carry a letter from your host club or hunt indicating that you have been invited. In addition, you will always be expected to have with you some proof of identification – do not leave your passport in the hotel. Member States

---

[25] For those who are interested in this topic, there is a useful Wikipedia article which sets out the various categories in more detail: https://en.wikipedia.org/wiki/European_Firearms_Directive.

can 'opt out' of the whole or part of this regime[26] and deem it necessary to have prior authorisation for all, or some, categories of weapons. Readers may not be surprised to learn that the UK has given such notice and European visitors to the UK (as set out above) must not only be in possession of an appropriate European Firearms Pass, but must also have acquired in advance a visitor's firearm or shotgun permit, as appropriate.

PURCHASES IN THE EUROPEAN COMMUNITY

7.22   Again, this will disappear on Britain leaving the EU.

7.23   Regulations made to implement the European Weapons Directive contain detailed provisions about buying section 1 firearms and their ammunition in other Member States of the European Community.[27] This is commonly known as an 'Article 7 Authority' and permits the holder to purchase a firearm in another (usually specified) EU country, subject to a number of conditions:

(a)   The holder does not have a certificate for the firearm under UK law.
(b)   The firearm falls within Category B of the EU Directive.
(c)   The holder does not propose to bring the firearm into Great Britain.[28]

7.24   The police will obviously wish to satisfy themselves that the applicant for an Article 7 Authority is a fit person, but that person does not have to be a British certificate holder. Further, this authority permits the purchase of items such as pistols ('small firearms') and self-loading rifles which are not permitted in Great Britain. This procedure is a way of getting a 'certificate of good standing' from your local police for those who wish to purchase and use firearms in other EU countries. Although it is not the concern of the British police, you may well find that the local authorities in the country of purchase will wish to be satisfied that proper arrangements have been made for storage of the weapons (e.g. with a firearms dealer in the country in question) when not in use.

---

[26]   By giving notice under Art 8(3) of the Directive.

[27]   Details of the provisions may be found in the Firearms Acts (Amendment) Regulations 1992, regs 5 and 9, which inserted ss 18A, 32A, 32B and 32C into the FA 1968.

[28]   FA 1968, s 32A(2).

Chapter 8

Security of Firearms and Ammunition

INTRODUCTION

8.01   All firearms and shotguns will be held on certificate subject to conditions as to them being held and used securely. 'Firearms or shotguns to which a certificate relates must be stored securely at all times so as to prevent, so far as is reasonably practicable, access to the guns by unauthorised persons'.[1]

8.02   On a firearm or shotgun certificate the relevant statutory conditions are expressed as follows:[2]

   (4)   That the firearms and ammunition to which the certificate relates must at all times (except in the circumstances described in (5) below) be stored securely so as to prevent, so far as is reasonably practicable, access to them by unauthorised persons.

   (5)   That, where a firearm or ammunition to which the certificate relates—

      (a)   is in use;[3] or
      (b)   the certificate holder has the firearm with him for the purpose of cleaning, repairing or testing, or for some other purpose connected with its use, transfer[4] or sale; or

---

[1]   Firearms Rules 1998.

[2]   Firearms Rules 1998, r 3(4). Further conditions can be imposed in the case of specialised weapons and ammunition, such as humane killers, shot pistols and starting pistols, restricting their use to their special purposes (Firearms Rules 1998, r 3(5)).

[3]   In a case decided under the earlier Firearms (Dangerous Air Weapons) Rules of 1969, which referred to 'actual use', it was held that live ammunition concealed in the back of an unattended car for about half an hour was not in actual use nor kept in a secure place with a view to preventing access to it by unauthorised persons (*Marsh v Chief Constable of Avon & Somerset, The Independent*, 8 May 1987, DC).

[4]   'Transfer' is defined to include let on hire, give, lend and part with possession (FA 1968, s 57(4)).

(c)   is in transit to or from a place in connection with its use for any of the
purposes at (b) above,

reasonable precautions must be taken for the safe custody of the firearm or
ammunition.

8.03   Similar conditions are imposed on RFDs, auctioneers, shooting clubs,
museums and those who hold the Secretary of State's authority to possess
prohibited weapons. In some of these cases the conditions relating to security may
also require the firearms in question to be stored at particular premises (such as
the RFD's place of business, or the clubhouse, as appropriate), unless in use.
There are a large number of technical specifications, such as the thickness of the
steel from which a gun cabinet should be made and the type of alarm that might
be appropriate in particular circumstances, but these details are outside the scope
of this book.[5] It should be said that while the law requires 'safekeeping', how that
is to be achieved is not set out in the law. It is a matter of interpretation in each
individual case and there is a wide discretion left to individual police forces. Set
out below is some general guidance as to what is likely to be expected.

8.04   When considering the question of security, it is important to bear in mind
two matters. Firstly, it is a criminal offence to fail to comply with a condition of
your certificate, and so if you were found to be in breach of the security
requirements you are liable to be prosecuted. Secondly, failure to take security
seriously is likely to lead the police to believe your possession of firearms might
pose a danger to public safety or the peace and will lead to the loss of your
certificate.

8.05   Following the two conditions set out above, there are two different sets of
circumstances that need to be considered, with two different levels of security
required.

STORAGE

8.06   As indicated at para 3.81 and Chapter 4, when you apply for a firearm or
shotgun certificate you will be visited by an enquiry officer who will inspect your
security arrangements for the storage of your firearms and ammunition. This will
not only include checking that your cabinet is properly fixed to the wall, but good
practice suggests that the officer should carry out a review of your general home

---

[5]   For those who require greater detail as to the specific requirements see *Firearm Security
Handbook*, 2005 (Home Office); *Consolidated Guidance on Firearm Security*, 1999 (Home
Office and ACPO) – this is the one the police are most likely to look at – and *Guide*, Chapter 19
and Appendix 7.

security as well. This is the most important examination of your security and although you will receive a visit at every renewal, your security arrangements may not be examined again in detail, unless, for example, you apply to increase the number of guns you hold. The enquiry officer will look for window locks, secure doors and no other easy means of access for intruders. All firearms and shotguns must be stored in a lockable steel cabinet which is securely fixed to the fabric of your building. This also applies to section 1 ammunition, but not section 2 (shotgun) ammunition. There is no safekeeping requirement for ordinary shotgun ammunition, although most certificate holders choose to keep it under lock and key if they have the room. Although it is very difficult to generalise, the following will usually be considered necessary:

(a) If possible the cabinets should be within an occupied building, not for example in an outhouse or garage.
(b) Cabinets should be securely fixed to a wall, brick being preferable to breezeblock. If this is not possible, consideration should be given to a floor fixing.
(c) Security always involves an element of discretion and cabinets should be located so as not to be seen by casual visitors to the property.

It is also acceptable to have a 'gunroom' if you are lucky enough to have sufficient space to spare. This will be expected to have a solid construction and a reinforced metal door.

8.07   The actual level of security the police require will depend on a large number of factors. Circumstances such as the building often being unoccupied, a high crime area, a large number of firearms, particularly ones which might be used in crime, and so on, are all factors which will increase the amount of security sought. Applicants sometimes feel that the police are being unreasonable in their approach. Disputes of this type can be difficult to resolve. If, for example, the police insist on an alarm being installed, this can cause major additional expense to the applicant. Such a request is usually made where an applicant wishes to hold a large number of firearms, usually over 12 in one premises. In some cases the police will ask for a 'central station alarm', where a call centre is automatically notified in the event of the alarm being triggered. If the police refuse a certificate because of the applicant's insistence that the security required is too great, then it is possible to appeal that decision. However, it is advisable to try to reach a compromise. The costs of installing an alarm system required by the police may well be less than the legal costs for an appeal to the Crown Court to resolve the dispute.

8.08   Bear in mind that it is also good practice, if possible, to keep ammunition apart from suitable firearms and to store rifle bolts separate from the rifle.

8.09   Unless your weapons are actually 'in use' as defined in Condition 5, they are expected to be locked up. Leaving them out overnight with a view to cleaning them in the morning is not considered acceptable, and most enquiry officers would revoke your certificate if they found you had that loaded shotgun propped up in the corner of the room in case you spotted a rabbit out of the window. In the second example you might argue that the gun was 'in use', but we have seen plenty of certificate holders lose their certificates in similar circumstances. Most breaches of security only come to light as a result of the theft or loss of a firearm or ammunition. As the certificate holder is under a duty to notify such a loss within 7 days (14 if abroad),[6] it will quickly become apparent as to what has occurred and the police will conduct exhaustive enquiries as to the circumstances of the loss.

8.10   Note that Condition 4 does not require the certificate holder to always keep his firearms and ammunition in the approved cabinet at home; they simply have to be 'stored securely'. This could be, for example, in a similar cabinet at the owner's country house or with a gun dealer. The requirement is simply that they should be stored securely 'so far as is reasonably practicable' to prevent access by unauthorised persons. Bear in mind, however, that placing guns in a friend's cabinet, to which the friend retains a key, would in law be giving possession to an unauthorised person, although in the case of shotguns this is acceptable if your friend is also a shotgun certificate holder, and it is for less than 72 hours.

8.11   Because of the fact that the vast majority of certificate holders follow these requirements, the number of firearms subject to theft and loss in Great Britain is very small indeed. It is said that less than 1 per cent of firearms used in armed crime were taken unlawfully from their rightful owners.

'Unauthorised persons'

8.12   Bear in mind that the stated purpose of Condition 4 is 'to prevent, so far as is reasonably practicable, access to them by unauthorised persons'. In the case of a section 1 firearm, the only person authorised to have possession is the certificate holder, and not, for example, his spouse or family, however much the holder might trust them. It is not unknown for the police to express concerns where it becomes apparent to them that the certificate holder's spouse has access to the keys to the gun cabinet. This applies equally to shotguns, with the single exception that another shotgun certificate holder can take possession (for up to 72 hours without entering it onto his certificate) of a shotgun without committing

---

6   F(A)A 1997, ss 34 and 35. It is a criminal offence to fail to notify a loss, whether in Great Britain or abroad.

an offence.[7] Readers can decide for themselves how realistic this is in practice. What is the certificate holder to do when he is asleep, or in the shower? Does the spouse not know where the keys are likely to be?

IN USE

8.13 'In use' covers all the situations set out in Condition 5 where your firearms are not being stored in the approved cabinet at home. Such circumstances obviously vary widely and we cannot comment on every situation. Condition 5(b) is widely drafted and covers most normal situations where a certificate holder might take a firearm or ammunition with them. We would suggest it covers any situation where you have taken your guns with you, so long as it is for a purpose reasonably connected with your ownership of them.[8] At its 'nearest' it covers the owner cleaning his guns on the kitchen table; at its furthest it is perhaps a 2-week trip to the Highlands to go stalking. What is required is for the owner to take 'reasonable precautions' for the safe custody of the firearm or ammunition. This is obviously going to be a matter of individual judgment in each set of circumstances. Examples of 'reasonable' precautions may include taking rifle bolts with you if the rifles are to be left unattended; securing guns in a hotel safe or strong room, or alternatively using a steel security cable to attach them to some immovable object (radiator perhaps?) in the hotel room. If firearms have to be left in a vehicle for any length of time, they must be out of sight. The *Guide* recommends that if firearms are to be regularly carried in a vehicle it might be appropriate to have a steel cable or cage attached to the chassis.[9]

8.14 In a recent case[10] a shooter travelled from his home address in Northumberland to Kirkham Abbey near York with his rifle and ammunition for the purpose of pest control. He then attended a county court hearing in York before intending to travel on further to Banbury in Oxfordshire, again for the purpose of pest control. At the court he placed his rifle in his locked Subaru Forester in the rear of his vehicle under clothing and bags. The safety catch was on; there was a round in the breech and eight rounds in the magazine. He placed his ammunition in the compartment between the front seats; he deliberately parked his car outside the county court rather than in a public car park. There was a dog in the vehicle, so he left a window partly open. The vehicle was unattended

---

[7] The question of 'possession' is considered in detail at para 3.13 *et seq*, 'When do I need a firearm certificate?'.

[8] In any event it is an offence to have a firearm and suitable ammunition together in a public place without a reasonable excuse, FA 1968, s 19. See para 15.47 *et seq* for more details.

[9] *Guide*, Chapter 19.

[10] *DPP v Frank Houghton-Brown* [2010] EWHC 3527 (Admin), Silber J. We are grateful to barrister Jerome Silva for details of this case.

for 3 hours and the presence of the gun was discovered by a police officer who was concerned about the dog, it being a hot day. Mr Houghton-Brown was prosecuted for breach of the security conditions on his licence, the terms being identical to those in Condition 5(b) and (c). He was found not guilty by the magistrates. The police then appealed and the decision of the magistrates to find him not guilty was upheld. Two questions were posed for the High Court. First, was he 'in transit'? The appellants (the police) conceded that he was, given that he intended to travel on to Oxfordshire for more shooting. This is a sensible decision on their part and demonstrates the point that 'in transit' means what it says; a given journey does not have to be limited only to the purposes of shooting. The second question was that if he were in transit, had he taken reasonable precautions to ensure the safe custody of his firearm and ammunition? The High Court stated that this was 'a fact sensitive matter' and there was nothing to suggest that the magistrates had come to a conclusion which was not reasonable on the evidence. It should be remembered that the burden is on the prosecution in a criminal trial to show beyond a reasonable doubt that the defendant did *not* take reasonable precautions. It was made clear in the judgment that all cases such as this must be decided on their own individual facts and the judge observed that 'many people will regard him as having been fortunate'. We would respectfully agree with that observation and in all cases certificate holders are advised to err on the side of caution.

'Reasonable precautions'?

8.15   If there is a loss, the police are likely to suggest that the precautions clearly weren't reasonable. This is not necessarily correct. Those who lost items when the Covent Garden Safety Deposit Company was broken into had undoubtedly taken reasonable precautions for the security of their possessions. Those precautions were defeated. The fact that security arrangements were breached does not mean reasonable precautions were not being taken and it is important to distinguish between the two criteria.

Air weapons

8.16   Although not subject to licensing in England and Wales, it is an offence for a person in possession of an air weapon to fail to take 'reasonable precautions' to prevent someone under the age of 18 from gaining unauthorised access to it.[11] For further details of this offence, and the defences to it, see para 14.29.

---

[11]   FA 1968, s 24ZA, as amended by the Crime and Security Act 2010, s 46, in force 10 February 2011. Maximum penalty £1,000 fine.

Chapter 9

Imitation Firearms

IMITATION FIREARMS

9.01   It is an offence under the FA 1968 to commit a number of criminal offences with an imitation firearm, such as committing indictable offences (e.g. robbery), or resisting arrest, and is punishable in the same way as if the offender had used a real firearm. Details of such offences can be found at para 15.37 *et seq*, para 15.71 *et seq* and para 15.93. Further, if an imitation firearm can be 'readily converted' to fire with lethal effect, possession of these is controlled in the same way as if they were real firearms of the same classification under the Firearms Acts.

9.02   Those reading this chapter because they are considering an item which has the appearance of a firearm may also wish to look at para 1.30, 'Deactivated firearms'.

9.03   An imitation firearm is defined as: 'any thing which has the appearance of being a firearm (other than such a weapon as is mentioned in section 5(1)(b) of this Act) whether or not it is capable of discharging any shot, bullet or other missile'.[1] It does not therefore include stun guns and CS gas canisters, but it does include items which are capable of working as a firearm, so it cannot be argued that 'it is not an imitation firearm because it is a firearm'. A banana in a carrier bag can be an imitation firearm.

---

[1]   FA 1968, s 57(4).

IMITATION FIREARMS WHICH ARE 'READILY CONVERTIBLE'

9.04   Increasing concern about the use of imitation firearms for criminal purposes, and uncertainty about the extent to which the FA 1968 applied to them,[2] led to the passing in 1982 of a Firearms (Amendment) Act, which was brought into force on 1 November 1983. The expressed purpose of the Act is to apply (with some exceptions and qualifications) the provisions of the FA 1968 to imitation firearms if they fulfil certain conditions.[3]

9.05   An imitation firearm is defined in the FA 1982, by reference to the FA 1968, to mean anything which has the appearance of being a section 1 firearm (whether or not it is capable of discharging any shot, bullet or other missile) other than a weapon designed or adapted for the discharge of any noxious liquid, gas or other thing.[4]

9.06   There are two conditions, both of which must be fulfilled. First, that the imitation firearm shall have the appearance of being a section 1 firearm.[5] This is obviously a question of fact. In this context, component parts and accessories have been excluded.[6]

9.07   The second condition is that the imitation firearm shall be so constructed or adapted as to be 'readily convertible' into a section 1 firearm.[7] The FA 1982 goes on to say that the firearm shall be regarded as readily convertible if:

(a)   it can be converted without any special skill on the part of the person converting it in the construction or adaptation of firearms of any description; *and*

(b)   the work in converting it does not require equipment or tools other than such as are in common use by persons carrying out works of construction and maintenance in their own homes.[8]

---

2   See, e.g., the cases discussed at para 1.73 *et seq.*

3   FA 1982, s 1(2).

4   FA 1968, ss 5(1)(b), 57(4); FA 1982, s 1(3). See para 2.05 for details of such weapons.

5   FA 1968, s 1; FA 1982, s 1(1)(a), (4)(a); F(A)A 1988, s 25(7). For the definition of 'section 1 firearm' see para 3.01 *et seq.* Note: for these purposes this will include having the appearance of any prohibited weapon such as a handgun or a machinegun, which are section 1 firearms as well as being section 5 prohibited weapons.

6   FA 1968, s 57(1); FA 1982, s 1(3), (4)(b).

7   FA 1968, s 1(3); FA 1982, s 1(1)(b).

8   FA 1982, s 1(6).

The Home Office explain that the equipment and tools referred to are taken to mean tools and equipment that are normally on sale in retail tools shops, in do-it-yourself shops and from mail order suppliers or discount catalogues. They include, the Home Office adds, electric or hand-powered drills, with or without speed control and with or without vibratory or hammer device, hacksaws, rotating abrasive discs and wheels, high speed twist drills, tungsten carbide masonry drills, hacksaw blades, hammers, drifts, punches, files, etc. It would not include, for example, a lathe.

9.08   If these two conditions are fulfilled, a readily convertible imitation firearm will be subject to all the provisions of the FA 1968 which apply to firearms (other than those applying specifically to shotguns and air weapons), but excluding the provisions mentioned below.[9] The main effect is to require a firearm certificate to be obtained for the handling, etc of imitation firearms in those circumstances where it would be needed for a real firearm, and the provisions described in Chapter 3 will apply, as will the later provisions in that chapter referring to section 1 firearms. A readily convertible imitation firearm will also be a firearm for the purposes of the offences considered in Chapter 15.

9.09   The provisions of the FA 1968 which do not apply to imitation firearms (so far as those provisions are discussed in this book) are those dealing with:

(a)   conversion into a firearm of anything incapable of discharging a missile;[10]
(b)   carrying a firearm in a public place;[11]
(c)   police powers in connection with item (b) above.[12]

It follows, then, from what has been said above that, with the exclusions just mentioned, the provisions contained in Chapters 2, 3, 6, 7, 8, 14, 15 and 16 apply to imitation firearms meeting the required conditions in the same way as they apply to real firearms, unless the provisions refer specifically to shotguns or to air weapons. The same offences may be committed, and the exceptions to those offences, where relevant, will apply.[13]

9.10   The FA 1982 includes an important defence which is available in any prosecution involving an imitation firearm. It applies when the accused can show[14] that he did not know and had no reason to suspect that the imitation

---

[9]   FA 1982, ss 1(2), (4), 2(1).
[10]   FA 1968, s 4(3); FA 1982, s 2(2)(a).
[11]   FA 1968, s 19; FA 1982, s 2(3), applied by Anti-social Behaviour Act 2003, ss 37(1), 93. For such a carrying, see paras 15.47–15.65.
[12]   FA 1968, s 47(1), (3)–(5); FA 1982, s 2(3). For these powers, see Chapter 15.
[13]   FA 1982, ss 1(2), 2(1).
[14]   I.e. can convince the court before which he is prosecuted.

firearm was so constructed or adapted as to be readily convertible (as described above) into a firearm to which the Act applies.[15]

9.11   In conclusion, it may assist to highlight in summary form the points to be considered in deciding whether an imitation firearm is to be treated as a firearm for the purpose of the provisions of the FA 1968:

(a)   It must have the appearance of being a section 1 firearm.
(b)   Component parts and accessories of imitation firearms are excluded.
(c)   It is readily convertible into a real firearm.
(d)   It does not need to be readily convertible to be treated as a firearm in respect of those offences which are committed with an imitation firearm, such as robbery and carrying a firearm in a public place. For offences which can be committed with an imitation firearm this will also include a deactivated firearm as that will certainly have the appearance of a firearm..

The position regarding imitation firearms, court cases about guns which were incapable of being fired, and the FA 1982 is also dealt with para 1.30 *et seq*, dealing with deactivated firearms, which are for these purposes imitation firearms.

9.12   Note that to come within the FA 1982 as an item which is readily convertible, and therefore in law a firearm, it has to have the appearance of a section 1 firearm. As already noted, this will include prohibited weapons as they will also qualify as lethal barrelled weapons. Shotguns and air weapons are not covered, unless they are 'specially dangerous'.[16] So there is no such thing as a readily convertible imitation shotgun. This is in contrast to the position where other offences are committed with an imitation firearm where it can have the appearance of any type of firearm, including a shotgun and a low-powered air weapon, including the banana in the bag.

REALISTIC IMITATION FIREARMS

9.13   Not content with the provisions set out above regarding imitation firearms, Parliament made further provision in 2006 to prohibit the manufacture, sale, modification or importation into Great Britain of a 'realistic imitation firearm'.[17] A realistic imitation firearm is an imitation firearm that is 'so realistic as to be

---

[15]   FA 1982, s 1(5). Contrast this defence with the absence of a corresponding defence if the firearm is a real one under the ruling in *R v Hussain* [1981] 1 WLR 416, (1980) *The Times*, 28 November 1980; see para 3.19 *et seq*, 'When do I need a firearm certificate?', footnotes and the related text.

[16]   FA 1982, s 1(4)(a).

[17]   VCRA 2006, s 36.

indistinguishable, for all practical purposes, from a real firearm'.[18] This does not, however, cover deactivated firearms, or things that are classified as antiques under the Firearms Acts. The difference between an imitation firearm under the FA 1982 and a realistic imitation firearm under the VCRA 2006 is that the first Act prohibits items which are readily convertible to be a real firearm, the second prohibits those which have the appearance of a real firearm, convertible or not. A realistic imitation firearm is not to be regarded as distinguishable from a real firearm if it can only be distinguished by an expert, on close examination, or by attempting to load or fire it.[19] The court is entitled to take into account the size, shape and principal colour in deciding the issue, although regulations[20] provide approved sizes and colours. In limited circumstances there are defences available on a prosecution under section 36. These are that the manufacture, sale, importation, etc was for the purpose only of placing the item in a museum or gallery; or for theatrical productions and rehearsals or film production (this would include TV). There is also a defence for the organisation and holding of historical re-enactments by persons approved under the regulations by the Secretary of State.[21] Further, it is a defence to do such things by way of trade or business, if you intend to modify the realistic imitation firearm in such a way as it ceases to be a realistic imitation firearm. This would provide you with a defence if you imported realistic imitation firearms with the intention of painting them bright purple, or some other 'approved' colour and then selling them as toys. Readers will have seen toy guns which have an orange cap on the 'muzzle'. This does not provide a defence in Great Britain, although it does in the State of California, and was widely copied here before the introduction of the VCRA 2006. The purpose of the Act is to eventually reduce the number of imitation firearms (toys or otherwise) that are in circulation. Possession, however, is not an offence, unless you are committing some ulterior criminal offence with the realistic imitation firearm where it will simply be classified as an imitation firearm. The use of any type of imitation firearm in furtherance of another offence is punishable in the same way as if you had a real one, with one exception. The penalty for carrying an imitation firearm contrary to section 19 of the FA 1968 is less than for other types of weapon, see para 15.52 for more details.

---

[18] VCRA 2006, s 38(1).

[19] VCRA 2006, s 38(2).

[20] The Violent Crime Reduction Act 2006 (Realistic Imitation Firearms) Regulations 2007 (SI 2007/2606). The size has to be less than 38 mm high and 70 mm long. Colours such as bright pink are permitted, or transparent, but black and silver do not appear in the list!

[21] VCRA 2006, s 37(2).

IMPORTATION OF REALISTIC IMITATION FIREARMS

9.14   Items intercepted by the UK Border Agency[22] on arrival into Great Britain which they consider are realistic imitation firearms and do not meet the approved criteria in the regulations are liable to seizure and forfeiture.[23] If the goods are intercepted, the owner will be served with a Notice of Seizure. This will initially invite you to make representations (if you wish) as to why the goods should not have been seized. If you wish to appeal against the legality of the seizure you must submit a notice of claim giving your reasons within one calendar month of the date of seizure. Be warned this time limit is absolute and any claim received later will be rejected.

9.15   Provided you submit a notice of claim challenging the legality of the seizure within the time limit, Border Force will then be obliged to issue 'condemnation proceedings' in a magistrates' court, usually the one closest to where your items were seized. This will give you the opportunity to put your case before a court of law as to why your goods should not have been seized and should be returned to you. If the court does not find in your favour, or you do not lodge an appeal against seizure within the time limit, then your realistic imitation firearm will be 'condemned', i.e. forfeited to the Crown.

9.16   You are entitled to rely on the defences in section 36, set out at para 9.13, when arguing that the seizure was not lawful. So if you are importing a realistic imitation firearm for use in a theatrical play (which is a permitted reason to import it), you will be allowed to make the claim on that basis. What does lead to some confusion is that the Notice 12A, mentioned at para 9.19, suggests that the 'defences' available under the VCRA 2006 cannot be argued. That is strictly true when Border Force are considering restoration, but not condemnation.

9.17   In the Notice of Seizure you will also be offered the option of seeking 'restoration'. This is an application to Border Force to have your goods returned, even if you accept the seizure was, or may have been, lawful. Any request for restoration must be put in writing no later than 45 days from the date of seizure. Restoration is considered by an officer of the Border Agency who will be independent of the officers who initially made the seizure. If you are dissatisfied with the decision notified to you, there is an option within 45 days to request a review. If following the review you are still dissatisfied, you can appeal within 30 days to an independent tribunal. In our experience there is little point in asking

---

22   Formerly border controls were administered by HM Customs, now by Border Force.

23   VCRA 2006, s 39(6).

for restoration; it is usually refused as a matter of policy, an approach which has been approved by the courts.

9.18 You can apply for restoration either alone or in conjunction with condemnation proceedings, i.e. an appeal against the legality of the seizure. We would generally recommend doing both. Owners of goods often ignore 'condemnation' and ask only for 'restoration' at their peril. This can be a big mistake, as your best prospect of getting your property back will usually be by having the matter heard in court. Perhaps not surprisingly, our experience is that where goods are considered by Border Force to have been lawfully seized, they are unlikely to agree to restore them.

9.19 You will receive with the Notice of Seizure an information Notice 12A outlining your rights of appeal. This claims to be written in plain English, but those who have no previous experience of such matters may not appreciate from reading this leaflet the distinctions between condemnation and restoration proceedings, and the consequences of pursuing one route rather than the other. If the items are valuable and you want them back, this is an area where you really need to consult a specialist solicitor quickly.

IMPORTATION OF KNIVES

9.20 We should add that while we have dealt with the process for appealing against seizure of goods by Border Force in the context of importation of realistic imitation firearms, the above paragraphs apply equally to challenging the seizure by Border Force of any other type of goods on entry into the UK, such as firearms and knives. Items such as flick knives are illegal to import. This also includes a number of other offensive weapons listed in the Criminal Justice Act 1988 (Offensive Weapons) Order 1988.[24] Those interested in this topic should also note that there is an Offensive Weapons Bill currently before Parliament which, if enacted, will alter the definition of flick knife to include spring-assisted knives – the button will no longer need to be on the handle. This will also make simple possession of any of the items in the Offensive Weapons Order an offence; at the moment they can be possessed, but not carried in public without a reasonable excuse. The Bill will also introduce further controls on the sale of knives to those under 18 and on the sale of corrosive substances.

---

[24] SI 1988/2019.

Chapter 10

Shooting Game

WHAT IS MEANT BY 'GAME'?

10.01 There are several Acts of Parliament dealing with the shooting of game. In some of those Acts the term 'game' is defined; however, the definitions are not always consistent. In some Acts there is no definition of the term. The definition, or the lack of it, is mentioned in this chapter when each of the statutory provisions is dealt with.

10.02 It is also important to note that under the legislation the word 'game' is not always given its everyday meaning; for example, rabbits (which are also referred to as conies) are included in the definition in some Acts.[1] Further, the expression will include, where appropriate, dead game[2] as well as live, and tame game as well as wild.[3]

10.03 Strictly speaking, deer cannot be regarded as game but, since most of the law in this chapter applies to game and deer, both are dealt with in the one chapter. The law relating specifically to the shooting of deer can be found in Chapter 12.

10.04 Finally, the reader will find references made to various different types of game such as black game, red game, moor game and ground game. These terms are taken from the legislation, which on the whole does not seek to define them, and so we are left to apply a common sense approach as to what might be included in these various types of game.[4]

---

[1] E.g. in the Poaching Prevention Act 1862 (PPA 1862), s 1.

[2] *Loome v Bailey* (1860) 3 E & F 444; though the Game Act 1831 (GA 1831) does not apply to game killed abroad (*Guyer v R* (1889) 23 QBD 100).

[3] *Cook v Trevener* [1911] KB 9, 74 JP 469. But tame pheasants are not 'game' within the meaning of the Night Poaching Act 1828 (NPA 1828) (*R v Garnham* (1861) 2 F & F 34).

[4] The exception is ground game which is defined: Ground Game Act 1880 (GGA 1880), s 8. See further Chapter 13.

WHEN CAN I SHOOT GAME?

10.05 There are periods of the year, known as 'close seasons', during which game and deer[5] must not be shot.[6] These periods vary according to the bird or animal protected.[7] For this purpose, 'game' means: pheasants, partridges, black game, grouse/red game or bustards.[8] A table of close seasons is set out in Appendix C.

10.06 Furthermore, there are certain days and times, outside the close seasons, during which game must not be killed. Game must not be killed on a Sunday or on Christmas Day.[9] For this purpose, the term 'game' includes: hares, pheasants, partridges, grouse, heath or moor game and black game.[10] Since the word 'includes' is used, it is possible that other birds and animals may fall within the provision if they can be described as game.[11]

10.07 In addition to the different definitions of game, there is a further distinction between shooting out of season and shooting on a Sunday or on Christmas Day. In both instances, in the Game Act 1831 (GA 1831), the words 'kill or take' are used, but in respect of Sundays and Christmas Day there are the added words: 'or use any dog, gun, net, or other engine or instrument[12] for the purpose of killing or

---

[5] For this purpose deer are the species listed in section 3 of Appendix C (Deer Act 1991 (DA 1991), s 2(2) and Sch 1).

[6] GA 1831, s 3; DA 1991, s 2(1); Game (Scotland) Act 1772 (G(S)A 1772), s 1.

A general exception arises under Agriculture Act 1947 (AA 1947), s 98. In this instance government ministers may require a person having the right to do so to take steps to kill particular birds and animals which are causing damage, even though they may be out of season. The only animals which may presently be the subject of this requirement are deer, though other animals and birds may be nominated by government order.

For special exceptions relating to deer, see para 12.21 and, in the case of deer, the maximum punishment on summary conviction is a fine at level 4 on the standard scale (currently £2,500), or 3 months' imprisonment, or both (DA 1991, s 9(1)). If an offence involves more than one deer, the maximum fine shall be regarded as if there was a separate offence against each deer (DA 1991, s 9(2)).

In the case of game, the maximum penalty on summary conviction is a fine at level 1 on the standard scale (currently £200), for every head of game illegally taken (GA 1831, s 3; G(S)A 1772, s 1).

[7] GA 1831, s 3; DA 1991, s 2(2) and Sch 1.

[8] GA 1831, s 3. In Scotland, G(S)A 1772, s 1 creates close seasons applicable to muir fowl, tarmagan (old spelling of ptarmigan), heath fowl, partridge or pheasant.

[9] GA 1831, s 3. The maximum punishment on summary conviction is a fine at level 1 on the standard scale (currently £200).

[10] GA 1831, s 2.

[11] However, the word 'includes' has been interpreted in some statutory contexts to mean exclusively the items mentioned after it.

[12] E.g. a snare.

taking any game'. This distinction has significance, as to shoot at and miss a pheasant on Christmas Day is an offence, but to do so on a weekday during the close season is not.

10.08 There are also restrictions on shooting game at night. You must not unlawfully[13] take or destroy any game[14] or rabbits at night[15] on any open or enclosed land.[16] By a later Act[17] this restriction was extended to include any public road, highway or path or the sides thereof and the openings, outlets or gates from any open or enclosed land leading onto any public road, highway or path.

GAME LICENCES

10.09 Game licences have now been abolished throughout the UK. Since 1 August 2007, there has no longer been any requirement to hold a game licence to shoot game in England and Wales.[18] The change was brought about as the cost of game licences had not kept up with inflation, and the requirements were not strictly adhered to, meaning that game licences did not generate significant revenue for the Crown. The fee payable for a game licence varied, depending on whether it was to be valid for a full year or part thereof, but the maximum fee in 2007 was as little as £6, having not been increased in many years, and even thereafter remained unaltered for Scotland and Northern Ireland, where game licences continued to be required for several more years. It is perhaps unsurprising, therefore, that game licences were also finally abolished in both Scotland and Northern Ireland by legislation passed in 2011. In Northern Ireland the requirement to hold a game licence in order to shoot game ceased with effect

---

13   I.e. without having the game rights. Thus, a tenant not having these rights could be convicted under this provision for these activities on land within his tenancy (*Liversedge v Whiteoak* (1893) 57 JPN 692; although this case does not specifically refer to night poaching, the principle is of general application).

14   'Game' includes hares, pheasants, partridges, grouse, heath or moor game and black game (NPA 1828, s 13). As to 'includes', see fn 11.

15   This is from one hour after sunset to one hour before sunrise (NPA 1828, s 12).

16   NPA 1828, s 1. To do so is an offence with a maximum punishment on summary conviction of a fine at level 3 on the standard scale (currently £1,000). For an interpretation of 'enclosed land', though in another context, see para 12.25 and fn 109 thereto.

17   Night Poaching Act 1844 (NPA 1844), s 1.

18   The Regulatory Reform (Game) Order 2007 (SI 2007/2007) (RR(G)O 2007). This repealed in its entirety the Game Licences Act 1861 in respect of England and Wales and likewise the Hares Act 1848. Certain provisions of the GA 1831 were repealed, and various other consequential amendments made to legislation, to remove references to the requirement for a game licence in England and Wales. See RR(G)O 2007, art 2 and Sch, Pt 1.

from 13 June 2011.[19] Scotland closely followed suit, with the change coming into force there from 29 June 2011.[20]

10.10 As a result of these changes in the law, we do not discuss the extensive learning on the topic of having taken game without a licence. For those who might find it useful, it is set out in the 1999 edition of *Gun Law*, an earlier version of this book.

SALE OF GAME

10.11 Prior to the abolition of game licences and the repeal of associated legislation, the law restricted the sale of game at certain times. It was illegal to sell, or indeed buy, a game bird[21] after the expiration of 10 days from the beginning of its close season.[22] Of those 10 days, one was inclusive so that, for example, in the case of partridges, a sale after 11 February was illegal, the close season for partridges beginning on 1 February. This rule did not apply to foreign game birds,[23] or to live birds bought or sold for rearing or exhibition purposes or for sale alive.[24]

10.12 In England and Wales, hares and leverets, unless imported, still must not be sold or exposed for sale during the months of March to July inclusive.[25] Although it is no longer an offence for dealers to buy, sell or possess game birds after 10 days from the beginning of the close season,[26] the sale of game birds in

---

[19] The Wildlife and Natural Environment (Northern Ireland) Act 2011, s 35 provides that Part 4 of the Miscellaneous Transferred Excise Duties Act (Northern Ireland) 1972 (game licences and game dealers' licences) shall cease to have effect. The Wildlife and Natural Environment (2011 Act) (Commencement No 1) Order (Northern Ireland) 2011 (SI 2011/215) brought s 35 into force on 13 June 2011.

[20] The Wildlife and Natural Environment (Scotland) Act 2011 received Royal assent on 7 April 2011. Part 2 of Sch 1 to that Act repeals various Acts and provisions relating to the requirement for game licences in Scotland. The Wildlife and Natural Environment (Scotland) Act 2011 (Commencement No 1) Order 2011 (SI 2011/279) brought those repeals into force on 29 June 2011.

[21] 'Game' is defined in GA 1831, s 2 as including pheasants, partridges, grouse, heath or moor game, black game.

[22] GA 1831, s 4; for close seasons, see Appendix C.

[23] *Guyer v R* (1889) 23 QBD 100.

[24] GA 1831, s 4. The maximum penalty on conviction is at level 1 on the standard scale (currently £200) for each head of game.

[25] Hare Preservation Act 1892 (HPA 1892), ss 2, 3. The maximum penalty on conviction is at level 1 on the standard scale (currently £200); this probably applies to each head of game. This Act has now been repealed in Scotland under the Wildlife and Natural Environment (Scotland) Act 2011.

[26] RR(G)O 2007, which repealed GA 1831, s 4.

England and Wales is not without limitation. It is now an offence for any person to sell or offer or to expose for sale, or to have in his possession or transport for the purposes of sale, any bird of game, which has been taken or killed in circumstances which constitute an offence under the Night Poaching Act 1828 (NPA 1828), the GA 1831, the Poaching Prevention Act 1862 (PPA 1862), or Part 1 of the Wildlife and Countryside Act 1981 (WCA 1981), where the person concerned knows or has reason to believe that it has been so taken or killed.[27]

OWNERSHIP OF GAME AND NEIGHBOURS' RIGHTS

10.13 While birds and animals are in a wild state they cannot be completely owned by anyone,[28] but in the following three cases there can be qualified ownership:

(a) A person who lawfully takes, tames or reclaims a wild animal or bird may claim it as his property until it regains its natural liberty.[29]

(b) An owner of land has a right to the young of wild animals or birds born on his land until they can run or fly away.[30]

(c) A landowner also has the right[31] to shoot or otherwise take wild animals or birds while on his land.[32]

10.14 Tame or domesticated birds and animals may be owned, as can wild birds kept in captivity or tamed.[33] The Theft Act 1968 (TA 1968) creates an offence of theft of wild creatures. The offence is committed if:

---

[27] GA 1831, s 3A. As of 17 August 2011, a similar offence exists in Northern Ireland under s 36 of the Wildlife and Natural Environment (Northern Ireland) Act 2011.

[28] While there can only be qualified property in wild animals while they are alive, there can be absolute property in such animals when they are dead. This right is vested in the owner of the land, or the grantee of shooting rights over the land, and this is so even if the animals are not killed by them but by a trespasser.

[29] Known as qualified property obtained *per industriam, Halsbury's Laws of England*, 5th Edition Reissue, Vol 2, para 712.

[30] Known as qualified property *ratione impotentiae et loci, Halsbury's Laws of England*, 5th Edition Reissue, Vol 2, para 713; a claim of trespass will lie for young so born *Case of Swans* (1592) 7 Co Rep 15b at 17b; *Blades v Higgs* (1865) 11 HL Cas 621.

[31] For the cases when this right will be shared with or let to a tenant, see Chapter 13.

[32] Known as qualified property *ratione soli* in respect of landowners and *ratione privilegii* in respect of grantees of those rights *Halsbury's Laws of England*, 5th Edition Reissue, Vol 2, para 714, *Blades v Higgs* (1865) 11 HL Cas 621.

[33] *Oke's Game Laws* (5th Edition, 1912) p 17. Note: there are a number of references to *Oke's Game Laws* in these chapters. The current authors have been unable to obtain a copy of this great work

(a)   they are domesticated, tamed or ordinarily[34] kept in captivity; or

(b)   their carcass has been reduced into possession[35] by or on behalf of another person and possession of them has not since been lost or abandoned; or

(c)   another person is in the course of reducing them into possession.[36]

10.15   Difficult questions may arise when game (or other wild birds or animals) are put up on one person's land and are killed there or elsewhere. A person who puts up and kills game on another's land does not thereby own the carcass; it belongs to the person having the shooting rights over that land. But if you put up game on your land and kill it on or over another's land, the ownership is yours. Similarly, though for different reasons, if you, being a trespasser, start game on A's land, follow it on to B's land and there kill it, you are the owner of the game.[37] Mere ownership of the carcass will not necessarily entitle the owner to retrieve it, and he must take care that he does not commit the offence of trespassing in pursuit of game.[38] Simply to discharge your gun at game over your neighbour's land does not make you liable for this offence,[39] but personal entry to retrieve the game may do so. Unfortunately, the law on this point is confused, as is illustrated by the following four court decisions:

(a)   M, on land where he had a right to shoot, shot at and killed a pheasant on the ground on adjoining land occupied by U and over which M had no shooting rights. M then went on to U's land and picked up the pheasant. The court decided that M should be convicted of trespassing in pursuit of game, since the shooting and picking up of the game was one transaction constituting the pursuit.[40]

(b)   A pheasant rose from H's land and, when it was over T's land, H, being on his own land, shot at it. The pheasant fell on T's land. H went on to T's land to pick up the pheasant, which was then dead. The court decided there was no offence of trespass in pursuit of game. The offence refers to the pursuit of live game only.[41]

---

in order to verify these references. We assume they are correct, given that they appeared in the previous six editions of *Gun Law*, presumably with corrections as appropriate.

[34]   I.e. the offence can be committed while they are temporarily out of captivity.

[35]   No statutory definition is given for the phrase 'reduce into possession'. It is suggested that this is akin to appropriation and means the doing of some act by the other person to assert his ownership, e.g. putting the carcass in his game bag or car or hiding it in some place.

[36]   TA 1968, s 4(4). Upon conviction on indictment for the offence, the maximum term of imprisonment is 7 years (TA 1968, s 7).

[37]   *Blades v Higgs* (1865) 34 LJCP 286, and cases there cited.

[38]   As to this offence, see Chapter 11.

[39]   Although, technically, you will be committing the civil wrong of trespass.

[40]   *Osbond v Meadows* (1862) 26 JP 439, 31 LJMC 238.

[41]   *Kenyon v Hart* (1865) 29 JP 260, 34 LJMC 87.

(c) T, one of a party shooting pheasants, saw pheasants that had been shot fall into the adjoining wood of S. Two days afterwards, T went into S's wood to pick up the pheasants, believing them to be dead. The court decided that if the pheasants were dead, or if T believed them to be dead, there was no offence, but it would be otherwise if the pheasants were alive or believed to be alive.[42]

(d) R stood on his own land and fired at and killed a grouse sitting on the adjoining land of G. Some hours later, R went on to G's land to pick up the bird, which had in the meantime been picked up by somebody else, namely the gamekeeper. The court decided that the shooting and searching were sufficiently connected to form a continuous act and together constituted the pursuit of game. R was therefore guilty of the offence, and it mattered not whether the grouse was dead or alive when searched for.[43]

10.16 In all cases the entry on the adjoining land without permission will constitute the civil wrong of trespass, as opposed to the criminal offence of trespass in pursuit of game. Permission to enter and retrieve game may not, however, easily be obtained.

SHOOTING GAME ON THE FORESHORE AND OVER WATER

10.17 The majority of the foreshore,[44] the bed of the sea for some distance below low-water mark, and the beds of estuaries, arms of the sea and tidal rivers are owned by the Crown Estate. The Crown has granted some of these lands to private individuals and other bodies, such as local authorities. Whether or not such a grant has been made, the only general rights of the public which may be exercised in these areas are rights of fishing and of navigation and their attendant rights, for example, anchoring and mooring. The public has no general right of shooting or otherwise taking game and other birds and animals.[45] However, it has been suggested that the Crown, where it is the owner of the foreshore, would effectively acquiesce in the exercise of a right to shoot by the public when no mischief or injury is likely to arise from the exercise of that right.[46]

---

[42] *Tanton v Jervis* (1879) 43 JP 784.

[43] *Horn v Raine* (1898) 62 JP 420; 67 LJQB 533.

[44] 'Foreshore' in England, Wales and Northern Ireland is generally defined as the land between the high water mark of medium high tides and the low water mark: *Halsbury's Laws of England*, 5th Edition Reissue, Vol 100, para 34. In Scotland the 'foreshore' is defined as the land between the mean high water of spring tides and the mean low water of spring tides.

[45] *Halsbury's Laws of England*, 5th Edition Reissue, Vol 100, para 52.

[46] *Halsbury's Laws of England*, 5th Edition Reissue, Vol 100, para 53.

10.18 For a private individual to have the right of shooting in the areas mentioned, he must be able to show that:

(a) he owns or has acquired a title to the land or to the right of shooting by long uninterrupted usage;[47] or
(b) he is entitled to the benefit of a grant from the Crown of the land in question.[48]

Non-tidal waters are treated as if they were land not covered with water; for example, the right to shoot over a lake depends upon whether the area of the lake forms part of the land within the shooting. Where the land is bounded by a river or stream, the general rule is that the boundary of the land is the middle of the water.

---

[47] The acquisition of the right in this way is governed by strict legal rules and it is not, e.g., sufficient for a claimant to say merely that he has shot over a particular stretch of foreshore for many years.

[48] The right to shoot and take birds on the foreshore is a *profit à prendre*: *Halsbury's Laws of England*, 4th Edition Reissue, Vol 14, paras 240 *et seq*, and *Halsbury's Laws of England*, 5th Edition Reissue, Vol 100, para 52.

Chapter 11

Poaching

INTRODUCTION

11.01 In addition to seeking a prosecution,[1] the owner or occupier may take civil action against a poacher under the ordinary rules relating to trespass of the land.[2] If a person is trespassing on land, that is to say, is on land where he has no right to be, the owner or occupier of that land may order that person to leave at once. If the person does not leave, the owner, the occupier or others under the direction of the occupier or owner, may use force to expel him provided that they only use such force as is necessary to remove him.[3] The occupier may also sue the trespasser in the civil courts for any damage caused while trespassing and, if that person is a persistent trespasser, may be able to obtain an injunction[4] against him.

11.02 Acts of Parliament have created a number of poaching offences whose ingredients and penalties vary according to whether the offences are committed in the daytime or by night, whether the poacher is alone or with others, whether or not he is armed, and whether he resists or co-operates when detected.

---

[1]   A prosecution may be instituted by anyone, whether he is interested in the land trespassed on or not (*Halsbury's Laws of England*, 5th Edition Reissue, Vol 2, para 798).

[2]   Though, where a prosecution for daytime poaching has been started, civil proceedings for trespass cannot be brought against the offender for the same act by a person at whose instance or with whose concurrence or assent the prosecution was instituted (GA 1831, s 46).

[3]   *Halsbury's Laws of England*, 5th Edition Reissue, Vol 2, para 779.

[4]   I.e. an order of the court forbidding him to commit further trespass, the penalty for non-compliance usually being a fine or imprisonment.

POACHING IN THE DAYTIME

11.03 If you 'commit any trespass[5] by entering or being[6] in the daytime[7] upon any land in search or pursuit of game[8] or woodcocks, snipes ... or conies',[9] you will commit an offence.[10] If five or more of you together do the same thing, each of you will upon conviction be liable to a greater penalty.[11]

11.04 If you are caught in the circumstances just mentioned by any one of a number of specified persons, you must, if asked to do so, leave the land at once and supply your full names and address. The persons who are entitled to make these requests are:[12]

(a) the person having the right of killing game on the land;
(b) the occupier of the land, whether or not he has the right of killing game on it;
(c) the gamekeeper or other servant of, or any person authorised by, either of the persons described in (a) and (b) above;
(d) a police constable.

11.05 If you refuse to give your real name and address, or give such a general description of your place of abode 'as shall be illusory for the purpose of discovery', or wilfully continue or return upon the land, you may be apprehended by the person making the request, or by anybody acting by his order and in his aid, and later charged before a magistrate.[13] Any person so apprehended must be released if he is not brought before a magistrate within 12 hours.[14] Any of the

---

[5] I.e. entry without the prior permission of the occupier of the land or, where the shooting rights are held by some other person, of that other person (GA 1831, s 30).

[6] An entry or presence by a person is necessary to constitute the offence. The sending of a dog on to the land is not enough (*Pratt v Martin* [1911] 2 KB 90).

[7] This lasts from the beginning of the last hour before sunrise to the end of the first hour after sunset (GA 1831, s 34).

[8] The word 'game' includes hares, pheasants, partridges, grouse, heath or moor game and black game (GA 1831, s 2).

[9] I.e. rabbits.

[10] GA 1831, s 30. The maximum penalty on summary conviction is a fine at level 3 on the standard scale (currently £1,000).

[11] GA 1831, s 30. The maximum penalty on summary conviction is a fine at level 4 on the standard scale (currently £2,500). Any vehicle used by you in committing the offence may be forfeited by order of the convicting court (Game Laws (Amendment) Act 1960 (GL(A)A 1960), s 4A).

[12] GA 1831, ss 31, 31A.

[13] GA 1831, ss 31, 31A. You will be liable on summary conviction to a maximum fine at level 1 on the standard scale (currently £200).

[14] GA 1831, ss 31, 31A.

persons listed above may also demand from you any game[15] in your possession which appears to have been recently killed and, if this is not delivered to them, they may seize it from you for the use of the person entitled to it.[16]

11.06 If five or more of you together are found on land in pursuit of game, woodcock, snipe or rabbits in the daytime,[17] one or more of you having a gun, and you prevent or try to prevent 'by violence, intimidation or menace' any of the persons described in items (a) to (d) at para 11.04 from approaching for the purpose of requiring you to leave the land or giving them your particulars, you will commit a further offence.[18]

POACHING BY NIGHT

11.07 As discussed a para 10.08, there are certain restrictions against shooting game at night. Additionally, Parliament has created a more serious offence to deal with armed trespass at night in pursuit of game by three or more persons. An offence is committed if persons in such numbers are or enter on any land[19] unlawfully[20] by night[21] for the purposes of taking or destroying game[22] or rabbits and any of them is armed[23] with a gun, crossbow, firearm, bludgeon or any other

---

[15] This will be 'game' as defined in fn 8. Thus the power of seizure will not extend to woodcock, snipe and rabbits, which are the other birds and animals that may be the subject of daytime poaching. But see also the police powers of seizure at para 11.14.

[16] GA 1831, s 36, although this section does not expressly refer to a police constable having the power to demand game.

[17] This lasts from the beginning of the last hour before sunrise to the end of the first hour after sunset (GA 1831, s 34).

[18] GA 1831, s 32. The maximum fine on summary conviction is at level 5 on the standard scale (currently £5,000). If you aid or abet the commission of the offence you are likewise liable. This is so even though you may be on a road, and not on the land being trespassed upon (*Stacey v Whitehurst* (1865) 18 CB NS 344).

[19] This includes any public road, highway or path and the sides thereof, and the openings, outlets and gates from any land into them (NPA 1844, s 1).

[20] I.e. without having any necessary permissions or the right to take game.

[21] This means from one hour after sunset to one hour before sunrise (NPA 1828, s 12).

[22] This includes hares, pheasants, partridges, grouse, heath or moor game, black game and bustards (NPA 1828, s 13).

[23] If one of the party is armed, all are deemed to be so (*R v Goodfellow* (1845) 1 Car & Kir 724 CCR).

offensive weapon;[24] each of the party in these circumstances will be guilty.[25] It is not necessary that all of the party should enter the land; if all are associated for a common purpose and some enter while others remain near enough to assist, all of them may be convicted.[26] Nor is it necessary that all of them should be on the same piece of land or on land in the same occupation or ownership,[27] but they must have a plan in common;[28] and they may be convicted even though they may have abandoned their arms before being arrested.[29]

11.08   There are also the offences of unlawfully by night: taking[30] or destroying game or rabbits on any land; or entering[31] or being on any land with any gun, net, engine[32] or instrument for the purpose of taking or destroying game.[33] Any person found upon land committing either of these offences may be seized and apprehended by any of the following people who may also apprehend him in any other place to which he may have escaped and been pursued:

(a)   The owner or occupier of the land.

(b)   The lord of the manor or reputed manor in which the land lies.

---

[24]   This can include a large stone, provided it is capable of inflicting serious injury if used offensively and brought and used for that purpose (*R v Grice* (1837) 7 C & P 803) and, if taken with the intention of it being used offensively, a stick (*R v Fry & Webb* (1837) 2 Mood & R 42). A definition of 'offensive weapon' is given in another Act of Parliament as 'any article made or adapted for use for causing injury to the person, or intended by the person having it with him for such use by him or by some other person' (Prevention of Crime Act 1953 (PCA 1953), s 1(4)). See para 15.69 for a full discussion of offensive weapons.

[25]   NPA 1828, s 9. Criminal Law Act 1977 (CLA 1977), s 15(4) provides that this offence is triable summarily only and the maximum punishment on summary conviction is 6 months' imprisonment, or a fine at level 4 on the standard scale (currently £2,500), or both. Originally the offender could have been transported overseas for 7 to 14 years or sentenced to hard labour!

[26]   *R v Whittaker and Others* (1848) 2 Car & Kir 636 CCR.

[27]   *R v Uezzell and Others* (1851) 2 Den 274 CCR.

[28]   There must be a joint act for each to be guilty of the offence: *R v Nickless* (1839) 8 C & P 757; in modern criminal law a 'joint enterprise'.

[29]   *R v Nash & Weller* (1819) Russ & Ry 386.

[30]   Taking does not necessarily involve the offence of theft. It means, not to take away, but to catch, e.g. catching game in a snare with a view to keeping or killing it (*R v Glover* (1814) Russ & Ry 269, CCR).

[31]   Personal entry is necessary (*R v Pratt* (1855) 4 E & B 860); thus, the sending of a dog on to land to drive out game does not constitute entry (*Pratt v Martin* [1911] 2 KB 90).

[32]   The words 'engine' and 'instrument' include a snare (*Allen v Thompson* (1870) LR 5 QB 336 at 339). This case was concerned with the use of a snare on a Sunday but is of general application. Further, it was held that leaving a trap or snare is sufficient; there is no need for the person to be present when it is operated.

[33]   NPA 1828, s 1. The maximum punishment on summary conviction for this offence is a fine at level 3 on the standard scale (currently £1,000).

(c)   Any gamekeeper or servant of any of the persons listed at (a) and (b).

(d)   Any person assisting such gamekeeper or servant.

The person so apprehended must be delivered as soon as possible into the custody of a police officer to be brought before the magistrates.

11.09   If the offender assaults, or offers any violence to, a person so authorised to arrest him with any gun, crossbow, firearm, bludgeon, stick, club or any other offensive weapon whatsoever, he commits an offence.[34]

11.10   The powers to demand and seize game, which have been discussed above in relation to daytime poaching, apply equally to offences of nocturnal poaching.[35]

POACHING BY DAY OR NIGHT

11.11   If you obtain game[36] by unlawfully going on any land, in search or pursuit of game, you will commit an offence.[37] 'Unlawfully in search or pursuit of game' means a trespass by the offender on land of which he is neither the owner, nor occupier, nor the gamekeeper nor the servant of either, nor having any *bona fide* right to kill the game thereon; the trespass being also without the consent of the owner, or of any person having the right to kill game there, or of any person having any right to authorise the offender to enter or be upon the land for the purpose of searching for or pursuing game.[38]

---

[34]   NPA 1828, s 2. CLA 1977, s 15(4) provides that this offence is triable summarily only and the maximum punishment on summary conviction is 6 months' imprisonment or a fine at level 4 on the standard scale (currently £2,500), or both.

[35]   GA 1831, s 36.

[36]   'Game' includes hares, pheasants, partridges, woodcocks, rabbits, snipe, grouse and black or moor game (PPA 1862, s 1). As to 'includes', see para 10.05 *et seq*, 'When can I shoot game?', text and related footnotes.

[37]   The maximum penalty on summary conviction is a fine at level 3 on the standard scale (currently £1,000). Game, guns and ammunition in the offender's possession may also be forfeited by order of the court (PPA 1862, s 2; Game Laws (Amendment) Act 1960 (GL(A)A 1960), s 3(2)).

[38]   GA 1831, s 30.

11.12 If you use[39] any gun, part of a gun, cartridges or other ammunition, or nets, traps, snares or other devices of a kind used for the killing or taking of game, for unlawfully killing or taking game, that will be an offence.[40]

11.13 A person who is an accessory[41] to either of the last two offences is liable to the same penalties as the offender himself.[42]

POWERS OF POLICE

11.14 The powers of the police to arrest suspected persons are governed by the Police and Criminal Evidence Act 1984 (PACE 1984), which is of general application. However, statutes dealing with poaching contain a number of provisions enabling the police to stop and search suspected persons and their vehicles, to arrest suspected persons and to seize and detain things found on those arrested. If a police officer has reasonable grounds for suspecting that a person is committing an offence of poaching in the day or at night he may enter on that land to arrest him.[43] A police officer may, in any highway or public place, search any person whom he has good cause to suspect of coming from land where he has been unlawfully in search or pursuit of game,[44] or any person aiding or abetting him, and of having in his possession any game unlawfully obtained, or any gun, part of gun, cartridges or other ammunition, or any nets, traps, snares or other devices of a kind used for the taking of game.[45] The police officer has the power to seize any game or rabbits, or any gun or article used for killing or taking game or rabbits, which are in his possession.[46] The police officer also has the power to stop and search any cart or conveyance in or on which the officer suspects any such game or article is being carried.

---

[39] So far as this offence is concerned, a gun may be said to be used for these purposes, even though it has not been fired. If you go onto land with a gun for the purposes of shooting game with that gun, then you are deemed to be using that gun for the purpose of taking game within the meaning of the Act (*Gray v Hawthorn* [1961] Crim LR 265).

[40] The maximum penalty on summary conviction is a fine at level 3 on the standard scale (currently £1,000). Game, guns and ammunition in the offender's possession may also be forfeited by order of the Court (PPA 1862, s 2; GL(A)A 1960, s 3(2)).

[41] An accessory is one who assists an offender before, during or after the commission of the offence.

[42] See fn 40.

[43] GL(A)A 1960, s 2(1)(a), (b) (amended by PACE 1984, Sch 6, para 10; and the Serious Organised Crime and Police Act 2005, s 111, Sch 7, para 52(2)).

[44] 'Game' for these purposes means: hares, pheasants, partridges, eggs of pheasants and partridges, woodcocks, snipes, rabbits, grouse, black or moor game, and eggs of grouse, black or moor game (PPA 1862, s 1).

[45] PPA 1862, s 2; GL(A)A 1960, s 3(2).

[46] GLA(A) 1960, s 4(1).

Chapter 12

Protected Birds and Animals

INTRODUCTION

12.01 Wild birds and animals are protected by a number of Acts of Parliament. The principal measure is the WCA 1981[1] which contains wide-ranging provisions protecting most kinds of wild birds and animals. Deer, seals and badgers are each singled out for individual protection in their own Acts.

12.02 Less important are: the Criminal Damage Act 1971 (CDA 1971), which affects wild creatures no longer in a wild state; and the Wild Mammals (Protection) Act 1996 (WM(P)A 1996), which is concerned with the unnecessary infliction of suffering on wild animals.

12.03 The following sections of this chapter consider each of the foregoing measures in turn. Except for the last section, discussion is confined to those measures which relate to shooting and to those wild creatures which may be the subject of shooting.

WILDLIFE AND COUNTRYSIDE ACT 1981

12.04 It is first necessary to look at a number of definitions which the WCA 1981 uses. A 'wild bird' is defined as any bird of a species which is ordinarily resident in, or is a visitor to, the European territory of any EU Member State in a wild state, but does not include poultry or (except of the types mentioned in this paragraph) any game bird.[2] Within this definition, further terms are defined: 'poultry' means domestic fowls, geese, ducks, guinea-fowls, pigeons and quails, and turkeys; a 'domestic duck' and a 'domestic goose' mean, respectively, any

---

[1] In Northern Ireland the relevant legislation is the Wildlife (Northern Ireland) Order 1985 (SI 1985/171).

[2] WCA 1981, s 27(1). This exception relating to game birds has been repealed in Scotland pursuant to Wildlife and Natural Environment (Scotland) Act 2011, s 2(b).

domestic form of duck or goose; 'game bird' means any pheasant, partridge, grouse (or moor game), black (or heath) game or ptarmigan.[3] A wild animal is defined as any animal (other than a bird) which is or was (before it was killed or taken) living wild.[4] The Act's provisions extend to the Scilly Isles and the territorial waters adjacent to Great Britain.[5]

12.05   With the exceptions set out at para 12.06, it is an offence[6] to intentionally kill, injure or take any wild bird[7] or to intentionally or recklessly kill, injure or take any of the animals listed in Schedule 5 to the Act.[8] These animals collectively are referred to at para 12.06 *et seq* as listed animals.

12.06   The exceptions to these offences are:

(A)   A person shall not be guilty of an offence under section 1 by reason of the killing or taking of a bird included in Part I of Schedule 2 outside the close season for that bird, or the injuring of such a bird outside that season in the course of an attempt to kill it,[9] except:

---

[3]   WCA 1981, s 27(1). This definition has been repealed in Scotland pursuant to Wildlife and Natural Environment (Scotland) Act 2011, s 2(a).

[4]   WCA 1981, s 27(1).

[5]   The breadth of territorial waters adjacent to Great Britain is 12 nautical miles (1 nautical mile = 1,852 metres). The baselines from which this measurement is taken are to be laid down by Orders in Council from time to time (Territorial Seas Act 1987, s 1).

[6]   The offence in respect of wild birds is set out in WCA 1981, ss 1(1) and 9(1) in respect of wild animals. WCA 1981, s 18(1) provides that anyone who attempts to commit such offences will be punishable in a like manner for the offence. The maximum punishment on summary conviction for either of these offences is a term of imprisonment not exceeding 6 months and/or an unlimited fine. Where more than one animal or bird is involved in an offence, the maximum fine is as if the offender were convicted of a separate offence for each bird or animal (WCA 1981, s 21(1) and (5)).

[7]   In this instance 'wild bird' does not include any bird which is shown to have been bred in captivity unless it has been lawfully released into the wild as part of a re-population or re-introduction programme. A bird shall not be treated as bred in captivity unless its parents were lawfully in captivity when the egg was laid (WCA 1981, ss 1(6), 27(2)).

[8]   WCA 1981, s 9(1) and Sch 5. The listing may be varied by government order (WCA 1981, s 22(3), (4)). In proceedings for an offence these animals will be presumed to have been wild unless the contrary is shown (WCA 1981, s 9(6)).

[9]   WCA 1981, s 2(1).

(i)   in Scotland on Sundays and Christmas Day,[10] and

(ii) in England and Wales in any area prescribed for the purpose by government order.[11]

The names of the birds so listed and the close seasons for them are given in Appendix E. Both may be varied by government order, and orders may be made giving special protection to any listed bird, which have the same effect as a close season for it. Prior to making an order giving any special protection, the Secretary of State shall consult a representative of persons interested in the shooting of birds of the kind proposed to be protected by the order.[12]

(B) To prevent damage to crops, pasture, animal or human foodstuffs, livestock,[13] trees, hedges, banks or any works on land, government ministers may require the person having the right to do so to kill wild birds and animals causing such damage. Such a killing or an injuring of a wild bird or a listed animal is excused in these circumstances.[14]

(C) Any act done in pursuance of the provisions of the Animal Health Act 1981 or of any order made under it is excused.[15]

(D) A person shall not be guilty of the killing of a wild bird or listed animal if it is shown that it had been so seriously disabled, otherwise than by his unlawful act, that there was no reasonable chance of its recovering.[16]

---

[10] The Wildlife and Natural Environment (Scotland) Act 2011, s 3(8) introduces Part 1A to Sch 2 in respect of Scotland. This Part lists a number of species of birds which cannot be shot in Scotland on Sundays or Christmas Day. See Appendix E.

[11] WCA 1981, s 2(3).

[12] WCA 1981, ss 2(5)–(7), 22(1). Notice of the making of all orders must be published in the *London Gazette*, or the *Edinburgh Gazette* for orders affecting Scotland (WCA 1981, s 26(5)).

[13] 'Livestock' includes any animal which is kept: for the provision of food, wool, skins or fur; for the purpose of its use in the carrying on of any agricultural activity; or for the provision or improvement of shooting or fishing (WCA 1981, s 27(1)).

[14] AA 1947, s 98 and in respect of Scotland, Agriculture (Scotland) Act 1948, s 39; WCA 1981, ss 4(1)(a), 10(1)(a).

[15] WCA 1981, ss 4(1)(b) and (c), 10(1)(b); Animal Health Act 1981, ss 21 and 22. This does not apply in all instances to wild birds listed in WCA 1981, Schs ZA1 and 1, for which see Appendix D.

[16] WCA 1981, ss 4(2)(b), 10(3)(b). However, a person shall not be permitted to rely on the defence under s 10(3)(c) as respects anything done in relation to a bat otherwise than in the living area of a dwelling house unless he had notified the conservation body for the area in which the house is situated or, as the case may be, for the area where the act is to take place, or of the proposed action or operation, and has allowed them a reasonable time to advise him as to whether it should be carried out and, if so, the method to be used (WCA 1981, s 10(5)).

Similarly, he shall not be guilty of taking a wild bird or listed animal if it is shown that the animal had been disabled otherwise than by his unlawful act and was taken solely for the purpose of tending it and releasing it when no longer disabled.[17]

(E) Any act done if it is shown that the act was the incidental result of a lawful operation[18] and could not reasonably have been avoided.[19]

(F) The killing, injuring or taking of a wild bird (except one included in Schedule 1 of the Act)[20] by an authorised person[21] shall not be an offence if it is shown that it was necessary for the purpose of preventing serious damage to livestock,[22] foodstuffs for livestock, crops, vegetables, fruit, growing timber, fisheries or inland waters.[23]

But this exception cannot be relied on if any of the following apply:

(i)   the authorised person was unable to show that, as regards the purpose of preventing the serious damage, there was no other satisfactory solution;

(ii) it had become apparent, before the time of killing or injuring, that that action would prove necessary for the purpose of preventing the serious damage and either:

---

[17] WCA 1981, ss 4(2)(b), 10(3)(a).

[18] E.g. an accidental killing or injury of a wild bird or listed animal by a moving vehicle or by a shot lawfully fired at something else.

[19] WCA 1981, ss 4(2)(c), 10(3)(c). However, note the point made in fn 16 above regarding bats.

[20] For the birds listed in Sch 1, see Appendix D.

[21] An 'authorised person' means: the owner or occupier, or any person authorised by the owner or occupier, of the land on which the action authorised is taken; any person authorised in writing by the local authority for the area within which the action authorised is taken; a person authorised in writing by certain authorities and other statutory bodies who may also authorise persons for this purpose. (WCA 1981, s 27(1)).

[22] 'Livestock' includes any animal which is kept: for the provision of food, wool, skins or fur; for the purpose of its use in the carrying on of any agricultural activity; or for the provision or improvement of shooting or fishing (WCA 1981, s 27(1)).

[23] WCA 1981, s 4(3)(c). The expression 'inland waters' means: (a) inland waters within the meaning of the Water Resources Act 1991; (b) any waters not falling within paragraph (a) which are within the seaward limits of the territorial sea; (c) controlled waters within the meaning of Part II of the Control of Pollution Act 1974 other than ground waters as defined in s 30A(1)(d) of that Act (WCA 1981, s 27(1)).

(1) a licence[24] authorising the action had not been applied for as soon as reasonably practicable after the fact had become apparent; or

(2) an application for a licence had been determined;[25]

(iii) the authorised person, as respects any action taken at any time, does not notify the Ministry of Agriculture as soon as reasonably practicable after that time that he had taken the action.[26]

(G) The killing or injuring by an authorised person[27] of a wild animal listed in Schedule 5 to the Act if it is shown that that was necessary for the purpose of preventing serious damage to livestock,[28] foodstuffs for livestock, crops, vegetables, fruit, growing timber or any other form of property or to fisheries.[29]

But this exception cannot be relied on if it had become apparent before the time of killing or injuring that that would prove necessary for the purpose of preventing serious damage of any of the kinds described, and either:

(i) a licence authorising the action had not been applied for as soon as reasonably practicable after that fact had become apparent; or

(ii) an application for a licence had been determined.[30]

(H) The killing or injuring by an authorised person[31] of a wild bird (except one included in Schedule 1 to the Act)[32] if it is shown that that was necessary for

---

[24] For licences, see item (I) below.

[25] To meet the requirements of paragraphs (ii)(1) and (2) of item (F) above, it appears that it is only necessary to apply for a licence promptly.

[26] WCA 1981, s 4(3)–(6).

[27] An 'authorised person' means: the owner or occupier, or any person authorised by the owner or occupier, of the land on which the action authorised is taken; any person authorised in writing by the local authority for the area within which the action authorised is taken; a person authorised in writing by certain authorities and other statutory bodies who may also authorise persons for this purpose (WCA 1981, s 27(1)).

[28] 'Livestock' includes any animal which is kept: for the provision of food, wool, skins or fur; for the purpose of its use in the carrying on of any agricultural activity; or for the provision or improvement of shooting or fishing (WCA 1981, s 27(1)).

[29] WCA 1981, s 10(4).

[30] WCA 1981, s 10(6).

[31] An 'authorised person' means: the owner or occupier, or any person authorised by the owner or occupier, of the land on which the action authorised is taken; any person authorised in writing by the local authority for the area within which the action authorised is taken; a person authorised in writing by certain authorities and other statutory bodies who may also authorise persons for this purpose (WCA 1981, s 27(1)).

[32] For the birds listed in Sch 1, see Appendix D.

the purpose of preserving public health, or public or air safety, or preventing the spread of disease.[33]

(I)   Any killing or injuring of a wild bird or listed animal, or an attempt to kill or injure either, which is done under and in accordance with the terms of a licence granted by the appropriate authority.[34] Licences are obtainable only for particularised purposes, and those which may be relevant to shooting are listed in Appendix F, along with details of the authorities from whom they can be obtained.[35]

12.07   It is an essential ingredient of the offence of killing or injuring a wild bird, or attempting to do so, that there was intent to kill or injure. Therefore, if there is no such intent, no offence is committed. However, the offence of killing or injuring a listed animal has been drafted to include a reckless basis also. Therefore, it is not necessary to prove intent; it is sufficient to show that the killing or injuring of the animal was a foreseeable consequence of the action taken.

12.08   The WCA 1981 creates a number of other offences which are connected directly or indirectly with shooting, and these, together with the available defences, will now be considered. This Act has also been amended on a number of occasions, including by the Natural Environment and Rural Communities Act 2006 and various statutory instruments. These changes have introduced provisions to protect matters such as biodiversity, but are largely outside the scope of this work.

12.09   It is an offence to intentionally or recklessly disturb any wild bird included in Schedule 1 to the WCA 1981[36] while it is building a nest or is in, on or near a nest containing eggs or young, or to intentionally or recklessly disturb the dependent young of such a bird.[37] Similarly, it is an offence to intentionally or recklessly damage or destroy any structure or place which any listed animal uses for shelter or protection, or to intentionally or recklessly disturb any listed animal

---

[33]   WCA 1981, s 4(3)(a), (b).

[34]   WCA 1981, s 16(1)–(3).

[35]   Game birds, for which see para 12.04, may be the subject of a licence (WCA 1981, ss 16, 27(1)). Although, pursuant to Wildlife and Natural Environment (Scotland) Act 2011, s 2 game birds may not be the subject of a licence in Scotland.

[36]   The birds included in Sch 1 are listed in Appendix D. The Sch 1 listing may be varied by government order (WCA 1981, s 22(1)).

[37]   WCA 1981, s 1(5). WCA 1981, s 18(1) provides that anyone who attempts to commit such an offence will be punishable in a like manner for the offence. The maximum punishment on summary conviction for this offence is a term of imprisonment not exceeding 6 months and/or an unlimited fine. Where more than one bird, nest or egg is involved in an offence, the maximum fine is as if the offender were convicted of a separate offence for each bird, nest or egg (WCA 1981, s 21(1) and (5)).

while it is occupying a structure or place which it uses for shelter or protection or to obstruct access to any such place.[38]

12.10 The exceptions listed at items (C) and (E) in para 12.06 apply to all the above offences, and the disturbance of a bird or animal as the result of such a requirement by the Ministry of Agriculture as described in item (B) in the same paragraph will also be an exception.[39] Any disturbance of a listed animal shall not be unlawful if it takes place in a dwelling house[40] except where the listed animal is a bat, which has been disturbed in a place other than the living area of a dwelling house. In that instance, the conservation body for the area in which the house is situated should be notified.[41]

12.11 The WCA 1981 prohibits certain methods of killing wild birds and wild animals. Some methods are prohibited only in respect of the kinds of wild animal set out in Schedule 6 to the Act reproduced in Appendix G,[42] whereas other prohibited methods apply to all wild birds and to all wild animals respectively. There is some duplication of the methods prohibited in respect of wild birds and wild animals; therefore, for convenience, the prohibited methods have been organised into the four groupings, which appear below.

12.12 The list of prohibited methods may be varied by government order.[43] However, in respect of any method of killing or taking wild birds which involves the use of a firearm, or any method of killing or taking wild animals, that power shall not be exercised, except for the purpose of complying with an international obligation.[44] To use a prohibited method, or knowingly to cause or permit the use of such a method, is an offence[45] unless approved by a licence issued by the

---

[38] WCA 1981, s 9(4)(a), (b), (c). WCA 1981, s 18(1) provides that anyone who attempts to commit such an offence will be punishable in a like manner for the offence. The maximum punishment on summary conviction for this offence is a term of imprisonment not exceeding 6 months and/or an unlimited fine. Where more than one animal is involved in an offence, the maximum fine is as if the offender were convicted of a separate offence for each animal (WCA 1981, s 21(1) and (5)).

[39] WCA 1981, ss 4(1), (2)(c), 10(1), (3)(c). Although the exception under s 10(3)(c) shall not apply where the listed animal concerned is a bat unless the relevant conservation body have been notified (WCA 1981, s 10(2), (5)).

[40] WCA 1981, s 10(2).

[41] WCA 1981, s 10(2), (5).

[42] The listing may be varied by government order (WCA 1981, s 22(4)(a)).

[43] WCA 1981, ss 5(2), 11(4).

[44] WCA 1981, ss 5(3), 11(4).

[45] WCA 1981, ss 5(1), 11(1). WCA 1981, s 18(1) provides that anyone who attempts to commit such an offence will be punishable in a like manner for the offence. The maximum punishment on summary conviction for this offence is a term of imprisonment not exceeding 6 months and/or an unlimited fine. Where more than one bird or animal is involved in an offence, the maximum

appropriate authority.[46] The prohibited methods, so far as they relate or may relate to shooting, are as follows:

(a) Methods applying to all wild birds[47] and to wild animals[48] listed in Schedule 6 to the WCA 1981:

    (i) Using for the purpose of killing:

        (1) any automatic or semi-automatic weapon;[49]
        (2) any device for illuminating a target or any sighting device for night shooting;
        (3) any form of artificial light or any mirror or other dazzling device.

    (ii) For the purpose of killing, using as a decoy any sound recording.
    (iii) Using any mechanically propelled vehicle[50] in immediate pursuit of a bird or animal for the purpose of killing or taking it.[51]

(b) Methods applying to all wild birds:[52]

    (i) Using, for the purpose of killing, any shotgun of which the barrel has an internal diameter at the muzzle of more than 1.75 inches.
    (ii) For the purpose of killing, using as a decoy any live bird or other animal whatever which is tethered, or which is secured by means of braces or other similar appliances, or which is blind, maimed or injured.[53]

---

fine is as if the offender were convicted of a separate offence for each bird or animal (WCA 1981, s 21(1) and (5)).

[46] WCA 1981, ss 5(1)(f), 11(2)(f), 16(1), (3). See Appendix F for the purposes for which licences may be obtained.

[47] In England and Wales, game birds are included in this instance and, for these purposes, 'game bird' means any pheasant, partridge, grouse (or moor game), black (or heath) game or ptarmigan (WCA 1981, ss 5, 27(1)). However, game birds will not be included in respect of Scotland pursuant to the Wildlife and Natural Environment (Scotland) Act 2011, s 2.

[48] In any proceedings for an offence the animal in question shall be presumed to have been wild unless the contrary is shown (WCA 1981, s 11(5)).

[49] 'Automatic weapon' and 'semi-automatic weapon' do not include any weapon the magazine of which is incapable of holding more than two rounds (WCA 1981, s 27(1)).

[50] The word 'vehicle' includes aircraft, hovercraft and boat (WCA 1981, s 27(1)).

[51] WCA 1981, ss 5(1)(c)–(e), 11(2)(c)–(e).

[52] In England and Wales, game birds are included in this instance and, for these purposes, 'game bird' means any pheasant, partridge, grouse (or moor game), black (or heath) game or ptarmigan (WCA 1981, ss 5, 27(1)). However, game birds will not be so included in respect of Scotland pursuant to the Wildlife and Natural Environment (Scotland) Act 2011, s 2.

[53] WCA 1981, s 5(1)(c)(iv), (d).

(c) Method applying to all wild animals:[54]
Using as a decoy, for the purpose of killing any wild animal, any live mammal or bird whatever.[55]

(d) Method applying to wild animals listed in Schedule 6 to the WCA 1981:[56]
Using any mechanically propelled vehicle[57] in immediate pursuit of an animal for the purpose of driving, killing or taking that animal.[58]

12.13 The WCA 1981 makes it an offence for a person to have in his possession,[59] for the purpose of committing any of the offences which have been described, anything capable of being used for committing one of those offences.[60] Many things so capable may be innocently possessed. However, it is an element of the offence, and hence must be proven beyond reasonable doubt, that the object in question was possessed for the purpose described; to that end, the prosecution would have to adduce evidence to demonstrate a link between possession and the commission, or intended commission, of one of the offences.

12.14 Constables,[61] with reasonable cause to suspect that a person is committing or has committed an offence under the WCA 1981, may without warrant stop and search the person, search and examine things the person has or is using and seize and detain things which may be evidence of an offence, or which may be forfeited by a convicting court.[62] They may also arrest the person suspected if he fails to give his name and address to the constable's satisfaction.[63] Constables may also enter any premises other than a dwelling to exercise these powers, and to make arrests if they reasonably suspect that an offence is being committed.[64] A constable will need to obtain a warrant from a justice of the peace to enter upon and search any premises where there are reasonable grounds to suspect that an

---

[54] In any proceedings for an offence the animal in question shall be presumed to have been wild unless the contrary is shown (WCA 1981, s 11(5)).

[55] WCA 1981, s 11(1)(c).

[56] The names of the animals in Sch 6 are listed in Appendix G.

[57] 'Vehicle' includes aircraft, hovercraft and boat WCA 1981, s 27(1).

[58] WCA 1981, s 11(2)(e).

[59] For commentary on the meaning of 'possession', see para 3.17 *et seq*.

[60] Anyone convicted of this offence shall be punished in like manner as for the offence for which it is alleged that the person had the thing in his possession to commit (WCA 1981, s 18(2)).

[61] As well as police constables, including special police constables, 'constables' includes others holding that office, e.g. harbour constables. The hallmark of a constable is his attestation as such before, usually, a magistrate.

[62] WCA 1981, s 19(1)(a), (b), (d). For police powers of general application, see paras 11.14 (poaching) and 12.25 (Deer Act 1991 (DA 1991)).

[63] WCA 1981, s 19(1)(c).

[64] WCA 1981, s 19(2).

offence has been committed and that evidence of that offence may be found on those premises.[65]

12.15 As well as imposing fines, a convicting court is compelled to order the forfeiture of any bird or animal in respect of which the offence was committed.[66] The court *may* also order forfeiture of any vehicle,[67] animal, weapon, or other thing which was used to commit the offence.[68]

DEER ACT 1991

Introduction

12.16 The earliest modern legislation specifically protecting deer was the Deer Act of 1963. Further protection was added by the Deer Acts of 1980 and 1987 and the Roe Deer (Close Seasons) Act of 1977, the 1980 and 1987 Acts legislating for the newer trends in deer farming, deer poaching and the selling of venison. These Acts have now been repealed and their provisions, with amendments, consolidated in the Deer Act 1991 (DA 1991).[69] The DA 1991 has recently been reformed in England and Wales by the Regulatory Reform (Deer) (England and Wales) Order 2007.

12.17 The shooting of deer is considered in the following pages under five headings: close seasons; killing deer at night; use of unlawful methods and illegal possession of objects; powers of police and powers of courts on conviction of offences; and deer poaching. The DA 1991 also legislates for licences for taking live deer and for trading in venison.[70] These, not being matters connected with shooting, are not further dealt with.

12.18 The provisions of the DA 1991 apply throughout to 'deer',[71] which term is defined as 'deer of any species and includes the carcass of any deer or any part thereof', unless the context otherwise requires; and 'species' includes any hybrid of different species of deer.[72] Thus, deer of either sex, of all ages and tame deer are included.

---

[65] WCA 1981, s 19(3).

[66] WCA 1981, s 21(6)(a).

[67] The word 'vehicle' includes aircraft, hovercraft and boat (WCA 1981, s 27(1)).

[68] WCA 1981, s 21(6)(b).

[69] In respect of Scotland the relevant legislation is the Deer (Scotland) Act 1996.

[70] DA 1991, ss 8, 10, 11.

[71] Except in relation to close seasons for particular species of deer.

[72] DA 1991, s 16.

Close seasons

12.19 There are close seasons for six species of deer, and these are shown in section 3 of Appendix C.

12.20 It is an offence to take or intentionally to kill deer[73] of these species, or to attempt to do so, during their respective close seasons,[74] except where one of the following defences (listed at A–E in para 12.21) is available.

12.21 The defences are as follows:

(A) That the deer was killed or taken or was injured in an attempt to kill or take it, by one of the persons described at (a) to (e) below by means of shooting, and the act was done on any cultivated land, pasture or enclosed woodland.[75] But this defence cannot be relied upon unless that person shows that:

   (i) he had reasonable grounds for believing that deer of the same species were causing, or had caused, damage to crops, vegetables, fruit, growing timber or any other form of property on the land;[76] and

   (ii) it was likely that further damage would be so caused and such damage was likely to be serious; and

   (iii) his action was necessary for the purpose of preventing any such damage.[77]

The above defence is available only to the following named classes of persons:

   (a) the occupier of the land on which the action is taken;

---

[73] The word 'deer' will include deer of either sex and all ages (*R v Strange* (1843) 1 Cox CC 58), and tame deer as well as wild deer.

[74] DA 1991, ss 2(1), 5(1). The maximum punishment on summary conviction is a fine at level 4 on the standard scale or 3 months' imprisonment, or both (DA 1991, s 9(1)). If an offence involves more than one deer, the maximum fine shall be regarded as if there was a separate offence against each deer involved (DA 1991, s 9(2)).

[75] DA 1991, s 7(1).

[76] I.e. the land upon which the act was done, being land of one of the three descriptions given earlier in the text.

[77] DA 1991, s 7(3)(a)–(c). Government ministers may by order add further conditions to those listed in paragraphs (i)–(iii) of item (A) in para 12.21 and may vary and delete such further conditions (DA 1991, s 7(5)(b)). For restrictions on the types of guns and ammunition which the authorised person may use, see item (c) in para 12.23 and item (D) in para 12.24.

(b) any member of the occupier's household[78] normally resident on the occupier's land, and acting with the occupier's written authority;

(c) any person in the ordinary service[79] of the occupier on the occupier's land, acting as above;

(d) any person having the right to take or kill deer on the land on which the action is taken; and

(e) any person acting with the written authority of a person at (d) above.[80]

(B) That the killing or attempting to kill was done for the purpose of preventing suffering by an injured or diseased deer.[81]

(C) That the taking or killing of the deer was because he reasonably believed that the deer had been deprived in any way (other than by an unlawful taking or killing by that person) of a female deer on which it was dependent; or was about to be deprived, by death from disease or a lawful taking or killing, of a female deer on which it is dependent.[82]

(D) That the killing or attempting to kill was done in pursuance of a government minister's requirement under section 98 of the Agriculture Act 1947 (AA 1947).[83]

(E) That the deer was killed by a person, or his authorised servant or agent, and that person, by way of business, kept the deer on land enclosed by a deer-proof barrier for the production of meat or other foodstuffs or skins or other by-products, or as breeding stock; and the deer so kept was conspicuously marked so as to identify it as kept by that person in the way described above.[84]

---

[78] As to household membership and 'ordinary service', see the discussion at para 13.05 and fns 16 and 18 thereto. Though derived from the law relating to ground game, those notes may serve as a guide pending any court decision on the words' meanings in this text.

[79] As above.

[80] DA 1991, s 7(4).

[81] DA 1991, s 6(2).

[82] DA 1991, s 2A.

[83] DA 1991, s 6(1). This is a reference to ministers' powers to require the person having the right to do so to kill deer (and other animals and birds) which are causing damage, even though they may be out of season.

[84] DA 1991, s 2(3).

Killing deer at night

12.22 It is an offence intentionally to kill a deer at night,[85] or attempt to do so,[86] except where one of the defences described at (B), (C) or (D) in para 12.21 is available.[87]

Use of unlawful methods and illegal possession of objects

12.23 Subject to the defences later described, the following acts done in relation to deer, and attempts to commit those acts, are offences:[88]

(a) Setting in position any trap, snare or poisoned or stupefying bait which is of such a nature or so placed as to be calculated to cause bodily injury to any deer coming into contact with it.[89]

(b) Using, for the purpose of taking or killing any deer, any trap, snare or poisoned or stupefying bait, or any net.[90]

(c) Using, or attempting to use, for the purpose of taking, injuring or killing any deer:

   (i)   any smooth-bore gun or any cartridge for use in it, or

   (ii) any rifle of a calibre less than 0.240 inches or a muzzle energy of less than 1,700-foot pounds (2,305 joules), or

   (iii) any bullet for use in a rifle, other than a soft-nosed or hollow-nosed bullet,[91] or

---

[85] 'Night' extends from the expiry of one hour after sunset to the beginning of one hour before sunrise (DA 1991, s 3).

[86] DA 1991, ss 3, 5(1). The maximum punishment on summary conviction is a fine at level 4 on the standard scale or 3 months' imprisonment, or both (DA 1991, s 9(1)). If an offence involves more than one deer, the maximum fine shall be regarded as if there was a separate offence against each deer involved (DA 1991, s 9(2)).

[87] DA 1991, s 6(1) and (2).

[88] The maximum punishment on summary conviction is a fine at level 4 on the standard scale, or 3 months' imprisonment, or both (DA 1991, s 9(1)). If an offence involves more than one deer, the maximum fine shall be regarded as if there was a separate offence against each deer involved (DA 1991, s 9(2)).

[89] DA 1991, ss 4(1)(a), 5(1).

[90] DA 1991, ss 4(1)(b), 5(1).

[91] The descriptions of guns and ammunition in item (c)(i)–(iii) in para 12.23 may be varied by order of the Home Office (DA 1991, s 4(3)).

(iv) any arrow, spear or similar missile, or

(v)   any missile, whether discharged from a firearm[92] or otherwise, carrying or containing any poison, stupefying drug or muscle-relaxing agent.[93]

(d) Discharging any firearm[94] or projecting any missile from any mechanically propelled vehicle[95] at any deer when the vehicle is moving or when its engine is running.[96]

(e) Using, or attempting to use, any mechanically propelled vehicle or aircraft for the purpose of driving deer.[97]

(f) Possessing[98] any object described at items (b), (c)(iv) or (v) above, or possessing any firearm or ammunition, for the purposes of committing any of the following offences: those described at items (a) to (e) above; or for the taking or killing certain deer during the close season; or for the killing or taking of deer at night.[99]

12.24 The defences to the offences listed above are:

(A) In the case of the offences at (a) and (b) in para 12.23, that any trap or net set in position or used was for the purpose of preventing the suffering of an injured or diseased deer.[100]

(B) A person shall not be guilty of the offences set out at (a), (b) and (c)(i)–(v) in para 12.23, by reason of the use of any reasonable means for the purpose of killing any deer if he reasonably believes that the deer has been so seriously injured, otherwise than by his unlawful act,[101] or is in such condition, that to kill it is an act of mercy.[102] For these purposes any

---

[92] The definition of 'firearm' examined at para 1.05 *et seq* applies (DA 1991, s 16; FA 1968, s 57(1)).

[93] DA 1991, ss 4(2), 5(1) and Sch 2. Schedule 2 contains a prospective provision prohibiting the using, or the attempting to use, for the purpose of taking, injuring or killing any deer, any air gun, air rifle or air pistol. This provision is not in force and as yet there is no date for it to be brought into force. Therefore, at the time of writing it is not an offence to use the items aforementioned.

[94] The definition of 'firearm' examined in Chapter 1 applies (DA 1991, s 16; FA 1968, s 57(1)).

[95] 'Vehicle' includes an aircraft, hovercraft or boat (DA 1991, s 16).

[96] DA 1991, ss 4(4)(a), 5(1).

[97] DA 1991, ss 4(4)(b), 5(1).

[98] For some notes on the meaning of 'possession', though in another context, see para 3.17 *et seq*.

[99] DA 1991, ss 4(1)(b), 4(2)(b), 4(2)(c), 5(2). To secure a conviction for this offence, it would be necessary for the prosecution to prove to the court's satisfaction a link between possession and the commission, or intended commission, of one of the offences.

[100] DA 1991, s 6(3).

[101] The words 'unlawful act' are not restricted to acts made unlawful by the DA 1991, and will thus, it seems, embrace acts which are otherwise unlawful, e.g. the improper use of a gun without a firearm or shotgun certificate.

[102] DA 1991, s 6(4).

'reasonable means' means any method of killing a deer that can reasonably be expected to result in rapid loss of consciousness and death and which is appropriate in all the circumstances (including in particular what the deer is doing, its size, its distance from the closest position safely attainable by the person attempting to kill the deer and its position in relation to vegetative cover).[103]

(C) In the case of the offence at (c)(i) in para 12.23, that the gun was used as a slaughtering instrument[104] to kill deer, provided the gun:

    (i)   was of not less gauge than 12 bore, and

    (ii)   had a barrel less than 24 inches (609.6 mm) in length, and

    (iii) was loaded with a cartridge purporting to contain shot none of which was less than 0.203 inches (5.16 mm) in diameter (size AAA or larger).[105]

(D) In the case of the offence at (c)(i) in para 12.23, if the gun is used for the purpose of taking or killing or injuring any Chinese water deer (*Hydropotes inermis*) or muntjac deer (*Muntiacus reevesi*), provided the gun:

    (i)   was a rifle having a calibre of not less than .22″ and a muzzle energy of not less than 1,356 joules (1,000 foot pounds), and

    (ii)   was loaded with a soft-nosed or hollow-nosed bullet weighing not less than 3.24 grammes (50 grains).[106]

(E) In the case of the offence at (c)(i) in para 12.23, that a smooth-bore gun of not less gauge than 12 bore was used by one of the persons described at items (A) (a)–(e) in para 12.21 to take or kill deer on any land, and the gun was loaded with:

    (i)   a cartridge containing a single non-spherical projectile weighing not less than 350 grains (22.68 grammes); or

    (ii)   a cartridge purporting to contain shot each of which was 0.203 inches (5.16 mm) in diameter (size AAA).[107]

---

[103] DA 1991, s 6(4A).

[104] Though the matter is not entirely clear, it appears that this defence is intended to apply when deer are killed preparatory to the use of their carcasses as venison, as on a deer farm.

[105] DA 1991, s 6(5).

[106] DA 1991, s 6(6). This is centre fire ammunition, either .222″ or .223″ or larger; .22″ rim-fire has insufficient muzzle energy.

[107] DA 1991, s 7(2). The Secretary of State and Agriculture Minister acting jointly may by Order either generally or in respect of a species of deer repeal this section or amend it by adding any firearm or ammunition or by altering the description of, or deleting, any firearm or ammunition for the time being mentioned in it (DA 1991, s 7(5)(a)).

But this defence cannot be relied upon unless the person using the gun can show he had reasonable grounds for believing that deer of the same species were causing, or had caused, damage to crops, vegetables, fruit, growing timber or any other form of property on the land; it was likely that further damage would be so caused and any such damage was likely to be serious; and his action was necessary for the purpose of preventing any such damage.[108]

(F)   In the case of the offences at (d) and (e) in para 12.23, that the prohibited act was done by, or with the written authority of, the occupier of any enclosed land[109] where deer are usually kept and was done in relation to deer on that land.[110]

Powers of police and powers of court on conviction of offences

12.25   Constables[111] are given wide powers by the DA 1991. They may, if they suspect with reasonable cause that a person is committing or has committed an offence under the Act, without a warrant, stop and search suspected persons, search or examine vehicles,[112] weapons, animals and other things for evidence, and seize and detain things which are such evidence and deer, venison,[113] vehicles, animals, weapons and other things which a court may order to be forfeited on conviction.[114] A constable may enter any land,[115] other than a dwelling house, to exercise the foregoing powers or to arrest a person under the general powers of

---

[108] DA 1991, s 7(2), (3), (4). The Secretary of State and Agriculture Minister acting jointly may by order, either generally or in respect of one species of deer, amend this proviso by adding any conditions which must be satisfied or by varying or deleting any conditions attached (DA 1991, s 7(5)(b)).

[109] No definition is given of 'enclosed land' but see *Jemmison v Priddle* [1972] 1 All ER 539 for a judicial interpretation in another context.

[110] DA 1991, s 4(4), (5).

[111] As well as police constables, including special police constables, 'constables' include others holding that office, e.g. harbour constables. The hallmark of a constable is his attestation as such before, usually, a magistrate.

[112] 'Vehicle' includes an aircraft, hovercraft or boat (DA 1991, s 16).

[113] 'Venison' includes imported venison and means: (a) any carcass of a deer; or (b) any edible part of the carcass of a deer which in either case has not been cooked or canned (DA 1991, s 16).

[114] DA 1991, s 12(1). For police powers of general application, see paras 11.14, 12.14 and 12.25.

[115] 'Land' includes building and other structures, land covered with water, and any estate, interest, easement, servitude or right in or over land (IA 1978, s 5 and Sch 1).

arrest available to him.[116] He may also sell any deer or venison[117] seized, and the net proceeds are to be forfeited in the same manner as the deer or venison sold.[118]

12.26 In addition to any sentence passed, a convicting court may order the forfeiture of:

(a) any deer or venison in respect of which the offence was committed or which was found[119] in the defendant's possession; and
(b) any vehicle,[120] animal, weapon or other thing which:

    (i) was used to commit the offence, or
    (ii) was capable of being used to take, kill or injure deer and was found in the defendant's possession.[121]

Deer poaching

12.27 The following acts are, subject to the exemptions mentioned below, made offences by the DA 1991:

(a) To enter land[122] in search or pursuit of any deer[123] with the intention of taking, killing or injuring it.[124]
(b) While on any land:

    (i) intentionally to take, kill or injure, or attempt to take, kill or injure, any deer; or
    (ii) to search for or pursue any deer with the intention of taking, killing or injuring it; or
    (iii) to remove the carcass of any deer.[125]

---

[116] DA 1991, s 12(2). For the powers of arrest, see PACE 1984, s 24.

[117] 'Venison' includes imported venison and means (a) any carcass of a deer; or (b) any edible part of the carcass of a deer which in either case has not been cooked or canned (DA 1991, s 16).

[118] DA 1991, s 12(3).

[119] 'Found' presumably refers to things found by a constable and seized or detained by him under the powers described in para 12.25.

[120] 'Vehicle' includes an aircraft, hovercraft or boat (DA 1991, s 16).

[121] DA 1991, s 13(1).

[122] 'Land' includes building and other structures, land covered with water, and any estate, interest, easement, servitude or right in or over land (IA 1978, s 5 and Sch 1).

[123] 'Deer' means deer of any species and includes the carcass of any deer or any part of the carcass (DA 1991, s 16).

[124] DA 1991, s 1(1).

[125] DA 1991, s 1(2).

But these offences are not perpetrated if the person committing the act:

(a)	has the consent of the owner or occupier of the land; or
(b)	has lawful authority[126] to do it;[127] or
(c)	believes that he would have the consent of the owner or occupier of the land if the owner or occupier knew of his doing the act and the circumstances of it; or
(d)	believes that he has other lawful authority[128] to do the act.[129]

12.28 If an authorised person[130] suspects with reasonable cause that another person is committing or has committed any of these offences on any land, he may require that person to give his full name and address and to leave the land at once; the failure to comply with those requests is an offence.[131]

12.29 The powers of convicting courts and of the police in relation to deer poaching are as given above, but, in addition, a court may cancel any firearm or shotgun certificate held by the convicted person.[132] Where a court cancels a firearm or shotgun certificate, the court shall give notice in writing to the chief officer of police by whom the certificate was granted. That officer shall require, by notice in writing, the holder to surrender that certificate. If the holder fails to surrender the certificate within 21 days from the date of that requirement, he shall be guilty of an offence.[133]

CONSERVATION OF SEALS ACT 1970

12.30 As of 31 January 2011, the Conservation of Seals Act 1970 (CSA 1970) has been repealed in respect of Scotland only. The regime for the protection of seals in Scotland is now dealt with by the Marine (Scotland) Act 2010 (M(S)A

---

[126] No definition or explanation of 'lawful authority' is given, but these words would cover acts by a tenant holding rights to kill or take deer on the land, or by Ministry of Agriculture officers acting under powers given to them to deal with animal diseases.

[127] DA 1991, s 1(1), (2).

[128] For the belief to be effective as a defence, it is suggested that, though the belief may be mistaken, it must be honestly and reasonably held.

[129] DA 1991, s 1(3).

[130] 'Authorised person' is defined as the owner or occupier of the land or a person authorised by either of them, and includes any person having the right to take or kill deer on the land (DA 1991, s 1(5)).

[131] DA 1991, s 1(4). This provision does not enable an authorised person to eject the suspected person, but an owner or occupier of the land, or an employee acting under their orders, may eject a trespasser at Common Law, using only such force as is necessary.

[132] DA 1991, s 13(2).

[133] DA 1991, s 13(3). The maximum punishment on summary conviction is a fine not exceeding level 2 on the standard scale (currently £500).

2010). This regime is considered at para 12.40 *et seq*. The CSA 1970 does not extend to Northern Ireland.

12.31 It is an offence to use, or attempt to use, for the purpose of killing, injuring or taking any seal,[134] any firearm[135] other than a rifle using ammunition[136] having a muzzle energy of not less than 600 foot pounds and a bullet weighing not less than 45 grains.[137] The following defences are available in respect of this offence:

(a)   In the case of killing a seal, that it had been so seriously disabled otherwise than by an act of the killer that there was no reasonable chance of its recovering.[138]
(b)   That the act done was authorised by a licence granted by the Home Office.[139]
(c)   That the act was done outside the seaward limits of the territorial waters adjacent to Great Britain.[140]

12.32 The annual close seasons for seals are as follows:

Grey seals (*Halichoerus grypus*)   1 September to 31 December
Common seals (*Phoca vitulina*)   1 June to 31 August[141]

It is an offence wilfully[142] to kill or injure, or attempt to kill or injure, these seals during their close seasons.[143] The killing, injuring or taking of seals is also an offence if done at any time of the year in an area designated for the conservation

---

[134]   Although this means all seals, the grey and common seals are the only species known to inhabit the coasts of Britain.

[135]   This word has the same meaning as in the FA 1968 (CSA 1970, s 15), as to which see para 1.05 *et seq*.

[136]   This word has the same meaning as in the FA 1968 (CSA 1970, s 15), as to which see para 1.42 *et seq*.

[137]   CSA 1970, ss 1(1), 8(1). The descriptions given of firearms and ammunition may be altered by order of the Home Office (CSA 1970, s 1(2)). The maximum punishment on summary conviction is a fine at level 4 on the standard scale (currently £2500) (CSA 1970, s 5(2)).

[138]   CSA 1970, ss 1(1), 9(2).

[139]   CSA 1970, ss 1(1), 10. For further details of such a licence, see para 12.34.

[140]   CSA 1970, s 17(2). For the extent of territorial waters, see para 12.04, fn 5.

[141]   CSA 1970, s 2(1). All dates are inclusive.

[142]   This means deliberately and intentionally, and not by accident or inadvertence (*R v Senior* [1899] 1 QB 283 at 290–91). Although this case involved offences concerning the welfare of children, it is submitted that the interpretation of the term 'wilfully' shall apply equally to animal welfare cases.

[143]   CSA 1970, ss 2(2), 8(1). The maximum punishment on summary conviction is a fine at level 4 on the standard scale (currently £2,500) (CSA 1970, s 5(2)).

of seals by way of a Home Office order.[144] One such order, which affects grey seals and common seals, is currently in force. In general terms, it extends to counties and metropolitan districts in England which border the North Sea and to their territorial waters.[145]

12.33 The following defences are available to an accused for either a close season offence or an offence contrary to the terms of a Home Office order:

(a) That the killing or injuring of the seal was unavoidable and the incidental result of a lawful action.[146]

(b) That the killing or attempted killing of any seal was to prevent it from causing damage to a fishing net or fishing tackle in the accused's possession or in the possession of a person at whose request he killed or attempted to kill the seal, or to any fish for the time being in such fishing net, provided that at the time of the killing or attempted killing the seal was in the vicinity of such net or tackle.[147]

(c) The defences described in items (a), (b) and (c) in para 12.31.[148]

12.34 The Home Office may grant a licence to any person to kill or take seals and, provided this is done within the terms and conditions of the licence, no offence will be committed. The purposes for which a licence may be given are:

(a) for scientific or educational purposes;
(b) for preventing damage to fisheries;
(c) for preventing a population surplus of seals for management purposes;
(d) for using a population surplus of seals as a resource; or
(e) for the protection of flora and fauna in certain areas.

12.35 In all cases, the licence will authorise a killing or taking in the area described in the licence which will also specify the means to be used and the number of seals to be killed or taken.[149] The licence may be revoked at any time

---

[144] CSA 1970, ss 3, 8(1). The maximum punishment on summary conviction is a fine at level 4 on the standard scale (currently £2,500) (CSA 1970, s 5(2)).

[145] Conservation of Seals (England) Order 1999 (SI 1999/3052). The order defines precisely the area in which it has effect. For the extent of territorial waters, see para 12.04, fn 5.

[146] CSA 1970, ss 2(2), 3(2), 9(1)(b).

[147] CSA 1970, ss 2(2), 3(2), 9(1)(c).

[148] CSA 1970, ss 2(2), 3(2), 9(2), 10, 17(2). A further defence is available to a person who takes or attempts to take a seal which has been disabled otherwise than by his act, if it was taken or to be taken solely for the purpose of tending it and releasing it when no longer disabled (CSA 1970, ss 2(2), 3(2), 9(1)(a)).

[149] CSA 1970, s 10(1). The use of strychnine cannot be authorised by a licence. The taking of seals for a zoological garden or a collection may also be covered by a licence.

by the Home Office.[150] A person who contravenes, attempts to contravene, or fails to comply with, any condition of the licence commits an offence.[151]

12.36 Any person, who, for the purpose of committing any of the offences described,[152] has in his possession,[153] or attempts to have in his possession, any poisonous substance or any prohibited firearm or ammunition[154] commits an offence.[155]

12.37 A court convicting a person of any of the offences described[156] may order the forfeiture of any seal or seal skin in respect of which the offence was committed, or any seal, seal skin, firearm, ammunition or poisonous substance in his possession[157] at the time of the offence.[158]

12.38 Constables[159] are given wide powers to enforce the Act. They may stop any person suspected by them with reasonable cause of committing any of the offences described and may:

(a) without warrant arrest that person if he fails to give his name and address to the constable's satisfaction;
(b) without warrant search any vehicle or boat which that person may be using at the time he is stopped by the constable; and

---

[150] No reasons for revocation are laid down, thus giving the Home Office a free hand in this respect. Before granting a licence, the Home Office must consult Natural England or Natural Resources Wales. The consent of these bodies is required prior to granting a licence in National Parks, sites of scientific interest or marine nature reserves except where the licence is granted to prevent damage to fisheries (CSA 1970, s 10(3)).

[151] CSA 1970, ss 8(1), 10(2). The maximum punishment on summary conviction is a fine at level 4 on the standard scale (currently £2,500) (CSA 1970, s 5(2)). Prosecution for this offence will not affect liability for another penalty under this or any other Act.

[152] And also the offences of wilfully obstructing or attempting to obstruct the entry on land or water of a person authorised in writing to enter by the Minister of Agriculture (CSA 1970, ss 8(1), 11(7)).

[153] For commentary on the meaning of 'possession', though in another context, see para 3.17 *et seq.*

[154] I.e. any firearm or ammunition other than the types described above as being permitted to use against deer.

[155] CSA 1970, ss 1(1)(b), 8. The maximum punishment on summary conviction is a fine at level 4 on the standard scale (currently £2,500) (CSA 1970, s 5(2)).

[156] And also the offences of wilfully obstructing or attempting to obstruct the entry on land or water of a person authorised in writing to enter by the Minister of Agriculture (CSA 1970, ss 8(1), 11(7)).

[157] For commentary on the meaning of 'possession', though in another context, see para 3.17 *et seq.*

[158] CSA 1970, s 6.

[159] As well as police constables, including special police constables, 'constables' includes others holding that office, e.g. harbour constables. The hallmark of a constable is his attestation as such before, usually, a magistrate.

(c)   seize any seal, seal skin, firearm, ammunition or poisonous substance which
       is liable to be forfeited by order of a court as described at para 12.37.[160]

12.39 A constable may also sell or otherwise dispose of any seal seized in this
way, and the net proceeds of sale are liable to forfeiture in the same manner as
the seal sold.[161]

MARINE (SCOTLAND) ACT 2010

12.40 Part 6 of the M(S)A 2010 now governs the conservation of seals in
Scotland. Killing, injuring or taking a live seal, either intentionally or recklessly,
is an offence.[162] However, it shall not be an offence for a person to end a seal's
life humanely (or to injure a seal when attempting to do so) provided that it has
been seriously disabled (otherwise than by the person's unlawful conduct), it has
no reasonable chance of recovering, and ending its life is the only satisfactory
way to end its suffering and is not detrimental to the maintenance of the
population of any species of seal at a favourable conservation status in their
natural range (within the meaning of Article 1(e) of the Habitats Directive).[163]

12.41 Similarly, it shall not be an offence to take a seal (or to kill or injure a seal
when attempting to take it) if it has been seriously disabled (otherwise than by the
person's unlawful conduct), it is to be taken only in order to tend it with a view
to releasing it when it is recovered or release it after it has been tended, it is taken
in a manner and in circumstances unlikely to cause the seal to suffer unnecessarily
and taking it is the only satisfactory way to help it recover, and is not detrimental
to the maintenance of the population of any species of seal at a favourable
conservation status in their natural range (within the meaning of Article 1(e) of
the Habitats Directive).[164] It is the duty of anyone killing or taking a seal lawfully
in the manner described above to report the matter to the Scottish Ministers
as soon as reasonably practical after doing so.[165] The failure to do so shall be
an offence.[166]

---

[160] CSA 1970, s 4(1).

[161] CSA 1970, s 4(2). For police powers of general application, see the end of paras 11.14 and 12.14.

[162] M(S)A 2010, s 107. A person guilty of this offence is liable on summary conviction to
       imprisonment for a term not exceeding 6 months or to a fine not exceeding level 5 on the standard
       scale (currently £5,000), or to both (M(S)A 2010, s 128(1)).

[163] European Council Directive No 92/43/EEC (Habitats Directive). M(S)A 2010, s 108(1).

[164] M(S)A 2010, s 108(2).

[165] M(S)A 2010, s 108(3).

[166] M(S)A 2010, s 108(4). A person guilty of this offence is liable, on summary conviction, to a fine
       not exceeding level 4 on the standard scale (currently £2,500) (M(S)A 2010, s 128(2)).

12.42 It shall not be an offence to kill or take a seal in accordance with a seal licence.[167] Scottish Ministers have the power to grant seal licences authorising the killing or taking of seals for a variety of reasons described in the Act.[168] A seal licence must specify the method which the licensee must use to kill or take seals and Scottish Ministers must not grant a seal licence authorising a person to kill seals by shooting unless they are satisfied that the person has adequate skills and experience in using firearms.[169]

12.43 A seal licence which authorises the killing of seals by shooting must impose conditions:

(a) specifying the type of firearm which must be used;
(b) specifying the weather conditions in which a person may attempt to shoot a seal;
(c) specifying how close a person must be to a seal before attempting to shoot it;
(d) prohibiting a person from attempting to shoot a seal from an unstable platform; and
(e) about the recovery of carcasses.[170]

There are reporting requirements for those who hold seal licences and the failure, without reasonable excuse, to send a seal licence report is an offence.[171] A seal licence may be varied or revoked at any time.[172]

12.44 Harassing a seal (intentionally or recklessly) at a haul-out site is an offence. The term 'haul-out site' is defined as any place which the Scottish Ministers, after consulting the Natural Environment Research Council, by order designate as such.[173]

12.45 A court convicting a person of any of the offences detailed above may order the forfeiture of any seal or seal skin in respect of which the offence was committed, or anything which the person possessed or controlled at the time of

---

[167] M(S)A 2010, s 109.

[168] M(S)A 2010, s 110.

[169] M(S)A 2010, s 111(1) and (2).

[170] M(S)A 2010, s 112(2).

[171] M(S)A 2010, s 113. A person guilty of this offence is liable, on summary conviction, to imprisonment for a term not exceeding 3 months or to a fine not exceeding level 5 on the standard scale (currently £5,000), or to both (M(S)A 2010, s 128(3).

[172] M(S)A 2010, s 114.

[173] M(S)A 2010, s 117. A person guilty of this offence is liable, on summary conviction, to imprisonment for a term not exceeding 6 months or to a fine not exceeding level 5 (currently £5,000) on the standard scale, or to both (M(S)A 2010, s 128(1)).

the offence which was capable of being used in connection with the offence.[174] A constable may stop any person whom he suspects with reasonable cause of committing any of the offences described above and may:

(a)   without warrant, search any vehicle or vessel which the constable reasonably believes to have been used in connection with the commission of the offence,

(b)   seize any seal, seal skin or other thing liable to be forfeited as described above.[175]

PROTECTION OF BADGERS ACT 1992

12.46 The Protection of Badgers Act 1992 (PBA 1992) states that it is an offence[176] wilfully[177] to kill or injure, or to attempt to kill or injure, any badger.[178] If, in a prosecution for attempt, there is evidence from which it could be reasonably concluded that at the material time the accused was attempting to kill or injure, he shall be presumed to have been so attempting unless the contrary is shown.[179] A number of defences are available and, so far as shooting is concerned, these are:

(a)   In the case of a killing or attempted killing, or in the case of injuring a badger in the course of attempting to kill it, that the defendant can show that his action was necessary for the purpose of preventing serious damage to land,[180] crops, poultry or any other form of property; *but* this defence is *not* available in relation to any action taken at any time if it had become

---

[174]   M(S)A 2010, s 127.

[175]   M(S)A 2010, s 126.

[176]   The maximum punishment on summary conviction is a term of imprisonment not exceeding 6 months and/or an unlimited fine, for each badger against which the offence is committed (PBA 1992, s 12(1), (2)).

[177]   This means deliberately and intentionally, and not by accident or inadvertence (*R v Senior* [1899] 1 QB 283 at 290–91). In addition in Scotland pursuant to the Wildlife and Natural Environment (Scotland) Act 2011, s 33, a person will be guilty of an offence if he knowingly causes or permits any act rendered unlawful by PBA 1992, s 1(1)–(3) to be done.

[178]   PBA 1992, s 1(1). Except that in Scotland the words to 'attempt to kill or injure' have been repealed by the Nature Conservation (Scotland) Act 2004 (N(C)SA 2004), s 26(2)(a), and attempts are now classified as offences pursuant to s 11 of the N(C)SA 2004. 'Badger' means any animal of the species *Meles meles* (PBA 1992, s 14).

[179]   PBA 1992, s 1(2). Except that this provision has been repealed with respect to Scotland by NC(S)A 2004, s 26(2)(b).

[180]   'Land' includes buildings and other structures and land covered with water (IA 1978, s 5 and Sch 1).

apparent, before that time, that that action would prove necessary for the purpose mentioned, and either:

(i)   a licence authorising that action had not been applied for as soon as reasonably practicable after the fact of the action proving necessary had become apparent; or
(ii)   an application for such a licence had been determined.

(b)   That it was a killing or attempted killing of a badger which appeared to be so seriously injured or in such a condition that to kill it would be an act of mercy.[181]
(c)   That it was an unavoidable killing or injuring as an incidental result of a lawful action.[182]
(d)   That the act was done under the authority of, and within the conditions of, a licence, the provisions for which are next considered.[183]

12.47   Licences related to shooting of badgers may be granted for the following purposes:

(a)   For scientific or educational purposes, to kill within the area and by the means described in the licence, or to sell or have in the licensed person's possession the number of badgers stipulated by the licence.
(b)   For the purpose of preventing the spread of disease, to kill badgers within the area and by the means described in the licence.
(c)   For the purpose of preventing serious damage to land,[184] crops, poultry or any other form of property, to kill badgers within the area and by the means described in the licence.[185]

In the first case, licences are granted by Natural England or, in Wales, Natural Resources Wales. In the last two cases, licences are issued by the Regional Offices

---

[181]   PBA 1992, s 6(b). Except that in Scotland the provision has been amended to read: 'killing or attempting to kill a badger which has been so seriously disabled otherwise than by his unlawful act that there was no reasonable chance of it recovering' (NC(S)A 2004, s 26(4)(b)).

[182]   PBA 1992, s 6(c). An example of this defence would be an accident between a vehicle and a badger on a road.

[183]   PBA 1992, ss 1(1), 10.

[184]   'Land' includes buildings and other structures and land covered with water (IA 1978, s 5 and Sch 1).

[185]   PBA 1992, s 10(1)(a), (2)(a), (b).

of the Ministry of Agriculture. A licence may be revoked at any time,[186] and breach of its conditions is an offence.[187]

12.48   The PBA 1992 creates a number of other offences related to badgers, some with special defences, which will now be considered.

12.49   Unless permitted by or under the PBA 1992,[188] it is an offence[189] for any person to have in his possession,[190] or under his control, any dead badger or any part of, or anything derived from, a dead badger,[191] but it is a defence if the person shows that:

(a)   the badger had not been killed;[192] or

(b)   it had been killed otherwise than in contravention of the PBA 1992 or the Badgers Act 1973;[193] or

(c)   the object in the person's possession or control had been sold (whether to him or any other person) and, at the time of purchase, the purchaser had no reason to believe that the badger had been killed in contravention of the Badgers Act 1973 or the PBA 1992.[194]

12.50   Described as offences of cruelty,[195] the following acts are forbidden:[196]

(a)   to cruelly ill-treat any badger;

(b)   to use any badger tongs in the course of killing, or attempting to kill, any badger;

---

[186]   Licences may not be unreasonably withheld or revoked (PBA 1992, s 10(9)) but otherwise the issuing authorities have a free hand in these respects.

[187]   PBA 1992, s 10(8). The maximum punishment on summary conviction is imprisonment of a term not exceeding 6 months and/or an unlimited fine for each badger against which the offence is committed (PBA 1992, s 12(1), (2)).

[188]   E.g. under the terms of a licence.

[189]   The maximum punishment on summary conviction is imprisonment of a term not exceeding 6 months and/or an unlimited fine for each badger against which the offence is committed (PBA 1992, s 12(1), (2)).

[190]   For commentary on the meaning of 'possession', though in another context, see para 3.17 *et seq.*

[191]   PBA 1992, s 1.

[192]   I.e. had died naturally.

[193]   The Badgers Act 1973, which was repealed by PBA 1992, s 15(2), contained substantially the same provisions as the PBA 1992.

[194]   PBA 1992, s 1(4)

[195]   PBA 1992, s 2.

[196]   The maximum punishment on summary conviction is a term of imprisonment not exceeding 6 months and/or an unlimited fine for each badger against which the offence is committed (PBA 1992, s 12(1), (2)).

(c) to use, for the purpose of killing or taking any badger, any firearm[197] other than a smooth-bore weapon of not less than 20 bore or a rifle using ammunition[198] having a muzzle energy of not less than 160 foot pounds and a bullet weighing not less than 38 grains.[199]

12.51 Constables[200] are given wide powers to enforce the legislation. If a constable has reasonable grounds for suspecting that any person is committing or had committed an offence under the Badgers Act 1973 or the PBA 1992 and that evidence of the commission of the offence is to be found on that person or any vehicle or article he may have with him,[201] he may:

(a) without a warrant stop and search that person and search any vehicle or article he may have with him; and

(b) seize and detain for the purposes of a prosecution under the Badgers Act 1973 or the PBA 1992 anything which may be evidence of the commission of the offence or which may be liable to be forfeited by a convicting court.[202]

12.52 On conviction of any offence under the Act the court *must* order forfeiture of any badger or badger's skin in respect of which the offence was committed, and *may* order forfeiture of weapons and articles connected with the offence.[203]

12.53 If any person is found on land committing any of the offences contrary to the PBA 1992, the owner or occupier of the land, or an employee of either, or a constable, may require that person to leave the land at once and give his name and address. If the person then deliberately remains on the land or refuses to give his particulars, he commits an offence.[204]

---

[197] The definitions of this word in the FA 1968 are applied (PBA 1992, s 4). For a discussion of it, see para 1.05 *et seq*.

[198] The definitions of these words in FA 1968 are applied (PBA 1992, s 4). For a discussion of them, see Chapter 1.

[199] PBA 1992, s 2(1). Digging for badgers is also forbidden unless permitted by or under the Act, e.g. by a licence (PBA 1992, s 2(1)(c)).

[200] As well as police constables, including special police constables, 'constables' includes others holding that office, e.g. harbour constables. The hallmark of a constable is his attestation as such before, usually, a magistrate.

[201] For an interpretation of the words 'have with him', though in another context, see para 14.26, fn 33.

[202] PBA 1992, s 11. For the powers of the police generally to make searches, etc., see paras 11.14 and 12.14.

[203] PBA 1992, s 12(4).

[204] PBA 1992, s 1(5). The maximum punishment on summary conviction for this offence is a fine at level 3 on the standard scale (currently £1,000) (PBA 1992, s 12(3)).
Note that this provision gives no right to the persons named forcibly to eject the offender from the land. If he is a trespasser, the common law powers of ejectment will apply.

OTHER LEGISLATION

12.54 It is an offence[205] to destroy or damage[206] wild creatures no longer in a wild state[207] 'without lawful excuse'.[208] A person shall be deemed to have a lawful excuse if at the time of the act he believed that the person or persons whom he believed to be entitled to consent to the destruction of or damage to the property in question had so consented, or would have so consented to it if he or they had known of the destruction or damage and its circumstances; or if he destroyed or damaged the property in order to protect property belonging to himself or another or a right or interest in property which was or which he believed to be vested in himself or another and that property was in need of immediate protection and the means of protection was reasonable in the circumstances.[209]

12.55 The WM(P)A 1996 lists several acts of cruelty against wild mammals which, if done with intent to inflict unnecessary suffering, constitute an offence.[210] Shooting is not one of those acts.

---

[205] The maximum punishment on conviction is 10 years' imprisonment (CDA 1971, s 4).

[206] The word 'damage' is used because the Act of Parliament creating the offence is primarily concerned with damage to lifeless property.

[207] I.e. tamed, ordinarily kept in captivity or otherwise reduced or being reduced into possession.

[208] CDA 1971, ss 1(1), (2), 5, 10(1)(a).

[209] CDA 1971, s (10)(2).

[210] WM(P)A 1996, s 1. The maximum punishments on summary conviction are a fine at level 5 on the standard scale (currently £5,000), or 6 months' imprisonment, or both (WM(P)A 1996, s 5(1)).

Chapter 13

The Tenant's Right to Shoot

COMMON LAW

13.01 Under Common Law, the right to possession of land carries with it the right to take all birds and animals naturally on the land, whether they be game or not.[1] Thus a landowner has such rights and he may reserve those rights to himself or grant them to another. When he grants such game rights, the grantee may exercise those rights in the same manner and to the same extent as the owner of the land. Where the owner, whether in occupation or not, has let the shooting rights, he has no right at Common Law to shoot over the land. However, an owner in occupation has a statutory right to shoot ground game.[2]

13.02 If the owner does not occupy his land but lets it to another under a tenancy then, unless the shooting is 'reserved' to the landlord, the tenant will have an absolute right to shoot as against any other person. Conversely, if the right to take game is 'reserved', the tenant will have no right to shoot at Common Law.[3] This rule is expressly preserved by the GA 1831.[4] Further, it is an offence under that Act for an occupier to pursue, kill or take game, or to permit another to do so, where the owner has reserved the game rights or granted them to another.[5] However, any reservation of rights will be void in so far as it purports to exclude the owner's rights to destroy ground game.[6] An occupier, such as a tenant, with

---

[1] Rare exceptions to this rule apply where sporting rights are given to lords of manors under Inclosure Acts and Awards.

[2] Ground Game Act 1880 (GGA 1880), s 1. 'Ground game' means hares and rabbits (GGA 1880, s 8).

[3] Unless he is expressly permitted to do so by the landlord.

[4] GA 1831, s 8, which also forbids the occupier to permit another person to shoot.

[5] GA 1831, s 1. The punishment for such an offence is a fine at level 1 on the standard scale, and a person can be fined such an amount for each head of game so killed or taken.

[6] GGA 1880, s 3.

full shooting rights may authorise any person to kill and take game and other birds and animals and may also let or assign his shooting rights.

GROUND GAME ACT 1880

13.03 As can be seen above, the position at Common Law was much altered by the Ground Game Act 1880 (GGA 1880). The objective of the Act was to allow tenants without shooting rights to protect their crops against hares and rabbits. It did so by permitting occupiers of land to kill and take ground game[7] on their land concurrently with any other person who may have the right to do the same thing.[8] Within certain limitations, tenants may also claim compensation from their landlords for damage to crops caused by any wild animals or birds.[9] There are some extensions to, and several limitations on, this right of the occupier to take ground game, and these will now be considered.

13.04 First, who shall be deemed an occupier for the purposes of the Act? Clearly, an occupying owner, tenant or sub-tenant of land will be. The Act says that a person having a right of common or 'an occupation for the purpose of grazing or pasturage of sheep, cattle, or horses for not more than nine months' will not be an occupier.[10] It would seem to follow from this that if the occupation for the purposes quoted exceeds 9 months, the occupier will be qualified under the Act. However, this proposition has been questioned and the contrary view put that the occupier must have the right to full possession of the land and not a limited right to its use, as in the case of a licensee.[11] Doubts also arise in cases where land is used for grazing other animals such as goats and pigs. Where there are joint occupiers, all are entitled to the rights conferred by the Act.[12]

---

[7]   'Ground game' means hares and rabbits (GGA 1880, s 8).

[8]   GGA 1880, s 1.

[9]   Agricultural Holdings Act 1986, s 20.

[10] GGA 1880, s 1(2).

[11] See *Oke's Game Laws*, 5th edition, p 103.

[12] *Oke's Game Laws*, 5th edition, pp 101–2.

13.05 In addition to the occupier, the occupier can authorise one other person in writing[13] to shoot[14] ground game.[15] This person can only be:

(a) a member of the occupier's household[16] resident[17] on the land in his occupation, the shooting authority extending only to that land; or
(b) a person in the occupier's ordinary service[18] on the land occupied, the shooting authority extending only to that land; or
(c) any other person *bona fide* employed by the occupier for reward[19] in the taking and destruction of ground game.[20]

More than one person from classes (a) and (b) above, but only one from class (c), may, at the same time, kill and take ground game otherwise than by shooting if, again, they are authorised in writing by the occupier.[21] Only one person, aside from the occupier himself, may be authorised by him to kill ground game with firearms.[22]

13.06 An authorised person must produce his written authority, if asked to do so, to any person having a concurrent right to take or kill ground game on the land or

---

[13] The authority need not be in any prescribed form, and no provision expressly requires it to be signed or dated, but it would be desirable for it to describe the person to whom it is given and precisely state the situation and extent of the land over which it is to operate.

[14] More than one person may, however, be authorised to take ground game otherwise than by using firearms.

[15] GGA 1880, s 1(1)(a). Where there are joint occupiers, it seems that all must give their authority to one other person to shoot and that each cannot authorise a different person (*Oke's Game Laws*, 5th edition, p 102).

[16] This will include servants who live and board at the house, but not those living in other houses on the farm (*Re Drax, Savile v Yeatman* (1887) 57 LT 475; *Ogle v Morgan* (1852) 1 De GM & G 359).

[17] This is a question of fact and could include a visitor staying at the house but presumably not one who comes for a day. A person invited to stay for a week and shoot rabbits for one week was held to satisfy the condition of residence (*Stuart v Murray* (1884) 12 R 9, Ct of Sess).

[18] 'Ordinary service' is not further defined in the Act but presumably means those in regular service so as to exclude casual labour but may include labour regularly employed for a certain season only.

[19] The fact of, e.g., a rabbit-catcher being allowed to keep all or some of the rabbits taken would probably be sufficient evidence of such employment for reward (*Bruce v Prosser* (1898) 35 Sc LR 433), but a similar gift to a friend asked to come and shoot would hardly be so. Further, the person must be definitely employed for this purpose; a verbal instruction to kill ground game is insufficient and shall be a trespass (*Richardson v Maitland* (1897) 34 SLR 426).

[20] GGA 1880, s 1(1)(b).

[21] GGA 1880, s 1(1)(b).

[22] GGA 1880, s 1(1)(a).

to any person authorised by the latter in writing to make the demand. In default, the authorised person's rights cease.[23]

13.07 In the case of moorlands and unenclosed non-arable land, except detached portions of either which are less than 25 acres in extent and adjoin arable lands, the time at which the right of the occupier to kill ground game may be exercised is limited. Between 11 December of one year and 31 March (both inclusive) of the following year the right may be exercised and ground game may be killed in any legal way by the occupier and persons authorised by him in accordance with the Act.[24] Between 1 April and 31 August (both inclusive) the right is suspended altogether. Between 1 September and 10 December (both inclusive) the right may be exercised otherwise than by the use of firearms.[25] The occupier may make an agreement with the owner of, or any other person having the right to take game on, lands of this description, for the joint exercise, or the exercise for their joint benefit, of the right to kill and take ground game within this period of the year.[26]

13.08 The occupier of land, *or* one other person[27] authorised by him, may now[28] use firearms[29] to kill hares and rabbits at night[30] on that land if:

(a)   the occupier has the exclusive right to kill and take hares and rabbits on the land; or

(b)   the occupier has the written authority[31] of the other person, or one of the other persons,[32] who has that right.[33]

---

[23]   GGA 1880, s 1(1)(c).

[24]   GGA 1880, s 1(3).

[25]   GGA 1906, s 2. This Act refers to the occupier only, whereas GGA 1880, s 1(3) also mentions persons authorised by him. Thus, it seems, only the occupier himself may take ground game, otherwise than by shooting, between 1 September and 10 December.

[26]   GGA 1906, s 3.

[27]   Who must be a person within one of the descriptions given in items (a)–(c) in para 13.05. As to the form of authority, there is no set form, but it is desirable for it to confirm the identity of the person concerned and the relevant land should be specified.

[28]   Since 16 February 1982 after the WCA 1981 came into effect. Previously, what is now permitted was, for occupying tenants, an offence.

[29]   The definition of 'firearm' discussed at para 1.05 *et seq* applies (FA 1968, s 57(1); WCA 1981, ss 12, 27(1) and Sch 7, para 1(1)).

[30]   From one hour after sunset to one hour before sunrise (WCA 1981, s 12 and Sch 7 para 1(1)).

[31]   Impliedly, this will be an authority to the occupier to use firearms at night for the purpose described; which need not, it is suggested, embrace others whom the occupier himself might authorise under this provision.

[32]   As to who these persons may be, see items (a), (b) and (c) in para 13.05.

[33]   WCA 1981, s 12 and Sch 7, para 1.

However, where the above does not apply, any occupier of land (other than the owner) who is entitled to kill ground game, either by virtue of the GGA 1880 or because the rights have not been reserved, uses firearms in the exercise of this right between the expiry of the first hour after sunset and the commencement of the last hour before sunrise, will be guilty of an offence.[34]

13.09 GGA 1880 is at pains to ensure that an occupier retains the shooting rights which it gives to him. Thus, if an occupier has the right to shoot hares and rabbits, otherwise than by the powers given to him by the Act, and he transfers that right to another person, he nevertheless retains his statutory shooting rights.[35] Again, any agreement, condition or arrangement which tries to divest the occupier of his rights under the Act, or which gives him an advantage in return for his forbearing to exercise those rights, is declared to be void.[36] As the Act twice declares,[37] the rights which it gives to the occupier are 'incident (*sic*) to and inseparable from' his occupation of the land.

13.10 On the other hand, nothing in the GGA 1880 operates so as to restrict the occupier's shooting rights to those rights which it gives to him. An occupier may still acquire, and exercise, the right to shoot ground game and other game and shall not be limited by the restrictions contained in the Act.[38] This means, for example, that an occupying tenant, whose lease does not reserve shooting rights to his landlord, may shoot ground game with freedom from the restrictions which the Act would impose if his right to shoot was acquired solely from the provisions of the Act.

13.11 Where the occupier has no shooting rights (except those given to him by the GGA 1880) and he shoots game,[39] other than hares and rabbits, or gives permission to any other person to do so, and does so without, in either case, the authority of the person who has the right of killing that game, then he shall commit an offence.[40]

---

[34] GGA 1880, s 6. The punishment for an offence of this nature is a fine not exceeding level 1 on the standard scale (currently £200).

[35] GGA 1880, s 2. This means that both persons have concurrent rights to shoot hares and rabbits.

[36] GGA 1880, s 3.

[37] GGA 1880, ss 1and 2.

[38] GGA 1880, s 2.

[39] Game in this context includes hares, pheasants, partridges, grouse, heath or moor game and black game (GA 1831, s 2). Note that 'includes' has been interpreted in some statutory contexts to mean exclusively the things mentioned after it.

[40] GA 1831, s 12. The maximum punishment on summary conviction is a fine at level 1 on the standard scale (currently £200) plus a similar fine for each head of game so taken.

Chapter 14

Young People and Guns

SUMMARY

14.01 To all the other regulations and restrictions affecting the use of guns and their ammunition Parliament has added special provisions for young people under 18 years of age.[1] These provisions vary according to age, depending upon whether the person is under 14, 15 or 18, vary again according to the kind of act done in relation to firearms and ammunition, and vary yet again according to the type of firearm or ammunition which is involved.

14.02 The principal sections of the FA 1968 regarding young persons are sections 22 to 24. The relevant official guidance can be found in Chapter 7 and Appendix 4 of the *Guide*.

Firearms

14.03 A firearm certificate may only be granted to a person aged 14 years or older. As well as not being able to obtain a firearm certificate under the age of 14, those under 14 cannot have possession of a section 1 firearm except when acting as a gun bearer or as a member of a Home Office-approved rifle club.

Shotguns

14.04 A shotgun certificate can be granted to persons of any age. A person under 18 is prohibited by section 22 of the FA 1968 (as amended by the VCRA 2006 and the Firearms (Amendment) Regulations 2010[2]) from purchasing or hiring any

---

[1]   FA 1968, ss 22–24A, as amended by VCRA 2006, ss 33(4); Firearms (Amendment) Regulations 2010 (SI 2010/1759) and VCRA 2006, s 33(5). A person attains a particular age expressed in years at the beginning of the relevant anniversary of the date of his birth (Family Law Reform Act 1969, s 9(1)). Thus, a person becomes 18 at the midnight immediately preceding his 18th birthday.

[2]   SI 2010/1759.

firearm or ammunition defined by section 57. Section 24A(1) of the FA 1968 also prohibits the purchase of imitation firearms by those under the age of 18.

14.05 Possession of shotguns and ammunition by those under 18 is permitted where they are a certificate holder at any age, or where they are being supervised by someone over 21. Supervision is not necessary where the shotgun is not assembled, or is in a suitable slip to prevent it being fired.

14.06 Further, it is an offence to gift a shotgun, or shotgun ammunition, to a person under 15, although those under 15 can purchase such items if they have a certificate. We had to advise that a shotgun offered as a prize by a well-known manufacturer in a high-level clay shooting competition could not be given to the winner, a certificate holder aged 14.

14.07 Although there is no age limit in respect of a shotgun certificate, in our experience, it would be highly exceptional for a shotgun certificate to be granted to a child aged less than 12.

Air weapons

England and Wales

14.08 Section 22(4) of the FA 1968 creates a prohibition on the possession of an air weapon by those under 18, and section 23 sets out the exceptions to that prohibition. A person under 18 is permitted to have possession of an air weapon on private premises when supervised by someone over 21, although he cannot fire it beyond the boundary of that land without the consent of the adjoining landowner. Possession of an air weapon under 18 is also permitted at any age at a miniature rifle range or as a member of a Home Office-approved club. Those who are under 18 but over 14 can use an air weapon on private premises with the consent of the owner, and there is no requirement to be supervised by a person over 21.

Scotland

14.09 In Scotland the Air Weapons and Licensing (Scotland) Act 2015, section 7 now requires a person under 18 to have a certificate to be in possession of an air weapon in that jurisdiction. To obtain a certificate the person must be over 14 and requires the consent of the parent or guardian. The applicant for an AWC must demonstrate a good reason for possessing such a weapon. A statutory condition for all AWCs for those under 18 is that the holder may not purchase, hire, accept a gift of or own, an air weapon. In order to obtain a certificate in Scotland an applicant of any age has to show a 'good reason', as with an application for a firearm certificate. For a young shooter at least one of the following conditions will then be applied to the certificate, dependent on what the police have accepted as a good reason. The six possible reasons for those under 18 are: for sporting purposes (including shooting quarry) on private land; target shooting on private land; taking part in events and competitions; target shooting as a member of an approved air weapon club; for the protection of livestock, crops or produce on land used for agriculture; or pest control.[3] At least one reason has to be conditioned on the licence, but it may be all six. The exceptions in section 23 which apply in England and Wales do not apply in Scotland, therefore no person under 14 can possess an air weapon in Scotland.

General exceptions

14.10 The general exceptions to firearms law in the cases of the Proof Houses and antique firearms, which are considered at para 1.51 *et seq* and para 1.53 *et seq* respectively, also apply to young people. It must be borne in mind that the possession of and other dealings with firearms by young people which are permitted under the headings now to be discussed will nevertheless in many cases be illegal unless covered by the necessary firearm or shotgun certificate, the need for which is discussed in Chapters 3 and 4.

14.11 So those under 18 cannot purchase:

- air weapons and ammunition for air weapons;
- imitation firearms, realistic imitation firearms and deactivated firearms;
- readily convertible replicas (as defined by section 1 of FA 1982);
- blank ammunition; and
- unless they hold a relevant certificate, section 1 firearms and ammunition or a smooth-bore gun or shotgun cartridges.[4]

Offences

14.12 As suggested by the above summary, a number of offences are created, many of them with exceptions. This produces a complex situation which may perhaps best be examined by considering each of the offences in turn and seeing how each applies to the different age groups and what exceptions each may have. For further clarity, a table is given in this chapter in an attempt to deal with all these offences in summary form.

Firearms and ammunition

14.13 Both these words are given lengthy definitions in FA 1968 and are fully discussed at para 1.05 *et seq* and para 1.42 *et seq* respectively. These definitions

---

[3] A breach of a condition on a Scottish AWC is punishable by a level 3 fine: Air Weapons and Licensing (Scotland) Act 2015, s 6(5).

[4] FA 1968, s 22(1A).

catch all ordinary kinds of firearms and ammunition (including, as we shall see, restrictions on air weapons) and, in the case of firearms, component parts and accessories for reducing noise or flash are included. Imitation firearms and realistic imitation firearms fulfilling the conditions described in Chapter 9 will also be subject to the following rules.

Buying or hiring

14.14 It is an offence:

(a) for a person under the age of 18 to purchase or hire an air weapon or ammunition for an air weapon;
(b) for a person under the age of 18 to purchase or hire a firearm or ammunition of any other description;[5]
(c) for a person under 18 to purchase an imitation firearm.[6]

Although they may hold a relevant certificate under 18, which allows them to acquire and possess a firearm or shotgun, they cannot purchase or hire one themselves. In other words there is an expectation that they will be gifted a gun by an adult, which provides some degree of supervision. An example of acquisition would be using a firearm under the supervision of a parent or guardian (provided they are of the correct age) or a firearm certificate holder aged 14 to 18 acquiring rifle ammunition from a parent or other adult certificate holder as a gift.

14.15 There are also corresponding offences for any person to sell[7] or let on hire any firearm or ammunition to a youngster under 18, or an air weapon or ammunition for it to a youngster under 18, or an imitation firearm to a youngster under 18,[8] unless the supplier can prove that he believed the youngster to be of or over that age, and had reasonable ground for the belief.[9]

---

5   FA 1968, s 22(1), as amended by the VCRA 2006, s 33. The maximum punishment on summary conviction is 6 months' imprisonment, or an unlimited fine or both (FA 1968, s 51(1), (2) and Sch 6, Part I).

6   FA 1968, s 24A(1), as amended by VCRA 2006, s 40. The maximum punishment on summary conviction is 6 months' imprisonment, or an unlimited fine, or both (FA 1968, s 51(1), (2) and Sch 6, Part I as amended by VCRA 2006, s 40(2)). Possession of a section 1 or 2 firearm if tried on indictment is punishable with a maximum of 5 years' imprisonment.

7   A sale, a condition of which is that the seller retains possession of the firearm and where the seller in fact retains subsequent physical possession, allowing the buyer only to have it to use at a rifle club, is nevertheless a sale for the purpose of this offence (*Watts v Seymour* [1967] 1 All ER 1044).

8   FA 1968, s 24(1) & 24A(2), as amended by the VCRA 2006, s 33 and 40.

9   FA 1968, s 24(1), (5) and, in relation to imitation firearms, s 24A(3) and (4). The maximum punishment for the supplier is the same as for the young person purchasing or hiring the relevant item.

Possession

14.16 Youngsters aged 14 or over may have section 1 firearms or section 1 ammunition[10] in their possession in accordance with the firearm certificate they have been granted.[11] Those who do not have a valid certificate for the firearm and ammunition, and those under 14, are only allowed to possess firearms and that ammunition (including muzzle-loading pistols and their ammunition) in the following situations:[12]

(a)   They may carry any firearm or ammunition belonging to a person holding a firearm certificate or shotgun certificate, the carrying being under instructions from, and for the use of, that person for sporting purposes only.[13]

(b)   As a member of an approved rifle club,[14] he may possess a rifle and ammunition for it, and use them, while engaged as such a member in connection with target shooting.[15]

(c)   For conducting or carrying on a miniature rifle range (whether for a rifle club or otherwise) or shooting gallery at which, in either case, no firearms are used other than air weapons[16] or miniature rifles not exceeding .23″ calibre, a person under 14 may have in his possession such miniature rifles and ammunition suitable for them; and he and other persons may use there those rifles and that ammunition.[17]

(d)   At a ground approved by the local chief of police under section 11(6) of the FA 1968 for shooting at artificial targets.

14.17 It is an offence for a person to part with the possession of section 1 firearms and section 1 ammunition to any child under the age of 14, except in those cases where the under-14 is allowed to have possession as described above.[18] It will be

---

[10]   For the meanings of 'section 1 firearm' and 'section 1 ammunition', see para 3.01 *et seq* and para 3.12 *et seq* respectively.

[11]   For commentary on the meaning of 'possession' see para 3.17 *et seq.*

[12]   Otherwise an offence is committed; FA 1968, s 22(2), as amended by the F(A)A 1988, s 23(4). The maximum punishment on summary conviction is 6 months' imprisonment, or an unlimited fine, or both, and, as with most firearms offences, is triable on indictment, for which a penalty of up to 5 years' imprisonment could be imposed.

[13]   FA 1968, s 11(1). This is intended to cover 'gun bearers' and only allows carrying but not use of the firearm and ammunition by the youngster. The shooting of rats in a barn is not shooting for a 'sporting purpose' (*Morton v Chaney* [1960] 3 All ER 632), although as Dr Barry Peachey, the wildlife expert, once observed of the judge who made this decision, 'His Lordship had obviously never tried it'!

[14]   As to the approval of rifle clubs, see para 3.30 *et seq.*

[15]   FA 1968, ss 22(2) and 11(3), as amended by F(A)A 1988, s 15.

[16]   This means any air gun, air rifle or air pistol, not being of a type declared by rules made by the Home Office to be specially dangerous (FA 1968, ss 1(3)(b), 57(4)).

[17]   FA 1968, ss 11(4), 22(2), e.g. at a fairground.

[18]   FA 1968, ss 11(1), (4), 22(2), 24(2)(b).

a defence for the accused person to prove that he believed the child to be aged at least 14 and had reasonable ground for the belief.[19]

14.18 It is an offence for a youngster under the age of 18 in possession of a firearm as the holder of a firearm or shotgun certificate to use it for a purpose not authorised by the European Weapons Directive.[20] The authorised purposes are: sporting purposes; shooting of vermin, or other activities in connection with the management of any estate, or other wildlife; target shooting; and competitions.[21]

Gifts

14.19 A person may not make a gift of or lend section 1 firearms or section 1 ammunition[22] to a youngster aged under 14. To do so is an offence[23] unless the person accused can prove that he believed the youngster to be 14 or over and had reasonable ground for that belief.

14.20 It is no longer expressly made an offence for a child under 14 to accept a gift or loan in a case where the donor or lender commits an offence though, technically, if the child assists the offender, the child is guilty as an accessory to the offence.

Shotguns and shotgun ammunition

14.21 The definition of 'shotgun' is given in Chapter 4. There is no control on possession of shotgun ammunition, as long as it comes within the exemption defined in section 1(4) of the FA 1968.

Gifts

14.22 A person may make a gift of a shotgun or shotgun ammunition to a youngster aged 15 or over, but not to one aged under 15.[24] Again, it is a defence if the accused person can prove that he believed the youngster to be 15 or over

---

[19] FA 1968, s 24(5).

[20] FA 1968, s 22(1A); Firearms Acts (Amendment) Regulations 1992, Reg 4(1). 'European Weapons Directive' means European Council Directive No 91/477/EEC.

[21] FA 1968, s 57(4A), Firearms Acts (Amendment) Regulations 1992.

[22] For the meanings of 'section 1 firearm' and 'section 1 ammunition', see para 3.01 *et seq* and para 3.12 respectively.

[23] FA 1968, s 24(2)(a). The maximum punishment on summary conviction is 6 months' imprisonment, or an unlimited fine, or both.

[24] FA 1968, s 24(3). The maximum punishment on summary conviction is a fine at level 3 on the standard scale (currently £1,000) (FA 1968, s 51(1), (2) and Sch 6, Part I).

and had reasonable ground for that belief.[25] A gift of a shotgun (but not cartridges) would be an offence of transferring a firearm to a person not authorised to possess it, unless the person held a relevant valid certificate, no matter what their age.

Having an assembled shotgun

14.23 A child aged less than 15 must not have an assembled shotgun with him[26] except while under the supervision of a person at least 21 years old or while the gun is so covered with a securely fastened gun cover that it cannot be fired.[27] Youngsters of 15 and over may have assembled shotguns with them without either of these restrictions. The person 'supervising' does not need to be a certificate holder (although the youngster has to be unless one of the exemptions such as being at a ground approved under section 11A of the FA 1968 applies), but we suggest the supervisor cannot be someone who is 'prohibited' under section 21 of the Act, see para 5.60 *et seq*.

Air weapons and air weapon ammunition

14.24 The following rules about young persons having air weapons and ammunition with them and about gifts of these to them relate only to air weapons not declared to be specially dangerous[28] and to air weapon ammunition generally.[29] If they are specially dangerous, they fall into the same category, for the purposes of this chapter, as section 1 firearms and must be considered under para 14.13, 'Firearms and ammunition'.

14.25 In the following paragraphs 'air weapon' means an air rifle, air gun or air pistol,[30] and will include an air weapon powered by compressed carbon dioxide.[31]

Having possession of an air weapon and its ammunition in a public place and elsewhere

14.26 No person under the age of 18 shall have with him[32] an air weapon or ammunition for it, unless:

---

[25] FA 1968, s 24(5). As the date of birth of the recipient is on their certificate, this could be a difficult defence to run where you are transferring a gun to them.

[26] It seems that the words 'with him' will cover the case of a gun being on or in a vehicle carrying a youngster. He will only be liable for conviction if he knew that the gun was with him (*R v Cugullere* [1961] 2 All ER 343).

[27] FA 1968, s 22(3).

[28] Firearms (Dangerous Air Weapons) Rules 1969.

[29] FA 1968, ss 22(4), (5), 23, 24(4), 57(4).

[30] FA 1968, ss 1(3)(b), 57(4).

[31] F(A)A 1997, s 48.

[32] It seems that the words 'with him' will cover the case of a gun being on or in a vehicle carrying a youngster. He will only be liable for conviction if he knew that the gun was with him (*R v Cugullere* [1961] 2 All ER 343).

(a) the youngster is engaged in connection with target shooting as a member of a rifle club or miniature rifle club, and that club is approved by the Home Office;

(b) the youngster is using the air weapon at a shooting gallery where the only firearms used are either air weapons which are not specially dangerous or miniature rifles not exceeding .23" calibre;[33] or

(c) the youngster may have with him on any premises an air weapon and ammunition for it, provided he is under the supervision of a person aged at least 21.[34] However, if the air weapon is used to fire a missile beyond those premises,[35] both the young person and the supervisor should be aware they will each be liable for an offence.[36] That said, it shall be a defence if it can be shown that the only premises into or across which the missile was fired were premises the occupier of which had given their consent to the firing of the missile (whether specifically or by way of general consent).[37]

Note in these circumstances there is no lower age limit. In relation to item (c) above, a child aged 14 or over does not require the supervision of an adult, provided he has the air weapon and ammunition with him on private premises and with the consent of the occupier.[38]

Scotland

14.27 As already observed in this chapter, in Scotland a person commits an offence at any age if he has possession of an air weapon without a certificate,[39] and a person under 18 may only be granted a certificate for certain 'good reasons'.

Parting with possession of an air weapon and its ammunition to a youngster

14.28 It is an offence to part with the possession of an air weapon or air weapon ammunition to a person under the age of 18, except where he is not prohibited

---

[33] FA 1968, ss 22(4), 23(2), as amended by VCRA 2006, s 33. It would appear that these two provisions permit the young person under 18 to have the air weapon and ammunition with them in a public place if they are in transit for either of these purposes.

[34] FA 1968, s 23(1).

[35] The word 'premises' is defined as including any land (FA 1968, s 57(4)).

[36] FA 1968, ss 21A and 23(1) as amended by VCRA 2006, s 34. The maximum punishment on summary conviction is a fine at level 3 on the standard scale (currently £1,000) (FA 1968, s 51(1), (2) and Sch 6, Part I).

[37] FA 1968, s 21A(2) as amended by VCRA 2006, s 34(2).

[38] FA 1968, s 23(3) as amended by VCRA 2006 s 34(2).

[39] Air Weapons and Licensing (Scotland) Act 2015, s 1. Punishable by a fine and up to 2 years' imprisonment.

from having it as set out at items (a) to (c) in para 14.26.[40] In addition, it will always be an offence to sell or let on hire an air weapon or ammunition for it to a person under the age of 18.[41] In any of these circumstances, the supplier of the air weapon or ammunition will have a defence if he can prove that he believed the youngster to be at least 18 and had reasonable ground for that belief.[42]

14.29 Yet another offence has recently been created, and that is where a person in possession of an air weapon fails to take reasonable precautions to prevent someone under the age of 18 from gaining unauthorised access to it.[43] A defence is provided where a person can show he had reasonable grounds for believing the other person to be aged 18 or over. It is not an offence under this section to permit someone under 18 to have possession of an air weapon in any of the permitted circumstances already set out here in this chapter; supervised by someone over 21, shooting galleries, etc. This places an onus on those who keep air weapons to prevent access to them by those under 18. There is no requirement to prevent access by adults. The guidance issued by the Home Office is very similar to the security advice they issue in relation to firearms. It is a matter of looking at each situation on the individual merits of the case. They suggest using steel cables, gun cabinets and the like. Further information on this topic is set out in Chapter 8. Given that the only risk that is required to be assessed is that from those under 18, the necessary steps that will need to be taken are obviously less stringent.

Gifts

14.30 A person may make a gift of an air weapon or air weapon ammunition to a youngster aged 18 or more, but not if under 18.[44] Again, the person making the gift has a defence if he can prove that he believed the youngster to be at least 18 and had reasonable ground for that belief.[45]

---

[40] FA 1968, ss 23, 24(4)(b) as amended by VCRA 2006, s 33. The maximum punishment on summary conviction is a fine at level 3 on the standard scale (currently £1,000) (FA 1968, s 51(1), (2) and Sch 6, Part I).

[41] FA 1968, s 24(1)(a). The maximum punishment on summary conviction is 6 months' imprisonment, or an unlimited fine, or both.

[42] FA 1968, s 24(5).

[43] FA 1968, s 24ZA, as amended by Crime and Security Act 2010, s 46, in force 10 February 2011. The maximum punishment on summary conviction is a fine at level 3 on the standard scale (currently £1,000).

[44] Except in circumstances (clubs, etc) set out above. FA 1968, s 24(4)(a) as amended by VCRA 2006, s 33. The maximum punishment on summary conviction is a fine at level 3 on the standard scale (currently £1,000) (FA 1968, s 51(1), (2) and Sch 6, Part I).

[45] FA 1968, s 24(5), as amended by VCRA 2006, s 33.

Table 14.1   Restrictions in relation to young persons

Restricted acts	Age				
	Up to and incl 13	*14*	*15 to 16 inc*	*17*	*18*
I. Acts by youngsters which are permitted					
1 Buying or hiring any section 1 firearm or shotgun or ammunition for either	No	No	No	No	Yes
2 Buying or hiring an air weapon or imitation firearm	No	No	No	No	Yes
3 Having an assembled shotgun with him in a secure slip	Yes D	Yes D	Yes	Yes	Yes
4 Possessing a section 1 firearm or ammunition	No B, C, E	Yes	Yes	Yes	Yes
5 Having with him an air weapon[46] or ammunition for one	No	No B, C, D	No B, C, D	No B, C, D	Yes B, C, D
6 Using a firearm for a purpose not authorised by the European Weapons Directive	No	No	No	No	Yes
7 Borrowing a firearm under section 11A	Yes	No	No	No	Yes
8 Borrowing a shotgun under section 11A (Lender must be over 18)	Yes	Yes	Yes	Yes	Yes
II. Acts by others[47] in relation to youngsters which are permitted[48]					
1 Selling or letting on hire a section 1 firearm or shotgun or ammunition for either	Yes	No	No	No	Yes

---

[46] The air weapon, and this applies to all references to air weapons in this table, must not be of a kind declared to be specially dangerous. If of such a kind, the rules relating to section 1 firearms apply.

[47] These may include other youngsters as well as adults.

[48] In the case of each of the acts under this heading, it will be a defence for the accused person to prove that he believed the youngster to be of or over the age of 14, 15 or 17 (as the case may be) and that he had reasonable ground for that belief.

Restricted acts	Age				
	Up to and incl 13	*14*	*15 to 16 inc*	*17*	*18*
2 Selling or letting on hire an air weapon or imitation firearm	No	No	No	No	Yes
3 Giving a shotgun or ammunition for a shotgun	No	No	Yes	Yes	Yes
4 Giving or lending a section 1 firearm or ammunition.	No	Yes	Yes	Yes	Yes
5 Parting with possession of a section 1 firearm or ammunition	No	Yes A, B, D	Yes	Yes	Yes
6 Giving an air weapon or ammunition for an air weapon	No	No	No	No	Yes
7 Parting with possession of an air weapon or ammunition for one	No A, B, C	No	No A, B, C	No A, B, C	Yes A, B, C

Exceptions

A. Member of a rifle club or miniature rifle club approved by the Home Office while engaged, as a member, in, or in connection with, target shooting. Section 15 of the F(A)A 1988.

B. Having the weapon or ammunition at a shooting gallery where the only firearms used are air weapons which are not specially dangerous or miniature rifles not exceeding .23″ calibre.

C. Supervision by a person at least 18 years old. Note there is no requirement for supervision in the case of a youngster aged 14 or over who has an air weapon with him if he is on private premises, and provided he is there with the consent of the occupier.

D. As a gun bearer a youngster under the age of 14 can carry a section 1 firearm for another's use but may not use it himself. The 'user' of the gun must be over 18.

14.31 By way of conclusion to this section, it is worth noting that the FA 1968 as originally enacted allowed youngsters aged 14 or over to purchase, be given or otherwise have in their possession air weapons and air weapon ammunition. However, the successive increases in that age limit firstly to 17 by virtue of the Anti-social Behaviour Act 2003 and then more latterly to 18 by virtue of VCRA 2006 have created a somewhat illogical situation. We are now left with the position where the possession by and transfer to under 18s of air weapons and their ammunition is on the face of it more tightly controlled than is the case in relation to section 1 firearms or shotguns. The counter view would be that any youngster aged under 18 will generally, although not always, have been assessed as to their suitability to hold a firearm or shotgun certificate before acquiring possession of the section 1 firearm or shotgun, whereas no corresponding vetting process will have taken place before a young person takes possession of an air weapon.

14.32 Upon conviction for an offence mentioned in this chapter (except an offence relating specifically to air weapons and the offence of having an assembled shotgun) the court may order the forfeiture or disposal of any firearm or ammunition found in the convicted person's possession,[49] and may cancel that person's firearm certificate or shotgun certificate.[50]

14.33 Many of the restrictions discussed above are complicated enough in themselves, but a greater difficulty is caused, when trying to find the answer in a particular case, by the considerable overlapping and duplication of the restrictions. In an attempt to overcome this, set out in summary form in Table 14.1 are the restricted acts which apply to the different age groups, and underneath the exceptions which operate in some cases. The word 'Yes' under the 'Age' heading indicates that the prohibited act may be done; the word 'No' shows it may not be, except where it is followed by a capital letter referring to an exception, in which case the prohibition is eased to the extent of the exception. The exceptions are set out underneath the table.

14.34 Great care must be taken when using the table. Because of the similarities of some of the expressions and the different descriptions of guns which are used, it is advisable, when considering any particular situation, to check the position under each of the prohibited acts. Most gun shops which sell firearms and air weapons should be able to advise you as to your particular circumstances; it is advisable to ask.

---

49   For commentary on the meaning of 'possession' see para 3.17 *et seq*.

50   FA 1968, s 52(1).

Chapter 15

Criminal Offences Relating to Firearms: General Restrictions on Shooting and Carrying Guns

INTRODUCTION

15.01 In addition to the requirements of the law referred to in earlier chapters relating to the possession of firearms, shotguns and specially dangerous air weapons, a number of criminal offences have been created relating to the possession and use of them and their associated ammunition. For these offences it matters not that you may be the lawful owner of the item found in your possession. Further, with the exception of the 'possession only' offences dealt with at para 15.05 *et seq*, it should be noted that where a firearm or shotgun certificate is required for the gun in question, even if you have been granted the relevant certificate, this will not provide you with a defence to these offences.

15.02 The usual range of penalties will be available to the criminal courts, which may include anything from a fine up to life imprisonment. Keep in mind that most, but not all offences that relate to the possession and use of prohibited weapons carry a minimum mandatory 5-year sentence, unless there are found to be exceptional circumstances which would make it 'unjust in all the circumstances' to impose such a sentence. The exceptional circumstances can relate to either the offence or the offender, as explained in the following section relating to 'possession'.

15.03 Depending on the length of the prison sentence, this may then result in a prohibition on possessing all types of firearms including air weapons, which could last for the rest of your life.[1] In addition, upon conviction for any of these offences, the court may also order forfeiture and disposal or destruction of the firearm and

---

[1] For further details on prohibition, see para 5.60 *et seq*.

any ammunition found in your possession at the time of the offence.[2] If that were not enough, if you are a certificate holder, the court may cancel your certificate, and even if the court does not, a conviction for any of these offences will almost certainly result in your certificate being revoked by the police. Your firearms licensing department may not wait until you are convicted to revoke your certificate and seize your guns. Indeed, even if the offence is ultimately not proved in the criminal court, the mere fact that you have been arrested on suspicion of such an offence may well be relied on as sufficient justification for revocation. Therefore, if you value your certificate, you would be well advised to avoid any activity that might put you under suspicion for these or indeed any other criminal offences.

15.04 This is not a criminal law textbook and therefore does not seek to address every possible detail relating to the offences. A summary of the more serious criminal offences that can be committed with a firearm is included with an emphasis on the particular issues which have arisen in recent years which are specific to these firearms offences. These may be of interest to the general reader and will assist practitioners. We also deal with some offensive weapons offences, as shooters often need to carry knives with them.

UNLAWFUL POSSESSION OF FIREARMS AND AMMUNITION

15.05 This section deals with what are referred to at para 15.01 as the 'possession only' offences. Chapters 1 to 4 explain in detail the classification of section 1 firearms, shotguns, prohibited firearms and the ammunition corresponding to each. Also set out in those chapters are the need for a firearm or shotgun certificate, as appropriate, and the exceptions where the person in possession will be exempt from the usual requirement to hold a certificate. Perhaps unsurprisingly, if you are found in possession of any such item without holding a valid certificate,[3] and you cannot demonstrate you fall within one of the exemptions, you will be liable for the offence of unlawful

---

[2]   FA 1968, s 52. This power is rarely used, perhaps because the police have usually already seized any weapons and ammunition. The power does not extend to air weapons. Note that the power to order forfeiture extends to any firearms and ammunition in the convict's possession, not just those involved in the offence.

[3]   This would include where your certificate has been cancelled, revoked or has expired and you have failed to promptly surrender your firearms to the police on demand, or to an RFD or other person authorised to possess them. In the case of renewals, provided you submitted your application for renewal in good time before the expiry of your certificate, it is unlikely the police would take action against you for this offence.

possession.[4] If you do hold a firearm or shotgun certificate, but possession of the particular firearm or ammunition in question is not authorised by it, and is not exempt from certification, you will similarly be guilty of unlawful possession of that item. In relation to ammunition for a section 1 firearm, bear in mind that the offence of unlawful possession can occur where you are in possession of a quantity that exceeds the amount authorised under your firearm certificate for that calibre. This would also apply to prohibited ammunition authorised under a certificate.

15.06   For these offences all that needs to be proved is that you were in possession of the firearm or ammunition in question, which is often not in dispute, and that in law it is classified as a section 1 firearm or ammunition, a shotgun, or as a prohibited firearm or prohibited ammunition, as charged. This will be enough for the offence to have been committed and there is no need to establish that you had it with you in a public place, fired it or did anything else with it, nor that you had any particular intent. Neither will it afford you a defence that you had the item in your possession in your own home or other private premises. These are therefore what lawyers refer to as offences of 'strict liability'.

POSSESSION OFFENCES

15.07   These are offences under sections 1, 2 and 5 of the FA 1968, depending on the category of the item in question.

'Possession'

15.08   Firearms law is unique in this country in respect of the level of knowledge that is necessary on the part of the defendant in order to be convicted of possession of firearms or ammunition. The mental element is none at all, as long as it can be proved the defendant was aware he had control of the container. If you have control of an item which is in fact a firearm you are guilty; knowledge as to the nature of the item is immaterial.

---

[4]   In the case of possession of a section 1 firearm or its ammunition, or a shotgun (but not shotgun ammunition, the possession of which does not require a certificate), the maximum punishment on summary conviction is imprisonment for 6 months or a fine of the prescribed sum or both; or on indictment, 5 years' imprisonment (unless it is a shotgun with a shortened barrel, in which case 7 years) or an unlimited fine, or both (FA 1968, ss 1,2, 51(1), (2) and Sch 6, Part I). Be aware that unless the court accepts that there are 'exceptional circumstances' committing this offence with most, although not all, categories of prohibited weapon or prohibited ammunition (see Chapter 2) attracts a *minimum* custodial sentence of 5 years, FA 1968, s 51A(1A), as amended by VCRA 2006, s 30.

15.09 Decided cases not only confirm this but explain the concept of dual possession. For example, in *Cotton and Treadwell*, C had left two of his shotguns with T for safekeeping while C and T went on holiday together and for later cleaning by T. The court held that during that holiday period C had 'proprietary possession' of the guns and T had 'custodial possession'.[5]

15.10 Further, if you are aware that you have possession of a friend's bag, even though you could not reasonably have known it contained a firearm, you are guilty.[6] This would be 'custodial possession'. In a drugs case you would at least have to believe that the bag contained *a* controlled drug, even if not the correct one. This anomaly has been pointed out to the courts, which have made it clear that in relation to firearms, the law will remain as it is for reasons of public policy, and this line of authorities will not be reopened,[7] so possession of a firearm (or component parts) without the correct certificate is an absolute offence. There is strong criticism of this decision, but it stands.

15.11 It is often helpful to ask the question 'Did he have control of the item?' That covers almost every situation.

15.12 If the court were to accept that a person had no knowledge that the firearm was in his possession, although no defence, it would likely result in an absolute discharge.

15.13 One recurring anomaly is the view taken by the police where a certificate holder has taken his guns to a dealer, or to a friend who has authority to hold them, commonly where his certificate is about to expire. Readers will appreciate that on expiry of a certificate the holder is in unlawful possession and commits an offence. Following the line of cases in the footnotes below, the owner will still have 'proprietary possession' of the guns, as he is still the owner, even if they are with the dealer. The police never consider the owner to be in possession in these circumstances. This is perhaps because the owner cannot have the guns returned to him without producing a valid certificate and therefore the 'possession' does not matter.

Exceptions and defences in possession cases

15.14 The most obvious exception is where a person has a valid certificate or authority (including an RFD or visitor's permit) to possess the firearm in question.

---

[5] *Hall v Cotton and Treadwell* [1986] 3 All ER 332. While the point at issue concerning possession was possession by T, who held no shotgun certificate, it is evident that the court was of the view that there was concurrent possession by C.

[6] *R v Waller* [1991] Crim LR 381, CA; *R v Steele* [1993] Crim LR 298, CA.

[7] *R v Vann & Davis* [1996] Crim LR 52, CA.

Investigating officers may have limited knowledge in this area, but the police firearms licensing department should be able to confirm the position through the NFLMS.[8] Police often find it helpful to know if a suspect had a certificate in the past; this system should help with that, but only back to about 2005. The NFLMS is 'searchable' in many ways: by type; calibre; manufacturer; serial number (or part thereof); area; address and so on.

15.15 There are a number of circumstances where possession of firearms is permitted without a certificate. These exceptions are set out in detail at para 3.22 *et seq*, but in short summary the principal exceptions are as follows:

(a) Organised clay pigeon shoots.
(b) Home Office-approved shooting clubs. Members can possess firearms and ammunition 'in connection with target practice and competition', not just at the club house, but anywhere where it would be reasonable to do so in connection with that activity.[9]
(c) Firearms and shotguns borrowed on private premises and gun bearers.
(d) Anyone can 'conduct' a miniature rifle range (.22″ rim-fire rifles only) and anyone can shoot a rifle at the range. A person conducting such a range can purchase and possess such rifles and ammunition without any other authority.
     These exemptions apply to everyone unless they are prohibited under the Act.
(e) An RFD[10] can usually possess any number of section 1 and section 2 firearms as part of his business. Servants of an RFD have the same entitlement.
(f) The Home Office issues authorities to possess prohibited weapons to both individuals and RFDs (as 'section 5 dealers'). In some circumstances holders of a firearm certificate can possess what would otherwise be prohibited weapons or ammunition.[11]

The possession offences themselves

15.16 In each case possession has to be proved, together with evidence that the item falls within the relevant section of the Act. Below are the maximum penalties on indictment. All firearms possession offences are triable either way, unless they carry a minimum mandatory sentence. In light of the guidelines in *Avis*,[12] the

---

[8]   In theory, the NFLMS is a complete database of all licensed firearms in the UK.

[9]   F(A)A 1988, s 15.

[10] Registered under s 33 and subsequent sections of the FA 1968.

[11] The principal exemptions are set out in the F(A)A 1997.

[12] *Avis & others* [1998] 1 Cr App R 420, [1998] 2 Cr App R (S) 178.

prosecution will normally seek a Crown Court hearing, and the court would normally agree:

(a)   Possession of section 1 firearms and ammunition – 5 years unless in the 'aggravated form', possessing a sawn-off shotgun, where the maximum is 7 years. Under 24 inches a shotgun becomes section1 and can be held on a certificate.

      As already mentioned, some signalling and line-throwing equipment, flare launchers and similar items are certainly lethal, but whether they fall to be classed as a weapon is debatable. Despite their size some are still within section 1 because of the exemption in section 5(1)(ae).

(b)   Possession of section 2 shotguns – 5 years.

      Prior to the coming in to force of section 7 of the F(A)A 1988 it was possible to bore out the rifling of an old section 1 rifle and hold it on a shotgun certificate.[13]

      A shotgun certificate permits the possession of an unlimited number of shotguns. A common mistake by police is to assume that someone who has failed to notify the acquisition of a shotgun (a summary offence) is in unlawful possession. They are not.

(c)   Possession of section 5 prohibited weapons – Maximum 10 years. Offences contrary to section 5(1) and 5(1A) attract a maximum sentence on indictment of 10 years' imprisonment: section 51 of, and Schedule 6 to, the FA 1968. Offences contrary to section 5(1)(a), (ab), (aba), (ac), (ad), (ae), (af) and (c), and section 5(1A)(a) attract the minimum sentence provisions in section 51A if, but only if, the indictment has a specific count alleging the relevant offence under section 5.[14] The minimum term for those under 18 is 3 years.

15.17 The remaining offences, i.e. those under section 5(1)(b) and section 5(1A)(b)–(g), do not attract a minimum sentence. Let us try and make this simple. All prohibited weapon offences carry a minimum of 5 years (3 years for offenders under 18[15]) except stun guns, CS gas, rockets and some military ammunition which explodes on or before impact, and the launchers for such items. Note that when dealing with prohibited ammunition it is the bullet head itself which is prohibited; it does not have to be a complete round of ammunition, hence no minimum sentence. The complete round does carry a minimum sentence. It is not uncommon for 'expanding' to be confused with 'exploding' when charging in relation to prohibited ammunition.

---

[13]   *R v Hucklebridge* [1980] 71 Cr App R 171, CA.

[14]   *Att-Gen's Reference (No 114 of 2004) (R v McDowell)* [2004] EWCA Crim 2954, [2005] 2 Cr App R (S) 6.

[15]   FA 1968, s 51A.

15.18   What is the position with a stun gun or CS gas canister disguised as another object under section 5(1A)(a)? The prosecution have a free choice, subject to the Code for Crown Prosecutors, which suggests that they should normally charge the more serious offence.

15.19   Possession of a stun gun, contrary to section 5(1)(b), usually merits a custodial sentence, but not always: *R v Kirby* [2009] EWCA Crim 14, [2009] 2 Cr App R (S) 49,; but will attract the 5-year minimum sentence provisions if the weapon is disguised and the offence is prosecuted under section 5(1A)(a). Prosecuting under the more serious section is not unfair: *R v Ramzan* [2012] EWCA Crim 2891, [2013] 2 Cr App R (S) 33 (where the Crown Prosecution Service had made, and later affirmed, their decision in light of the judgment in *R v Brereton* [2012] EWCA Crim 85, [2012] 2 Cr App R (S) 69 (where the court had said prosecution policy had been inconsistent as to which offence to charge, and as to whether or not to accept a plea to the lesser offence by way of disposing of a case charging the more serious offence), their own guidance in relation to stun guns, their charging practice and the Code for Crown Prosecutors). In *Ramzan* the court reduced the sentence to 3 years. In relation to possession of stun guns and CS gas canisters, it is possible to detect a certain reluctance to impose minimum mandatory sentences in respect of items that are deliberately non-lethal; after all that is why the police use them. It might be thought that sentencing should discourage possession of lethal weapons more than non-lethal.

15.20   Possession of 'Brococks' – section 5(1)(ae). This is a type of low powered air gun which uses a self-contained gas cartridge. They are not dangerous, but they can be easily converted to fire live .22" rounds, so they were prohibited in 2003.[16] To avoid having to pay compensation the government allowed those who possessed them prior to 30 April 2004 to retain them on a free firearm certificate. They could not be sold or gifted. Persons discovered with them now potentially face a conviction and minimum sentence, but a recent case has clarified the position. If you did possess the item before the cut-off date and failed to apply for a certificate, you have only committed an offence under section 1, not section 5(1)(af).[17]

15.21   We should also mention 'forward venting blank firing pistols'. These are not firearms and could therefore be freely possessed, but for the fact that in some European countries they are marketed as being able to discharge CS gas cartridges. It is therefore established policy, in accordance with FSS opinion, to prosecute those who possess them. Prior to 2015 they might have been classified within section 5(1)(b) of the Act, but this depended on whether they were

---

[16]   Anti-social Behaviour Act 2003, s 39(4).

[17]   *R v Goldsborough* [2015] EWCA Crim 1278, [2015] 2 Cr App R 29.

'*designed or adapted*' for the discharge of a noxious thing, following the wording of section 5(1)(b).

15.22 The Court of Appeal have now decided[18] that 'designed' should be equated with 'capability', and they are therefore items within section 5(1)(b) and this question of fact has been removed from the jury's consideration, assuming evidence is available that it is so capable. The only problem with this decision is that in Europe and elsewhere shotgun cartridges are available which discharge CS gas. Following this decision to a logical conclusion, everyone in Britain with a lawfully held shotgun (and any held illegally for that matter) is now in possession of a section 5(1)(b) prohibited weapon on the same basis. The term 'designed' is used a number of times throughout the Firearms Acts and it is respectfully submitted that the decision in *Rhodes* is not helpful, and may lead to unintended consequences and have to be further clarified in other cases.

15.23 As already observed in relation to shotguns, breach of a condition on a certificate will not necessarily place the holder in unlawful possession of the firearm. In a recent case,[19] however, it did render the defendant in unlawful possession. He had authority to possess a 'two shot' pistol' for vermin destruction. He had removed the obstructions so it would hold five rounds, thereby breaching a condition of the certificate. He was therefore guilty of the section 5(1)(aba) offence because the condition related to the *nature* of the firearm. It would not have been unlawful possession if he had, for example, used a rifle conditioned for target shooting to stalk deer. He would still be in lawful possession; he would simply have committed the offence of breach of a condition, as that only related to the *use* of the firearm.

OTHER OFFENCES RELATING TO POSSESSING FIREARMS

'Minding a weapon'

15.24 Introduced in section 28 of the VCRA 2006, this offence is committed by the owner of a 'dangerous weapon' who uses another to look after, hide or transport the item for him in circumstances which are intended to facilitate 'or likely to lead to' the commission of an offence. A 'dangerous weapon' is any firearm except an air weapon and includes any weapon that comes within section 141 of the Criminal Justice Act 1988 (CJA 1988).

---

[18] *R v Rhodes* [2015] EWCA Crim 155, [2015] Crim LR 445.
[19] *R v Shahabi-Shack* [2014] EWCA Crim 2842, [2015] 1 Cr App R 25.

15.25 If the possession of the item is itself an offence, for example, if it is a firearm, the criteria for the offence are automatically fulfilled. Otherwise it will be necessary to infer from the circumstances that the weapon in question was to be used in connection with a criminal offence.

15.26 The maximum penalty if the weapon is a knife or similar is 4 years.

15.27 If it is a section 1 or 2 firearm the maximum is 5 years, and if it is a prohibited firearm the maximum is 10 years, and if the offender is over 18 and the item is a prohibited firearm which would attract the 5-year minimum, that applies in relation to this offence in the same way.

15.28 This offence does not relate to the 'keeper' of the item in question who would fall to be prosecuted for possession if applicable.

Conversion of firearms

15.29 Section 4 of the FA 1968 creates an offence of 'converting a firearm'; this usually involves sawing off the barrel of a shotgun. The maximum penalty is 7 years.

Possession of articles for use in conversion of imitation firearms

15.30 Section 127 of the P&CA 2017 creates a new offence of possession of articles for use in connection with the conversion of imitation firearms. An imitation firearm is 'anything which has the appearance of being a firearm',[20] except those items covered by section 5(1)(b) (mainly CS gas and stun guns). This includes deactivated weapons. The offence is intended to deal with underworld armourers, although in most cases there would be other more serious offences which they would have committed. The article merely needs to be 'capable' of being used for this purpose rather than specifically designed or adapted for that use. However, the offence does also require proof of an intent on the part of the person in possession of the article to use it for this purpose. The maximum penalty is 5 years.

Dealing in firearms when not a registered firearms dealer

15.31 This is covered by section 3 of the FA 1968; the maximum penalty is 5 years.

---

[20] FA 1968, s 57(4).

15.32 In practice this now only refers to section 1 and 2 weapons and air weapons.

15.33 In cases relating to prohibited weapons this will now be covered by the next offence, manufacturing and supplying prohibited weapons.

Manufacturing and supplying prohibited weapons

15.34 Section 5(2A) was inserted into the Act in 2014:[21]

A person commits an offence if without authority—

(a) he manufactures any weapon or ammunition specified in subsection (1) of this section,
(b) he sells or transfers any prohibited weapon or prohibited ammunition,
(c) he has in his possession for sale or transfer any prohibited weapon or prohibited ammunition, or
(d) he purchases or acquires for sale or transfer any prohibited weapon or prohibited ammunition.

'Authority' can only be an authority from the Secretary of State. These offences carry a maximum sentence of life imprisonment and attract the minimum sentence provisions in section 51A.

15.35 Apart from proving that the defendant lacked authority, all that needs to be demonstrated is that the prohibited weapons were manufactured/supplied, or in (c) and (d) that he has the relevant intention to sell or transfer the prohibited weapon or ammunition. The Act does not suggest any further required *mens rea*. As with other firearms offences, a lack of knowledge that an item is a prohibited weapon is no defence.[22]

15.36 As with the offence under section 127 of the P&CA 2017, this offence deals with armourers to the criminal underworld and the like. In nearly every case guns supplied in these circumstances will be prohibited weapons. For a case at the top end of the scale where sentences with starting points up to 25 years were imposed, see *Stephenson & others*.[23]

---

[21] Anti-social Behaviour, Crime and Policing Act 2014, s 108(1), (7) and (8).

[22] *R v Bradish* [1990] QB 981, 90 Cr App R 271, CA.

[23] *Att-Gen's References (Nos 128–141 of 2015 and 8–10 of 2016) (R v Stephenson)* [2016] EWCA Crim 54, [2016] 2 Cr App R (S) 12.

OFFENCES CONCERNING THE USE OF FIREARMS

15.37 These offences can involve the use of any firearm, and in some case an imitation firearm. These offences should be the subject of a separate count on the indictment, particularly so if it is a prohibited weapon and a minimum sentence would be appropriate. This also allows the court to pass an appropriate sentence.

Possession of a firearm with intent to endanger life

15.38 This is covered by section 16 of FA 1968. The maximum sentence is life imprisonment.

15.39 Both possession and the intent to endanger life have to be proved. This only relates to 'real' firearms, and does not include suicide. Lawful self-defence and defence of others are defences.

Possession of a firearm or imitation firearm to cause someone to believe that unlawful violence will be used against them

15.40 This is covered by section 16A of FA 1968. It is indictable only, with a maximum of 10 years' imprisonment, and when committed with a prohibited weapon the minimum sentence applies. Self-defence is again a defence.

Possession of a firearm or imitation firearm to resist arrest

15.41 This is covered by section 17 of FA 1968. This applies not only where a suspect *uses* a firearm to resist arrest (section 17(1)), but also where he has possession of a firearm without it being for a 'lawful object' when he is arrested for any offence in Schedule 1 of the Act (section 17(2)). It is not necessary to prove that the ulterior offence was committed.

15.42 If the jury are not satisfied that an offence under section 17(1) has been committed, they can convict under section 17(2).

15.43 It is indictable only, with a maximum sentence of life imprisonment. Minimum sentence provisions apply if it is a relevant prohibited weapon.

15.44 As was observed by the court in *Bewley*,[24] had the defendant been charged with this offence the case would never have got to the Court of Appeal.

---

[24] *Bewley v Regina* [2012] EWCA Crim 1457, [2013] 1 All ER 1. See para 1.73 *et seq*.

Possession of a firearm with intent to commit an indictable offence

15.45 This is covered by FA 1968, section 18. The prosecution have to prove the necessary intent to commit the offence or resist arrest, or prevent the arrest of another. This includes imitation firearms. The suspect has to have the firearm 'with him' for the stated purpose. Possession at home would not be sufficient.[25]

15.46 The offence is indictable only, with a maximum life sentence. Minimum sentence provisions apply if it is a relevant prohibited weapon.

Carrying a firearm in a public place

15.47 This is covered by FA 1968, section 19.[26] This is identical to section 1 of the Prevention of Crime Act 1953 (PCA 1953) relating to offensive weapons, and similar considerations apply. It applies to persons carrying the following without lawful authority or reasonable excuse:

(a) a loaded shotgun;
(b) an air weapon (whether loaded or not);
(c) any other firearm (whether loaded or not) together with ammunition suitable for use in that firearm; or
(d) an imitation firearm.

Therefore, assuming you have a reasonable excuse, you can carry a shotgun and ammunition in public, even if the gun is loaded (a round in the chamber); an air weapon, whether loaded or not; any other firearm whether loaded or not and an imitation firearm.

15.48 This section does not apply to the carrying of an unloaded shotgun, even if you also have a box of ammunition with you, nor does it apply to carrying a firearm without any suitable ammunition.

15.49 The wording seems to suggest that if you *do* have a reasonable excuse, such as being on your way to a shoot, you can carry your guns loaded. Perhaps that is not what Parliament intended, although there will be circumstances where

---

25 *R v Pawlicki & Swindell* (1992) 95 Cr App R 246.

26 FA 1968, s 19, as amended by the Anti-social Behaviour Act 2003, s 37(1). The maximum punishment on summary conviction is imprisonment for 6 months or a fine of the prescribed sum or both; or (unless the firearm is an air weapon) on indictment, 7 years' imprisonment or an unlimited fine, or both (FA 1968, s 51(1), (2) and Sch 6, Part I). Be aware that unless the court accepts that there are 'exceptional circumstances', committing this offence with a prohibited weapon (see Chapter 2) attracts a *minimum* custodial sentence of 5 years, FA 1968, s 51A(1A), as amended by VCRA 2006, s 30.

persons legitimately will have loaded guns in a public place, crossing a country road for example.

15.50 The burden is on the defendant to show he had a reasonable excuse. A certificate is not 'lawful authority' for these purposes, although it might well be highly relevant when considering reasonable excuse, see the case of *Jones* cited at fns 27 and 28 and discussed at para 15.53.

15.51 The prosecution only have to prove possession with the same criteria already discussed. A lack of knowledge of the nature of the item is no defence. Similarly, it is not necessary to prove that the defendant knew the gun was loaded;[27] it is a question of fact for the court to decide.

15.52 This offence is triable either way, with a maximum sentence of 7 years, or 12 months in the case of an imitation firearm. Minimum sentence provisions apply if it is a relevant prohibited weapon.

15.53 '*Lawful authority*': these words are not defined in the Act, and there is no certain authority for their interpretation, but we suggest it would be taken to include the police and others in the service of the Crown and those other examples where persons have authority to possess firearms without a certificate, as set out in the first four chapters of this book. In relation to this offence it is not a defence likely to apply to private individuals. The grant of a firearm or shotgun certificate does not confer 'lawful authority' to carry it in public outside of the terms of the certificate.[28]

15.54 '*Reasonable excuse*': The carrying of a gun to a rifle range for shooting or the crossing of a public road with a gun during the course of a shoot are, it is suggested, examples of situations in which there is a reasonable excuse, as would be any other situation which is in accordance with the conditions of the relevant licence, if there is one. If a licence is not required, for example with an air weapon or an imitation firearm, then the facts of each case need to be examined. Although the meaning of the words is somewhat different, the question 'did you have a good reason for having the firearm in public?' is a good starting point. If the answer is 'yes' you may well have a reasonable excuse. It is obviously reasonable to take *both* the firearms and ammunition to go shooting, despite the wording of the Act implying that they should be kept separate. There is no requirement to make two trips each way! The certificate holder[29] in the case detailed at para 8.14 (relating to leaving his rifle in his car while he went to the county court) could

---

[27] *R v Harrison* [1996] 1 Cr App R 138. See also *R v Jones (T)* [1995] 1 Cr App R 262 for further discussion of the *mens rea*.

[28] *R v Jones (T)* [1995] 1 Cr App R 262, CA.

[29] Mr Houghton-Brown.

have been prosecuted under section 19 if the police had argued that he no longer had the gun with him in connection with its use. This does not seem to have been the position taken in that case, as it was accepted that he was on his way to Oxfordshire to shoot.

15.55 Apart from having a firearm and ammunition in a public place in connection with their use or ownership, other circumstances may arise where an owner might be tempted to take a gun into public. Self-defence, the defence of others and (perhaps) protection of property are all permitted in law, as long as the amount of force used (or threatened) is reasonable in the circumstances as you believe them to be. Certificate holders should be aware, however, that except in the most extreme cases the police will take a serious view of those who use lawfully held firearms 'to take the law into their own hands'. Not only would you risk revocation of your certificate, you would almost certainly be prosecuted for serious criminal offences. For there to be a reasonable excuse in respect of this offence under section 19, it must be shown that there was an imminent particular threat affecting the circumstances in which the weapon was carried. The constant carriage of a weapon on account of some enduring threat or danger, supposed or actual, to the carrier cannot be excused,[30] and neither can threatening the use of a weapon to enforce a private argument.[31] In short, do not do it.

15.56 *'The proof whereof shall lie on him'*: if charged, it will be enough for the defendant to satisfy the court of the probability of existence of the lawful authority or reasonable excuse, in other words, on the balance of probabilities.[32]

15.57 *'Has with him'*: this should be read as 'knowingly has with him'.[33] Thus, for example, the person is entitled to be acquitted if he can satisfy the court that the gun was in the vehicle he was driving without his knowledge. The words have a more restricted meaning than is implied by possession,[34] and extend to any situation where there is a close physical link between the defendant and the gun.[35]

15.58 *'A public place'*: this is defined in the Act as including any highway and any other premises or place to which at the material time the public have or are permitted to have access, whether on payment or otherwise.[36] This definition clearly covers places of public entertainment and hotels and public houses during

---

[30] *Evans v Hughes* [1972] 3 All ER 412.
[31] *Taylor v Mucklow* [1973] Crim LR 750. He had not paid his builder and threatened him with an air weapon when the builder started to demolish the extension he had built.
[32] *R v Carr-Briant* [1943] 2 All ER 156.
[33] *R v Cugullere* [1961] 2 All ER 343.
[34] For commentary on the meaning of 'possession', see para 3.17 *et seq*.
[35] *R v Kelt* [1977] 1 WLR 1365, [1977] Crim LR 556.
[36] FA 1968, s 57(4).

licensing hours and also, it is suggested, buses, trains, aeroplanes and ships running on scheduled services, and taxis while available for hire. The space behind the counter in a shop is a public place.[37]

15.59 *'Loaded'*: the Act declares that the weapon shall be deemed to be loaded if there is ammunition in the chamber or barrel or in any magazine or other device which is in such a position that the ammunition can be fed into the chamber or barrel by the manual or automatic operation of some part of the weapon.[38] In respect of firearms other than shotguns and air weapons, the offence arises if you have suitable ammunition with you, whether the gun is loaded or not.

15.60 *'Shotgun'*: is defined at para 4.01 *et seq*.

15.61 *'Air weapon'*: the Act defines this as an air gun, air rifle or air pistol, not being of a type declared by rules made by the Home Office to be specially dangerous.[39]

15.62 *'Firearm'*: the definition set out at para 1.05 *et seq* applies;[40] briefly, it includes virtually every type of gun, any component part of it and some accessories, and an imitation firearm.[41]

15.63 *'Ammunition'*: the definition set out at para 1.42 *et seq* applies;[42] but the point is that the ammunition is to be suitable for use in the firearm carried at the time.

15.64 In summary, this offence arises where a shotgun is loaded, but other firearms need not be, provided suitable ammunition is carried, and there is no reasonable excuse.[43]

15.65 Having an imitation firearm in public contravenes this section.[44]

---

[37] *Anderson v Miller and Spearman* [1976] Crim LR 743, DC.

[38] FA 1968, s 57(6)(b).

[39] FA 1968, ss 1(3)(b), 57(4).

[40] FA 1968, s 57(1).

[41] For imitation firearms, see Chapter 9.

[42] FA 1968, s 57(1).

[43] The offence under s 19 is in identical terms to that under PCA 1953, s 1, which concerns the carrying of offensive weapons in public. Many of the authorities regarding that legislation are equally applicable to this, and vice versa, as is obvious from the following paragraph.

[44] As amended by the Anti-social Behaviour Act 2003.

POSSESSION BY PERSONS PROHIBITED FROM POSSESSING FIREARMS

15.66   This is covered by section 21 of the FA 1968. Persons sentenced to life, or custody for 3 years or more are prohibited from possessing *any* type of firearm or ammunition for life. Persons sentenced to 3 months or more, including a suspended sentence, are prohibited for 5 years from their date of release. For those who receive a suspended sentence, the prohibition begins on the second day after the passing of the sentence to allow them to divest themselves of the items in question. For further details on the section 21 prohibition, see para 5.60 *et seq*.

15.67   This covers possession of air weapons and antiques as well as all types of firearm and none of the exemptions mentioned above will apply.

15.68   The offence is triable either way, with a maximum sentence of 5 years' imprisonment.

HAVING OFFENSIVE WEAPONS IN A PUBLIC PLACE

15.69   Any person who without lawful authority[45] or reasonable excuse, the proof whereof shall lie on him, has with him in any public place any offensive weapon commits an offence.[46] The term 'offensive weapon' is defined as 'any article made or adapted for use for causing injury to the person, or intended by the person having it with him for such use by him or by some other person'.[47] As the wording suggests, there are three categories of offensive weapon.[48] If an item was 'made (type 1) or adapted (type 2)' for causing injury, it is said to be an offensive weapon 'per se'. In these cases the offence is committed unless the person concerned demonstrates a reasonable excuse for having the item with him in public.[49] If the item is not offensive per se (e.g. an ordinary pocket knife, type 3), then the prosecution have to prove that the person had it with him with the intention of using it as a weapon of offence. Carrying an item with the intention to defend yourself with it comes within the Act; the 'intention' covers lawful as well as

---

45   The criteria are the same as for having a firearm in a public place under s 19; see para 15.47 *et seq*.

46   PCA 1953, s 1(1). The maximum punishments are: on indictment 4 years' imprisonment, or an unlimited fine, or both; on summary conviction, 6 months' imprisonment, or a fine of the prescribed sum (currently £5,000), or both (PCA 1953, s 1(1); CLA 1977, s 32(1)). Upon conviction the court may order the forfeiture or disposal of any weapon in respect of which the offence was committed (PCA 1953, s 1(2)).

47   PCA 1953, s 1(4).

48   *R v Simpson* (1983) 78 Cr App R 115.

49   For a recent decision on what a defendant needs to show to establish this defence and the difficulties when it is an offensive weapon *per se*, see *Garry v CPS* [2019] EWHC 636 (Admin).

unlawful injury, although the threat of imminent attack may be a reasonable excuse.[50] The fact that an item was used as a weapon of offence does not mean that it was being carried in contravention of the Act.[51] It is the intention before it is used as a weapon that is important; if the item is actually used this can be appropriately dealt with by prosecuting for one of the offences of violence under the Offences Against the Person Act 1861. Clearly, any gun is made or adapted for causing injury and therefore is offensive per se[52] and so, although the Act was aimed at persons with criminal inclinations, the ordinary citizen must beware lest he commits this offence while carrying a gun in a public place; in other words, he should be sure that he has 'lawful authority or reasonable excuse'. Many hunters will carry a knife for dealing with their quarry and so this offence should be borne in mind by all those who do so.

BLADED ARTICLES

15.70 The reader should also be aware that it is an offence to have an article with a blade or sharp point in a public place without 'good reason or lawful authority'.[53] This offence does not apply to a folding pocket knife with a cutting edge under 3 inches in length (7.6 cm). However, it covers a lock knife of any size. Lawful authority will have the same meaning as in the offences above. 'Good reason' can be any purpose, but is said to include use at work, for religious reasons or as part of any national costume.[54] It would include a knife for gutting game taken on a shoot. As above, it is for the person charged to prove the good reason on the balance of probabilities.

TRESPASSING WITH A FIREARM

15.71 It is an offence for any person who, while he has a firearm or imitation firearm[55] with him,[56] enters or is on any land[57] or in any building or part of a building as a trespasser and without reasonable excuse, the proof whereof shall

---

[50] *Evans v Hughes* [1972] 56 Cr App R 813.

[51] *R v Jura* [1954] 1 QB 503. This concerned a rifle at a miniature rifle range.

[52] As are swords, bayonets, 'death stars' and many other items used in martial arts, truncheons and knuckle dusters. Except with flick knives (which are offensive per se as a matter of law), it is a matter for the jury in each case to decide whether the item is made or adapted as an offensive weapon.

[53] CJA 1988, s 139.

[54] CJA 1988, s 139(5).

[55] For imitation firearms, see Chapter 9.

[56] But there will be no offence where there is no evidence that the firearm worked or could be made to work (*Grace v DPP* [1989] Crim LR 365, DC).

[57] 'Land' is defined to include land covered with water (FA 1968, s 20(3)).

lie on him.[58] This is a corresponding offence for private land and buildings to the last offence which related to public places. The same criteria largely applies, although the offence is committed with any firearm (including an air weapon), and whether loaded or not, or an imitation firearm.

15.72 Points arising on the words 'firearm', see para 1.05 *et seq*, 'without reasonable excuse', 'the proof whereof shall lie on him' and what is meant by a person having a firearm with him are discussed at para 15.54, but the following two small matters should be mentioned.

15.73 'Land', as the Act says,[59] includes 'land covered with water', so the mere fact that an offender is afloat will not enable him to escape the penalties of the law.

15.74 The word 'trespasser' is not defined. As well as having its ordinary meaning, for example, a person who is on premises without the permission of the occupier of the premises, it includes a person on a public road who is not using it for a legitimate purpose.

15.75 Lastly, it should be noted that the police have wide supporting powers in connection with the offences discussed under this head. These include[60] power to require a suspected person to hand over a firearm and ammunition to a constable[61] for examination;[62] power to search a suspected person and detain him for that

---

[58] FA 1968, s 20(1), (2). If the offence relates to a building, the maximum punishment on summary conviction is imprisonment for 6 months or a fine of the prescribed sum (currently £5,000), or both; or (unless the firearm is an air weapon or an imitation firearm), on indictment, 7 years' imprisonment or an unlimited fine, or both. Be aware that unless the court accepts that there are 'exceptional circumstances', committing this offence with a prohibited weapon (see Chapter 2) attracts a *minimum* custodial sentence of 5 years, FA 1968, s 51A(1A), as amended by VCRA 2006, s 30. If the offence relates to land, the maximum punishment on summary conviction is imprisonment for 3 months or a fine at level 4 on the standard scale (currently £2,500), or both (FA 1968, s 51(1), (2) and Sch 6, Part I).

[59] FA 1968, s 20(3).

[60] FA 1968, s 20 actually creates two separate offences, one relating to buildings or parts thereof and the other to land. The powers specified apply to one or other of the offences, but not necessarily to both of them.

[61] As well as police constables, including special police constables, 'constables' includes others holding that office, e.g. harbour constables. The hallmark of a constable is his attestation as such before, usually, a magistrate.

[62] Failure to do so is itself an offence carrying a maximum punishment on summary conviction of 3 months' imprisonment, or a fine at level 4 on the standard scale (currently £2,500), or both (FA 1968, ss 47(2), 51(1), (2) and Sch 6, Part I).

purpose; power to stop and search suspected vehicles; and power to arrest a suspected person and to enter any place.[63]

TRESPASSING WITH A WEAPON OF OFFENCE

15.76 A person who is on premises as a trespasser, after having entered as such, is guilty of an offence if, without lawful authority or reasonable excuse, he has with him on the premises any weapon of offence.[64] Several ingredients of this offence require individual examination.

15.77 The word 'premises' is defined to mean any building, any part of a building under separate occupation, any land ancillary to a building and the site comprising any building or buildings together with any land ancillary to the building or buildings.[65] The word 'building' in this definition is itself defined to extend its meaning to any structure other than a movable one, and to any movable structure, vehicle or vessel designed or adapted for use for residential purposes. Part of a building is to be treated as under separate occupation if anyone is in occupation or entitled to occupation of that part as distinct from the whole. Land is to be treated as ancillary to a building if it is adjacent to it and used or intended for use in connection with the occupation of that building or any part of it.[66]

15.78 A trespasser is, briefly, a person who is on premises without the permission of the occupier. Additionally, for the purpose of the offence now being considered, a person is treated as a trespasser if he enters or is on or in occupation of any premises 'by virtue of any title derived from a trespasser or any licence or consent given by a trespasser or by a person deriving title from a trespasser'.[67] The effect of the legal phraseology quoted here is that a person who is on premises by some arrangement with a trespasser is himself a trespasser; the word 'title' means entitlement to ownership or tenancy of premises, and 'licence' is used in the sense of leave or permission.

---

[63] FA 1968, ss 20, 47(1), (3)–(6), 50(2). For police powers of general application, see paras 11.14, 12.14 and 12.25.

[64] CLA 1977, s 8(1). The maximum punishment on summary conviction is an unlimited fine, or 3 months' imprisonment, or both (CLA 1977, s 8(3)).

[65] CLA 1977, s 12(1)(a).

[66] CLA 1977, s 12(2).

[67] CLA 1977, s 12(6).

15.79 Anyone who is on any premises as a trespasser does not cease to be a trespasser because he has been allowed time to leave the premises.[68]

15.80 The expressions 'without lawful authority or reasonable excuse' and 'has with him' are discussed at para 15.53 *et seq*.

15.81 'Weapons of offence' is defined to mean any article made or adapted for use for causing injury to or incapacitating a person, or intended by the person having it with him for such use.[69] Clearly, any gun capable of causing injury comes within this definition.

15.82 A constable[70] in uniform may arrest without warrant anyone who is, or whom he with reasonable cause suspects to be, in the act of committing the offence described.[71]

15.83 Though this offence was created primarily to deal with modern squatters who use offensive weapons to retain possession of property, those who, within the terms of the offence, trespass carrying guns in other circumstances may also be prosecuted.

SHOOTING ON OR NEAR THE HIGHWAY

15.84 The first point to bear in mind is that the only right which the public has on a public road is to pass to and fro on it and to use it for other purposes reasonably necessary to that right of passage (although case law has given the public rights of demonstration on public roads). Thus, roads are not places where anybody may shoot at will. The land on which roads are made belongs to the adjoining landowners, subject to the rights of road users and of the highway authority, or to the highway authority itself, or, in some cases, to the builder of the adjoining houses.

15.85 To this general proposition, Parliament has added a number of offences dealing with shooting on or near roads. First, under the Highways Act 1980 (HA

---

[68] CLA 1977, s 12(7).

[69] CLA 1977, s 8(2).

[70] As well as police constables, including special police constables, 'constables' includes others holding that office, e.g. harbour constables. The hallmark of a constable is his attestation as such before, usually, a magistrate.

[71] CLA 1977, s 8(4).

1980) it is an offence, without lawful authority[72] or excuse,[73] to discharge any firearm within 50 feet[74] of the centre of a highway which consists of or comprises a carriageway, as a consequence of which a user of the highway is injured, interrupted or endangered.[75]

15.86 A carriageway is defined in the Act as meaning a way constituting or comprised in a highway,[76] being a way (other than a cycle track) over which the public have a right of way for the passage of vehicles.[77] Thus, the offence will operate in the case of all public roads and will not apply to footpaths and bridleways.

15.87 A highway is generally taken to be the full width of the road between its boundary hedges or ditches and this will include wide verges in some cases. Additionally, for the purposes of this offence, a highway includes bridges and tunnels where it passes over or through them.[78]

15.88 Except in the Greater London area, an offence is committed[79] by any person who in any street[80] to the obstruction, annoyance or danger of its residents or passengers wantonly discharges a firearm.[81]

---

[72] See the comments on this phrase in para 15.53.

[73] In order to have a lawful excuse (which is to be distinguished from 'reasonable excuse') a person must show: (a) that he honestly, but mistakenly, believed on reasonable grounds that the facts were of a certain order; (b) that if those facts had been of that order, his conduct would have been lawful (*Cambridgeshire and Isle of Ely County Council v Rust* [1972] 3 All ER 232). An innocent motive alone will not be enough to establish a lawful excuse (*Dickens v Gill* [1896] 2 QB 310).

[74] This is to be measured in a straight line on a horizontal plane (IA 1978, s 8).

[75] HA 1980, s 161(2). The maximum punishment is a fine at level 3 on the standard scale (currently £1,000).

[76] I.e. a public road.

[77] HA 1980, s 329(1).

[78] HA 1980, s 328(2).

[79] The maximum fine on summary conviction is a fine at level 3 on the standard scale (currently £1,000) (Criminal Justice Act 1967 (CJA 1967), s 92(1) and Sch 3, Part I). A policeman may arrest an offender without warrant if the offence is committed in his sight (Town Police Clauses Act 1847 (TPCA 1847), s 28).

[80] The word 'street' includes any road, square, court, alley, thoroughfare or public passage (TPCA 1847, s 3). The word does not include a place from which the public may be excluded, such as a roadway to a station or other private property (*Curtis v Embery* (1872) LR 7 Exch 369).

[81] TPCA 1847, s 28; Public Health Act 1875, s 171; Local Government Act 1972 (LGA 1972), s 180 and Sch 14, paras 23, 26.

15.89 In the Metropolitan Police District[82] an offence is committed[83] by any person who in any thoroughfare or public place[84] wantonly discharges any firearm to the damage or danger of any person.[85]

SHOOTING BEYOND PREMISES

15.90 A person commits an offence if he uses an air weapon on any premises to shoot a missile beyond those premises,[86] although a defence is provided if you can show that the owner of the adjoining land consented. In those cases where the law requires a young person to be supervised while using an air weapon (see Chapter 14), the person supervising will commit an offence if he permits shooting onto adjoining land without consent.[87]

SHOOTING IN CEMETERIES AND BURIAL GROUNDS

15.91 In certain cemeteries and burial grounds[88] it is an offence to discharge firearms except at a military funeral.[89] In the case of cemeteries provided and maintained by local authorities no such offence exists,[90] but it is made an offence wilfully[91] to create a disturbance, to commit any nuisance or to play any game or sport;[92] depending on circumstances, shooting may constitute one of these offences.

---

[82] The District comprises Greater London (except the City of London and the Inner and Middle Temples) and parts of Essex, Hertfordshire and Surrey (LGA 1963, s 76(1)).

[83] The maximum fine is at level 2 on the standard scale (Metropolitan Police Act 1839 (MPA 1839), s 54). A constable belonging to the Metropolitan Police Force may arrest an offender without warrant if the offence is committed in his sight (MPA 1839, s 54).

[84] 'Public place' is not defined in this context. See para 15.58 for a description of places which might be considered as being within the meaning of the term.

[85] MPA 1839, s 54, para 15.

[86] FA 1968, s 21A as amended by VCRA 2006, s 34(2). The maximum punishment is a fine at level 3 on the standard scale (currently £1,000).

[87] FA 1968, s 22(1) as amended by VCRA 2006, s 34.The maximum punishment is a fine at level 3 on the standard scale (currently £1,000).

[88] These are cemeteries and burial grounds made under the authority of an Act of Parliament which incorporates the Cemeteries Clauses Act 1847 (CCA 1847, s 1).

[89] CCA 1847, ss 3, 59. The maximum punishment is a fine at level 1 on the standard scale (currently £200).

[90] LGA 1972, s 214(7), (8) and Sch 26, para 14.

[91] This means deliberately and intentionally, and not by accident or inadvertence (*R v Senior* [1899] 1 QB 283 at 290–91).

[92] Local Authorities' Cemeteries Order 1977, Art 18(1). The maximum fine is at level 2 on the standard scale (currently £500) (1977 Order, Art 19).

POSSESSION OF FIREARMS WHEN DRUNK

15.92 A person who is drunk[93] when in possession[94] of any loaded firearm[95] commits an offence[96] and may be arrested.[97]

POSSESSION OF A FIREARM, OR IMITATION FIREARM WITH INTENT TO CAUSE FEAR OF VIOLENCE

15.93 It is an offence to have in your possession a firearm (or an imitation[98]) with the intent to cause, or enable another person to cause, someone else to fear that unlawful violence will be used against him or another person.[99] 'Unlawful' is an important part of this offence. Doing acts such as defending yourself, or others, or your property, might be considered lawful in some circumstances.

REGULATORY OFFENCES REGARDING CERTIFICATES

15.94 These are mostly summary offences subject to a maximum penalty of 6 months' imprisonment and/or a fine. While these are not serious in terms of the calendar of criminal offences, and the police do not always even bother to prosecute the certificate holder, it will, in the majority of cases, lead to the certificate holder having his firearm and/or shotgun certificate revoked or not renewed, as it is often only on renewal that these offences come to light.

15.95 Below is a non-exhaustive list of what might be termed regulatory offences, i.e. offences arising from failure of certificate holders to comply with the duties and responsibilities imposed upon them by law.

---

[93] There is no test of drunkenness in this instance, and it will be for the magistrates to decide on the evidence before them whether the accused was drunk.

[94] It is suggested that a narrower meaning for 'possession' than that given at para 3.17 *et seq* would be applicable, i.e. that the defendant was carrying the firearm or perhaps had it within easy reach.

[95] The case of *Seamark v Prouse and Another* [1980] 3 All ER 26 decided that an air rifle is a firearm for this purpose.

[96] The maximum penalties are a fine at level 1 on the standard scale (currently £200) or one month's imprisonment.

[97] Licensing Act 1872, s 12. It appears that the offence is committed wherever the drunken person may be.

[98] See also Chapter 9.

[99] FA 1968, s 16A, inserted by the F(A)A 1994, s 1. Maximum penalty 10 years' imprisonment, and, if committed with some prohibited weapons, 5 years minimum.

15.96 The first in the list relates solely to firearm certificate holders, but the rest relate equally to anyone who holds either a firearm or shotgun certificate:

- acquiring or possessing ammunition in a calibre not authorised under the individual's certificate or in excess of the quantities authorised for that calibre;
- failure to comply with any of the certificate conditions, especially security requirements;
- failing to notify the police of the theft, loss, destruction, acquisition, disposal or loan of any firearm or shotgun within 7 days of the event (or 14 days if the event takes place outside UK), the only exception being that loans of shotguns for less than 72 hours do not need to be notified;
- continuing possession of firearm and shotguns licensed under certificate where the certificate has expired and not been renewed;
- buying, selling and hiring to or by persons aged under 18 of any firearms including air weapons and imitation firearms;
- giving false information in order to obtain a certificate;
- failure to surrender a certificate to police when required to do so;
- killing of protected birds and animals;
- taking of game during close seasons, in particular numerous offences created by the DA 1991;
- poaching;
- breach of certificate conditions such as:

  - failure to comply with standard conditions;
  - failure to sign certificate on receipt;
  - failure to notify change of address;
  - requirement to notify promptly all transactions;
  - theft, loss or destruction of certificates, guns or ammunition;
  - disposal, acquisition or loan, unless loan of shotguns and for less than 72 hours;
  - failure to abide by security conditions;
  - other failures to comply with certificate terms (firearm certificate holders only);
  - exceeding ammunition limits (regular stock check is recommended);
  - using firearm for purpose not authorised, for example, rifle granted for target shooting and using it for game shooting instead.

15.97 The breach of a certificate condition would usually mean you commit one of the possession offences, some of which would be considered serious. Some, such as forgetting to sign your certificate, are unlikely on their own to be a basis for revocation.

Chapter 16

Firearms Dealers

WHO IS A FIREARMS DEALER?

16.01 For the purposes of the regulations relating to firearms dealers, a firearms dealer is defined as a person who, by way of trade or business, manufactures, sells, transfers,[1] repairs, tests or proves any section 1 firearm[2] or section 1 ammunition[3] or a shotgun.[4]

16.02 Firearms dealers have come under increased scrutiny from the authorities in recent years as a result of a few bad apples and high-profile cases. Although a very small proportion of overall transactions in firearms, there have been instances of dealers providing firearms to criminals. In almost all cases these have in fact been items which were antiques (and therefore not subject to licensing) being supplied with suitable ammunition, or they have been deactivated firearms which have been reactivated. For obvious reasons, any firearm which is recorded on the NFLMS[5] and entered on to a dealers' register is traceable and so would be difficult to transfer to a criminal. This problem with a small number of dealers has been given the name 'Lawful to unlawful' by the National Ballistics Intelligence Service (NABIS) and the West Midlands Police.

16.03 As a result of these concerns the National Police Chiefs Council published a 7-page document entitled *Good Practice Guide for Registered Firearms*

---

[1] 'Transfer' is defined as including letting on hire, giving, lending and parting with possession (FA 1968, s 57(4)).

[2] For the meanings of these words, see para 3.01 *et seq*. An imitation firearm may also fall to be treated as a section 1 firearm (Firearms Act (FA) 1982, s 2(1)). See, further, Chapter 9.

[3] For the meanings of these words, see para 3.12. An imitation firearm may also fall to be treated as a section 1 firearm (FA 1982, s 2(1)). See, further, Chapter 9.

[4] FA 1968, s 57(4). The meaning of 'shotgun' includes any component part of it and any accessory to it designed or adapted to diminish the noise or flash caused by firing it (FA 1968, s 57(4)).

[5] The NFLMS; a computerised record of all lawfully held firearms in the UK.

Dealers (*Good Practice Guide*)[6] in 2017. This guide does not have force of law, and indeed some of the recommendations do not have a statutory basis. Having said that, all dealers would be well advised to be familiar with it and to follow the advice given. In cases of doubt you should seek the advice of your local licensing department, the Gun Trade Association (GTA), the British Association for Shooting & Conservation (BASC) or a lawyer who understands this area of law. Chapter 16 of the Home Office *Guide* also deals with the registration of dealers.

REGISTRATION OF FIREARMS DEALERS

16.04   The police are obliged to keep a register of firearms dealers and, with the exceptions mentioned in the list below, to enter in it the name and places of business of any person who, having or proposing to have a place of business in the police area, applies to be registered.[7] Application should be made to the local police firearms licensing department on a form provided by them if you are a firearms dealer within the definition discussed above.[8] Upon registration, a certificate will be issued to you.[9] A £200 fee[10] is payable on issue, not on application, although you send the cheque on application.[11] The certificate lasts for 3 years from the date on which it was granted,[12] unless the registration is cancelled under the provisions later to be considered at para 16.16 *et seq*. But in the following cases the police may, and in one case must, refuse registration:

(a)   Registration of the applicant *must* be refused where a court, following conviction of the applicant, has ordered that he shall not be registered.[13]

---

[6]   This should be available from your local licensing department or the GTA. It is helpfully placed on the BASC website: https://basc.org.uk/wp-content/uploads/2013/02/Good-Practice-Guide-for-Registered-Firearms-Dealers.pdf.

[7]   FA 1968, ss 33, 57(4). For form of register, see Firearms Rules 1998, r 10(3) and Sch 5, Part III.

[8]   FA 1968, s 33(3); Firearms Rules 1998, r 10(1) and Sch 5, Part I.

[9]   FA 1968, s 33(4).

[10]   The amount of the fee may be varied, or abolished altogether, by order of the Home Office (FA 1968, s 43(1)).

[11]   FA 1968, s 35(1), as amended by the Firearms (Variation of Fees) Order 1994. No fee is payable, however, when your only place of business was already registered in one police area and by boundary changes falls into a new police area, or when, being already registered in one police area, you propose transferring your only place of business to another police area (FA 1968, s 35(2)).

   If you apply to be registered for dealing at a game fair, trade fair or exhibition, agricultural show or similar event, and your principal place of business is registered in another area, the fee is £12 (FA 1968, s 35(1A); Firearms (Variation of Fees) Order 1994).

[12]   FA 1968, s 33(5); F(A)A 1988, s 13(1).

[13]   FA 1968, s 34(1). For the cases where a court in Great Britain may make such an order, see para 16.35. Courts in Northern Ireland may also make these orders.

(b) Registration of the applicant *may* be refused if the police are satisfied that the applicant cannot be permitted to carry on his business without danger to the public safety or to the peace.[14]

(c) Registration of a place of business *may* be refused if the police are satisfied that it is a place at which the applicant cannot be permitted to carry on business as a firearms dealer without danger to the public safety or to the peace.[15]

(d) Registration of the applicant *may* be refused unless the police are satisfied that the applicant will engage in business as a firearms dealer to a substantial extent or as an essential part of another trade, business or profession.[16]

16.05 There is an appeal to the Crown Court against a refusal of the police in any of these cases.[17] Notice of the appeal must be given within 21 days from the receipt of the decision of the police to refuse.[18]

16.06 An RFD must, on or before the expiration of 3 years from the date of its grant, surrender his certificate of registration to the police and apply on the appropriate form for a new certificate. If granted, it will cost £300[19] and will last for a further 3-year period unless the registration is cancelled under the provisions considered at para 16.16 *et seq*.[20] It can only be refused if the police are satisfied that the applicant is no longer carrying on business as a firearms dealer, or that he has ceased to have a place of business in the police area, or that he cannot be permitted to carry on such a business without danger to the public safety or to the peace.[21]

---

[14] FA 1968, s 34(2). There can, however, be no refusal on this ground where the applicant has been authorised by the Home Office to deal in prohibited weapons or prohibited ammunition, for which see FA 1968, ss 5, 34(3), 57(4); Transfer of Functions (Prohibited Weapons) Order 1968, arts 2(a) and 3(1)).

For some decisions on 'danger to the public safety or to the peace', see Chapter 4.

[15] FA 1968, s 34(4). See also the second part of point (b) in the list above.

[16] FA 1968, s 34(1A); F(A)A 1988, s 13(2).

[17] FA 1968, ss 34(5), 44(1), (2).

[18] FA 1968, ss 34, 44 and Sch 5, Part II. You should consult a solicitor at once if you are considering making an appeal.

[19] The amount of the fee may be varied, or abolished altogether, by order of the Home Office (FA 1968, s 43(1)).

[20] FA 1968, ss 33(5) and 35(3), as amended by the Firearms (Variation of Fees) Order 1994; F(A)A 1988, s 13(1).

[21] FA 1968, ss 33(5), 38(1). The last ground of refusal does not apply where the dealer has been authorised by the Home Office to manufacture or deal in prohibited weapons or prohibited ammunition, as to which see FA 1968, ss 5, 38(2); Transfer of Functions (Prohibited Weapons) Order 1968, Articles 2(a) and 3(1)).

For an interpretation of 'danger to the public safety or to the peace', see para 4.10 *et seq* and para 5.39 *et seq*.

16.07 It is an offence if:

(a) any person, by way of trade or business, manufactures, sells, transfers,[22] tests, proves, exposes for sale or transfer, or has in his possession for sale, transfer, repair, test or proof, any section 1 firearm,[23] section 1 ammunition[24] or shotgun[25] without being registered as a firearms dealer;[26]

(b) any person knowingly or recklessly makes a statement which is false in any material particular for the purpose of procuring the registration of himself or another person as a firearms dealer or of procuring, whether for himself or another person, the entry of any place of business in the register.[27]

16.08 Registration as a firearms dealer enables the dealer to do certain other things in relation to firearms and ammunition which others are not allowed to do. For example, the dealer may, within limitations, shorten the barrel of a shotgun and convert firearms and may possess, purchase and acquire,[28] firearms and ammunition without holding a firearm certificate or shotgun certificate.[29]

16.09 An applicant for registration can be an individual or a limited company.[30] In cases where a breach of condition or other offence is alleged against an RFD, it is the person, or company, who is registered as the dealer who commits the offence, not the director or manager. A person wishing to engage in business should not be deprived of the protection derived from limited liability simply because of this consideration.

CONDITIONS OF REGISTRATION

16.10 The police may at any time impose conditions on the registration of a person as a firearms dealer, and may, either on their own initiative or on the

---

[22] 'Transfer' is defined as including letting on hire, giving, lending and parting with possession (FA 1968, s 57(4)).

[23] For the definition of these terms, see para 3.01 *et seq.*

[24] For the definition of these terms, see para 3.12 *et seq.*

[25] For the definition of these terms, see para 4.01 *et seq.*

[26] FA 1968, s 3(1). The maximum punishment upon summary conviction is 6 months' imprisonment or a fine of the prescribed sum (currently £5,000), or both; and upon indictment, 5 years' imprisonment or an unlimited fine, or both (FA 1968, s 51(1), (2) and Sch 6, Part I).

[27] FA 1968, s 39(1). The maximum punishment upon summary conviction is 6 months' imprisonment, or an unlimited fine, or both (FA 1968, s 51(1), (2) and Sch 6, Part I).

[28] 'Acquire' means hire, accept as a gift or borrow (FA 1968, s 57(4)).

[29] FA 1968, ss 4(2), (3), 8(1).

[30] *Staravia Ltd v Gordon* [1973] Crim LR 298.

application of the dealer, vary or revoke any condition.[31] Where conditions are imposed on the issue of the certificate, they are to be written into it. When imposed, or varied or revoked, during the currency of a certificate, the police must give notice[32] to the dealer of the conditions or variations (giving particulars) or revocation. The notice may also require that the dealer deliver up the certificate to the police within 21 days from the date of the notice for the purposes of amending the certificate.[33] An appeal to the Crown Court can be made against the imposition or variation by the police of a condition or against their refusal to vary or revoke it on the dealer's application.[34]

16.11 The test to be applied on an appeal in relation to a condition imposed on an RFD is whether it is reasonable, or reasonably required, in the circumstances. These considerations will normally concern the security of firearms or ammunition or danger to public safety or the peace. Once a dealer has satisfied the criteria for registration, any conditions imposed should not be unduly restrictive or restrain the business without good reason. This principle is demonstrated by the fact that Parliament has provided a specific right of appeal in relation to conditions imposed on an RFD. This is in contrast to conditions imposed on a firearm certificate where there is no statutory right of appeal.

16.12 Failure to comply with any condition of registration is an offence,[35] and might be a basis for the police to cancel a registration.[36]

16.13 In considering any place of business proposed by a dealer, the police will consider whether appropriate arrangements are in place to secure the likely amount and types of firearms and ammunition to be stored there. An assessment will also be made of the area where the premises are situated, crime rate and other relevant factors.

---

[31] FA 1968, s 36(1).

[32] This notice may be sent by registered post or by recorded delivery service in a letter addressed to the dealer at his last or usual place of abode or at any place of business in respect of which he is registered (FA 1968, s 56). It may also, of course, be delivered to him personally, or alternatively can now be sent by email, provided the dealer has given the police his consent to be sent notices via electronic means (Firearms (Electronic Communications) Order 2011 (SI 2011/713)).

[33] FA 1968, s 36(2).

[34] FA 1968, ss 36(3) and 44.

[35] FA 1968, s 39(3). The maximum punishment upon summary conviction is 6 months' imprisonment, or an unlimited fine, or both (FA 1968, s 51(1) and Sch 6, Part I).

[36] FA 1968, s 38(3).

REGISTRATION OF A NEW PLACE OF BUSINESS

16.14 If a person is registered as a firearms dealer in a police area and he proposes to carry on business as such a dealer at a place of business in that area which is not entered in the register kept by the police, he must notify the police of the fact and supply them with certain particulars; a form for this can be obtained from the police.[37] The police must register the new place of business unless satisfied that it is a place at which the applicant cannot be permitted to carry on business as a firearms dealer without danger to the public safety or to the peace.[38] Again, there is a right of appeal to the Crown Court against any police decision to refuse a new place of business.[39]

16.15 An RFD[40] commits an offence if he has a place of business which is not entered in the register for the police area in which the place of business is situated and carries on business as a firearms dealer at that place.[41] Do note that section 8(1A) of the FA 1968 permits transactions taking place other than at the registered premises, as long as they are in the ordinary course of the dealer's business.

REMOVAL FROM REGISTER OF DEALER'S NAME OR PLACE OF BUSINESS BY THE POLICE

16.16 The name of a firearms dealer or his place of business is removable from the police register in the following circumstances:

(a) The police *shall* remove the dealer's name if, after giving reasonable notice[42] to the dealer, they are satisfied that:

    (i)   he is no longer carrying on business as a firearms dealer; or
    (ii) he has ceased to have a place of business in the police area; or

---

[37] FA 1968, ss 37(1), 57(4). Firearms Rules 1998, r 10(2) and Sch 5, Part II.

[38] FA 1968, s 37(1), (2).

[39] FA 1968, ss 37(3) and 44.

[40] An RFD is defined as one who is either registered in Great Britain or is registered in Northern Ireland under the Firearms Act 1920, s 8 or any enactment of the Parliament of Northern Ireland amending or substituted for that section (FA 1968, s 57(4)).

[41] FA 1968, s 39(2). The maximum punishment on summary conviction is 6 months' imprisonment, or an unlimited fine, or both (FA 1968, s 51(1) and Sch 6, Part I).

[42] This notice may be sent by registered post or by recorded delivery service in a letter addressed to the dealer at his last or usual place of abode or at any place of business in respect of which he is registered (FA 1968, s 56). It may also, of course, be delivered to him personally. Notice can alternatively now be sent via email.

(iii) he cannot be permitted to continue to carry on business as a firearms dealer without danger to the public or to the peace.[43]

(b) The police may, if satisfied that a dealer has failed to comply with any of the conditions of registration which have been imposed, remove from the register the dealer's name or any place of business of his to which the condition relates.[44]

(c) The police may remove a dealer's place of business from the register if satisfied that it is one at which the dealer cannot be permitted to carry on business as such without danger to the public safety or to the peace.[45]

(d) The police shall remove a dealer's name from the register if the dealer so desires.[46]

(e) The police shall remove the dealer's name from the register if:

    (i) the dealer fails, on or before its expiry, to surrender his certificate of registration to the police or to apply for a new certificate; and

    (ii) the police give written notice[47] to the dealer requiring him to do whatever he has failed to do under paragraph (i) above; and

    (iii) the dealer fails to comply with the written notice within 21 days from its date or such further time as the police may in special circumstances allow.[48]

Again, there is a right of appeal to the Crown Court in any of these cases.[49]

16.17 On removal of a dealer's name (but not his place of business) from the register, the police will require the dealer by written notice[50] to surrender his certificate of registration and his register of transactions. Failure to do so within 21 days from the date of the notice is an offence.[51] If an appeal is made against

---

[43] FA 1968, s 38(1). There can, however, be no removal under para (a) iii where the dealer has been authorised by the Home Office to deal in prohibited weapons or ammunition, as to which see Chapter 2 (FA 1968, ss 5, 38(2); Transfer of Functions (Prohibited Weapons) Order 1968, arts 2(a) and 3(1)).

[44] FA 1968, s 38(3).

[45] FA 1968, s 38(4).

[46] FA 1968, s 38(5).

[47] As to the methods by which such notice can be sent, see fn 50 below.

[48] FA 1968, s 38(6).

[49] FA 1968, ss 38(7) and 44. For appeals, see further Chapter 5.

[50] This notice may be sent by registered post or by recorded delivery service in a letter addressed to the dealer at his last or usual place of abode or at any place of business in respect of which he is registered (FA 1968, s 56). It may also, of course, be delivered to him personally, or now by email, Firearms (Electronic Communications) Order 2011.

[51] FA 1968, s 38(8); F(A)A 1988, s 13(3). The maximum punishment upon summary conviction is a fine at level 3 on the standard scale (currently £1,000) (FA 1968, s 51(1) and Sch 6, Part I).

the removal of the dealer's name from the register and is not successful, the period of 21 days will, instead, run from the date on which the appeal was abandoned or dismissed.[52]

16.18   In order to remove a dealer's name from the register, the police therefore have to write two letters to the dealer.[53] The first gives reasonable notice (usually 21 days) of the intention to remove and allows the dealer to make representations if he wishes. The second indicates that the name has been removed. Despite the clear guidance from the Home Office on this point, some forces remove the name from the register and seize all of the dealer's stock on the same day. This is unlawful.

THE REGISTER OF FIREARMS TRANSACTIONS

16.19   Every person who by way of trade or business manufactures, sells or transfers[54] firearms[55] or ammunition[56] must provide and keep a register of transactions[57] and must enter, or cause to be entered, in it certain prescribed particulars.[58] It is now both acceptable, and normal, for this to be a computerised record. An attempt in 2015 to require all RFDs to keep their registers on computer was abandoned, partly in recognition of the fact that in the case of some smaller dealers it was unreasonable expense, and was unnecessary for those who conduct relatively few transactions.

16.20   In the following cases, however, this requirement need not be complied with:

---

[52]   FA 1968, s 38(8) proviso.

[53]   As stated in *Guide*, para 16.52.

[54]   'Transfer' is defined as including letting on hire, giving, lending and parting with possession (FA 1968, s 57(4)).

[55]   As to the meaning of these words and for two general exceptions, see para 1.05 *et seq*. The register must now include sales of air weapons, VCRA, s 31(2).

[56]   This means section 1 ammunition, see para 3.12.

[57]   For form of register and directions for keeping it, see Firearms Rules 1998, r 10(4) and Sch 5, Part IV.

[58]   FA 1968, s 40(1). Failure to do so constitutes an offence, the maximum punishment for which on summary conviction is 6 months' imprisonment, or an unlimited fine, or both (FA 1968, ss 40(5), 51(1), (2) and Sch 6, Part I). The prescribed particulars, as amended by the Firearms Rules 1998, r 10(5), are reproduced in Appendix H. They may be further amended from time to time by rules made by the Home Office (FA 1968, ss 40(7), 53 and Sch 4).

(a)   When in England and Wales the firearms are component parts of, or accessories to, air weapons.[59]
(b)   When it is ammunition for a shotgun with more than five pellets, for an air weapon or is blank ammunition.[60]
(c)   When firearms or ammunition are sold by auction in accordance with the terms of a police permit issued to the auctioneer.[61]

16.21 The rules about keeping a register may be relaxed in the following situation. If it appears to the police that:

(a)   a person required to be registered as a firearms dealer[62] carries on a trade or business in the course of which he manufactures, tests or repairs component parts or accessories for shotguns,[63] but not complete shotguns; *and*
(b)   it is impossible to assemble a shotgun from the parts likely to come into that person's possession in the course of that trade or business; the police may, if they think fit, by written notice[64] given to that person exempt his transactions in those parts and accessories from all or any of the requirements for keeping a register. This exemption lasts 'so long as the notice is in force'.[65]

16.22 Every entry required to be made in the register must be made within 24 hours after the transaction to which it relates. In the case of a sale or transfer[66] of firearms or ammunition, the dealer[67] must, at the time, require the purchaser or

---

[59]   FA 1968, s 40(2) and Sch 4 to the Act. The VCRA 2006 prohibits anyone other than an RFD by way of trade or business, to sell, transfer, or expose for sale an air weapon (s 31), and requires such transactions to be face to face (s 32). It also amends the requirement to keep a register to include air weapons in the requirement (s 31(2)).

[60]   FA 1968, s 40(2).

[61]   FA 1968, ss 9(2), 40(6).

[62]   As to the persons required to be so registered, see the definition in para 16.01.

[63]   For the definition of 'shotgun', see para 4.01 *et seq*.

[64]   This notice may be sent by registered post or by recorded delivery service in a letter addressed to the dealer at his last or usual place of abode or at any place of business in respect of which he is registered (FA 1968, s 56). It may also, of course, be delivered to him personally, or alternatively can now be sent by email, provided the dealer has given the police his consent to be sent notices via electronic means (The Firearms (Electronic Communications) Order 2011 SI 713/2011).

[65]   FA 1968, s 41. It is not clear whether the notice should be given for a limited or unlimited time; if given for an unlimited time, it may presumably be cancelled by the police at any subsequent time by a further notice served in the same way as the original notice.

[66]   'Transfer' is defined as including letting on hire, giving, lending and parting with possession (FA 1968, s 57(4)).

[67]   Or his employee, or other person on his behalf (FA 1968, s 40(1), (3)).

transferee, if not known to him, to furnish particulars sufficient for identification[68] and must immediately enter those particulars in the register.[69]

16.23 A person keeping a register shall, unless required to surrender it to the police, keep it for such period so that each entry shall be available for inspection for at least 5 years from the date of the entry. In the past dealers tended to maintain manual registers, entering each transaction by hand. The F(A)A 1997 inserted new provisions into the FA 1968 enabling dealers to keep a computerised register, subject to the requirement that the register can be readily produced in a form in which it is visible and legible and can be taken away.[70]

16.24 A person keeping a register of firearms transactions must, if asked to do so by a constable[71] or a civilian officer[72] authorised in writing to make the demand by the chief officer of police, allow the constable or civilian officer to enter his premises to inspect all stock in hand. The register must be produced for inspection to any constable or civilian officer authorised in the same way and to any officer of customs and excise.[73] If asked to do so, the constable or civilian officer must produce their written authorisations.[74] In short, the authorities have the right to inspect a firearms dealer's premises and registers at any time. It is common practice for the licensing department to conduct an 'audit' of a dealers' register every year and check that registers are an accurate record of the firearms and ammunition held. The FEO who attends will normally sign the register to indicate that it has been inspected.

16.25 As the *Good Practice Guide* states: 'It is essential that your register has a clear audit trail for all firearms and ammunition recorded in it'.[75] This may seem obvious, but we have experience of a number of dealers falling out with their licensing department because of the way in which their registers had been maintained. It is common for the dealer to understand where everything is, but for this not to be so clear to the officers who attend to conduct the audit. Our advice

---

[68] It is suggested that the full names and address of the person concerned will be sufficient.

[69] FA 1968, s 40(3). Failure to comply with any requirement in this paragraph is an offence (FA 1968, s 40(5)).

[70] FA 1968, s 40(4A); F(A)A 1997 Sch 2, para 8(b).

[71] As well as police constables, including special police constables, 'constables' includes others holding that office, e.g. harbour constables. The hallmark of a constable is his attestation as such before, usually, a magistrate.

[72] A civilian officer is, briefly, a person employed by the police. Full details are in FA 1968, s 57(4).

[73] Failure to do so is an offence (FA 1968, s 40(5)). The maximum punishment on summary conviction is 6 months' imprisonment, or an unlimited fine, or both (FA 1968, s 51(1) and Sch 6, Part I).

[74] FA 1968, s 40(4).

[75] https://basc.org.uk/wp-content/uploads/2013/02/Good-Practice-Guide-for-Registered-Firearms-Dealers.pdf.

is that registers should be maintained so that there is a clear audit trail on the face of the register for those who do *not* work in the business. There are no fixed rules as to how a register should be set out, nor indeed whether there should be separate registers for firearms, shotguns, ammunition and air weapons, etc, but however it is done it should be easy to see whether an item is in stock, where it came from and, if it has gone, where it went.

16.26 It is an offence if a person knowingly makes any false entry in a register of firearms transactions.[76]

REGISTERED FIREARMS DEALERS' SERVANTS

16.27 Section 8 of the FA 1968 provides an exemption to allow servants of RFDs to possess firearms and ammunition 'in the ordinary course of that business' to the same extent, and subject to that same conditions, as the dealer or company themselves. Whether someone is a servant is a question of fact in each case. It does not have to be a permanent position of any sort; it can be someone helping out in the shop for the morning or making a delivery as a favour. The person does not have to be paid and such an appointment can be entirely informal. The dealer will no doubt wish to be careful that those who are his servants are responsible persons and are not prohibited from possessing firearms.

16.28 The *Good Practice Guide* recommends that dealers notify their local licensing department regarding prospective servants to confirm that 'there are no grounds for concern'. If a person is unknown to the dealer this may well be a good idea, but it is not a legal requirement. A person does not have to be 'registered' with the police before he can act as a servant. In reality most dealers will only use as servants persons they know, many will be certificate holders, and anyone who holds a certificate under the Act cannot be prohibited and is hopefully a suitable person.

REMOTE SALES

16.29 All sales of firearms are now required to be 'face to face'. If a customer wishes to purchase a firearm or shotgun from a dealer (perhaps having seen an advertisement in a magazine or on the internet) who is some distance away, the following procedure should be followed. The purchaser sends his certificate to the dealer who is selling the item. He enters the gun onto the certificate and returns the certificate to the purchaser. The purchaser then has to nominate a local dealer

---

[76] FA 1968, s 40(5).

to whom the seller has to send the gun. The seller has to enter the sale in his register and notify the purchaser's local police of the sale. Assuming payment has been received, the seller then sends the gun to the nominated dealer local to the purchaser. This second dealer is required to enter both the receipt of the gun and the eventual transfer to the purchaser into his register within 24 hours of those events occurring. On collecting the gun from his local dealer, the purchaser will have to produce his certificate, already completed by the first dealer. Finally, the purchaser will also notify his local police of the purchase within 7 days.

SALES FOR EXPORT

16.30 A person may buy from an RFD a firearm for export without holding a firearm or shotgun certificate. When this happens, the dealer must within 48 hours of the sale send[77] a notice of it to the chief officer of police in whose register the dealer's premises are entered.[78] The notice must contain the same particulars of the transaction as the dealer is required to enter in his register for other kinds of transaction.[79] The notice, and the particulars to be entered in the register, shall also include the number and place of issue of any passport held by the buyer of the firearm.[80]

CARRIERS

16.31 RFDs are entitled to use a common carrier for all section 1 and 2 firearms and ammunition. The carrier is exempt from the need to be licensed by virtue of section 9 of the FA 1968. Section 14 of the F(A)A 1988 requires a carrier to take reasonable precautions for the security of firearm sand ammunition.

16.32 The transportation of section 5 weapons and ammunition requires a carrier to hold a 'section 5 Transport Authority' from the Home Office. An RFD who also holds a section 5 authority can transport his own stock, subject to any conditions on his authority, but he cannot transport section 5 items for others unless he holds a specific authority to do so.

---

[77] The notice is to be sent by registered post or recorded delivery.
[78] F(A)A 1988, s 18(2). Failure to comply is an offence with a maximum punishment on summary conviction of 6 months' imprisonment, or an unlimited fine, or both (F(A)A 1988, s 18(5)).
[79] For those particulars, see Appendix H.
[80] F(A)A 1988, s 18(3), (4).

STORAGE OF EXPLOSIVES BY A FIREARMS DEALER

16.33 Be aware that the storage of shooter's powders, both black powder and nitro powder, and ammunition, is subject to overall limits. If these limits are exceeded, you will need an 'acquire and keep licence' under the Explosives Regulations 2014.[81] In all cases where the holder is an RFD, the licensing authority is the police licensing department for the area, and not the Health and Safety Executive. In reality the FEO who deals with your RFD will also deal with your explosives licence. You can store up to 15 kg of percussion caps or small arms ammunition or a mixture of them, or 10 kg of shooter's powders, without a certificate. This can only be a rough guide because you can only claim under one exemption for the same location, i.e. only ammunition *or* powder. With ammunition you will need to establish the net explosive mass; obviously only a small proportion of the weight of ammunition will be explosive.

16.34 The criteria for being granted an explosives licence are set out in regulation 11 of the Explosives Regulations 2014. The holder of a licence needs to be a fit person and there must be no danger to the public from the storage of explosives at the proposed location.

CONSEQUENCES OF CONVICTION OF FIREARMS DEALERS

16.35 When an RFD[82] is convicted of almost any offence[83] connected with firearms or ammunition, the convicting court has power to order that:

---

[81] SI 2014/1638.

[82] An RFD is defined as one who is either registered in Great Britain or is registered in Northern Ireland under the Firearms Act 1920, s 8 or any enactment of the Parliament of Northern Ireland amending or substituted for that section (FA 1968, s 57(4)).

[83] More precisely, the offences are: (i) offences against the enactments relating to customs or excise in respect of the import or export of any firearms or ammunition, except any of the types described in items (a) and (b) in para 16.20; (ii) all offences under FA 1968 except (briefly):

  (a) Obtaining or possessing a shotgun without a shotgun certificate and failing to comply with a condition of such a certificate (FA 1968, s 2).

  (b) A person under 15 handling a shotgun without an adult's supervision or while not covered with a gun cover (FA 1968, s 22(3)).

  (c) Giving a shotgun or ammunition for a shotgun to a person under 15 (FA 1968, s 24(3)).

  (d) An offence relating specifically to air weapons (FA 1968, s 45(2)).

  References above to a shotgun include references to component parts of a shotgun and to any accessories for diminishing its noise or flash (FA 1968, ss 45(2); 57(4)).

(a) the name of the dealer be removed from the register; and
(b) neither the dealer nor any person who acquires his business, nor any person who took part in the management of the business and was knowingly a party to the offence, shall be registered as a firearms dealer; and
(c) any person who, after the date of the court's order, knowingly employs in the management of his business the dealer convicted of the offence, or any person who was knowingly a party to the offence, shall not be registered as a firearms dealer or, if so registered, shall be liable to be removed from the register;[84] and
(d) any stock-in-hand of the business shall be disposed of by sale or otherwise in accordance with such directions as may be contained in the order.[85]

16.36 A dealer against whom such an order is made may appeal against it in the same way as he may appeal against his conviction, and the court may, if it thinks fit, suspend the operation of the order pending the appeal.[86]

ANONYMOUS SURRENDERS OF FIREARMS AND AMMUNITION FROM THE PUBLIC

16.37 Outside of official 'amnesties', it is a frequent occurrence for members of the public to take unwanted, unlicensed firearms into their local gun dealer. There is official guidance[87] as to how RFDs should deal with such hand-ins. If possible dealers are encouraged to obtain a name and address, or at least a vehicle registration number if applicable. This might be thought a little unrealistic. The view might be taken that it is better to remove unlicensed firearms from the street than to attempt to identify those who may have been in previous unlawful possession.

16.38 The dealer will be able to lawfully possess any item within section 1 or section 2 of the Act and will simply enter it into the register as an anonymous surrender. If the item falls within section 5, as it often will, the dealer is still encouraged to accept it and will take it in to pass on to the police or a dealer with a section 5 Authority. In all cases, dealers should notify their police licensing

---

[84] The evident purpose of an order that a person shall be 'liable to be removed from the register' is to enable a court subsequently, after proof of a conviction under this section, to remove from the register another dealer who chooses to employ the convicted dealer or any person who was knowingly a party to the convicted dealer's offence.

[85] FA 1968, s 45(1), (2).

[86] FA 1968, s 45(3). As to an appeal, see, further paras 16.16–16.18, and Chapter 5.

[87] From the National Police Chiefs Council.

department at the earliest opportunity and usually within 48 hours. In our experience, a failure to do so can result in difficulties for the dealer, particularly where the dealer is found in possession of section 5 weapons.

Chapter 17

Museum Firearms Licences

17.01 The F(A)A 1988 introduced provisions enabling the Home Office to issue licences to certain museums authorising them to acquire and possess firearms for exhibition.[1] The museums to which these arrangements apply are set out in Appendix B.

17.02 An application for a museum licence should be made in writing to the Operational Policing Policy Unit at the Home Office at 50 Queen Anne's Gate, London SW1H 9AT. There are no rights of appeal against a refusal to grant a licence. It is an offence knowingly or recklessly to make a statement which is false in any material particular in order to obtain the grant, renewal or variation of a licence.[2]

17.03 A licence will authorise the persons responsible for the management of the museum[3] and their employees, without holding a firearm or shotgun certificate, to possess, and purchase or acquire,[4] for the purposes of the museum, firearms and ammunition which are, or are to be normally, exhibited or kept at the museum or in particular parts of it which the licence may specify. A licence may also, in similar terms, cover prohibited weapons and prohibited ammunition[5] without the need to obtain the Home Office special authority which is normally required.[6]

---

[1]   F(A)A 1988, s 19 and Sch.

[2]   F(A)A 1988 Sch, para 4(1)(a). The maximum punishment on summary conviction is 6 months' imprisonment, or an unlimited fine, or both (F(A)A 1988 Sch, para 4(2)).

[3]   These persons are defined to mean the museum's board of trustees, governing body or other person or persons (whether or not incorporated) exercising corresponding functions (F(A)A 1988 Sch para 6).

[4]   'Acquire' is defined to mean hire, accept as a gift or borrow (FA 1968, s 57(4), F(A)A 1988, s 25(1)).

[5]   For the definitions of 'prohibited weapons' and 'prohibited ammunition', see Chapter 2.

[6]   F(A)A 1988, Sch para 1(2). As to the special authority, see Chapter 1.

17.04 A licence will not be granted or renewed unless the Home Office is satisfied, after consulting the police for the area in which the museum lies, that the arrangements for exhibiting and keeping the firearms and ammunition will not endanger the public safety or the peace.[7]

17.05 A licence may contain conditions to secure the safe custody of the firearms and ammunition.[8] The persons responsible for the management of the museum commit an offence if they fail to comply with a condition, or if they cause or permit another person to do so,[9] but it will be a defence for them to prove that they took all reasonable precautions and exercised due diligence to avoid commission of the offence.[10]

17.06 A licence will be granted for a 5-year period and can be renewed for successive 5-year periods.[11] It will continue in force for that time unless previously revoked or cancelled.[12] Revocation is effected by notice sent by the Home Office to the persons responsible for the management of the museum. A licence can be revoked if:

(a) the Home Office are satisfied that the continuation of the exemption conferred by the licence[13] would result in danger to the public safety or to the peace;[14] or

(b) the persons responsible for the management of the museum, or any of their employees, have been convicted of an offence under the licensing provisions;[15] or

---

[7]   F(A)A 1988, Sch para 1(3), (5). While some of the matters relating to endangering the public safety or the peace may be relevant, the Home Office's primary concern is likely to be the security arrangements for the firearms and ammunition.

[8]   F(A)A 1988, Sch para 1(4). There is evidently no power to impose other conditions.

[9]   F(A)A 1988, Sch para 4(1)(b). For maximum punishments, see fn 2. Special provisions about offences by a body corporate may be found in para 4(5) and (6) of the Schedule.

[10] F(A)A 1988, Sch para 4(4).

[11] The Home Office may by order substitute longer or shorter periods (F(A)A 1988, Sch, para 1(6)).

[12] F(A)A 1988, Sch para 1(5). A court convicting the licence holders of any of the offences mentioned in this chapter may order the cancellation of the licence (FA 1968, s 52(1); F(A)A 1988, s 25(5)).

[13] I.e. exemption from the need for a firearm or shotgun certificate or for an authority to hold prohibited weapons or ammunition, as the case may be.

[14] F(A)A 1988, Sch para 1(3), (5). While some of the matters reviewed at para 4.09 *et seq* in relation to endangering the public safety or the peace may be relevant, the Home Office's primary concern is likely to be the security arrangements for the firearms and ammunition.

[15] I.e. any of the offences mentioned in this chapter.

(c) the persons responsible for the management of the museum have failed to comply with a notice requiring them to surrender the licence on its variation by the Home Office,[16] as described at para 17.07.

A notice of revocation will require those persons to surrender the licence to the Home Office.[17] Failure to comply is an offence.[18]

17.07 A licence may be varied by notice from the Home Office in two ways: by varying its conditions, or by varying the licence itself so as to extend or restrict the buildings to which it applies.[19] The notice may require the persons responsible for the management of the museum to send the licence to the Home Office for variation within 21 days of the date of the notice.[20]

17.08 There is no right of appeal against the revocation or variation of a museum licence.

17.09 The fee for the grant or renewal of a licence is £200, though the Home Office may reduce this in particular cases. When a licence is extended to cover additional premises, the fee will be £75.[21]

17.10 The purchase, acquisition[22] or possession of antique firearms by a museum as items of curiosity or ornament will not require a licence.[23]

---

[16] F(A)A 1988, Sch para 2(2), (3).

[17] F(A)A 1988, Sch para 2(4).

[18] The maximum punishment on summary conviction is a fine at level 3 on the standard scale (currently £1000) (F(A)A 1988, Sch para 4(3)).

[19] F(A)A 1988, Sch para 2(1).

[20] F(A)A 1988, Sch para 2(2). Failure to return the licence is not made an offence, but is one of the grounds on which the licence may be revoked.

[21] F(A)A 1988, Sch para 3(1). The amounts of the fees may be varied, or abolished altogether, by Home Office order (FA 1968, s 43(1); F(A)A 1988, Sch para 3(2)).

[22] 'Acquire' is defined to mean hire, accept as a gift or borrow (FA 1968, s 57(4); F(A)A 1988, s 25(1)).

[23] FA 1968, s 58(2); F(A)A 1988, s 25(6). See, further, para 1.53 *et seq* where the difficulties of judging whether a firearm is an antique are considered.

Appendices

Appendix A

ANTIQUE FIREARMS: HOME OFFICE GUIDANCE TO THE POLICE[1]

This appendix sets out the current position with regards to antique firearms. As explained at para 1.53 *et seq*, the P&CA 2017 has brought in a new regime for defining such items. These regulations have not yet been published. The information below may be used as a guide in considering whether a firearm is to be regarded as an antique under the current regime, although it should be borne in mind that it is always a question of fact for a court as to whether a particular gun is an antique; see para 1.61 *et seq* for more details.

Antique firearms

The following will *usually* be considered antiques:

(a) All muzzle-loading firearms.
(b) Breech-loading firearms capable of discharging a rim-fire cartridge exceeding .23″ calibre (or its metric equivalent), but not 9 mm.
(c) Breech-loading firearms using ignition systems other than rim-fire or centre-fire. (These include pin-fire and needle-fire ignition systems.)
(d) Breech-loading centre-fire arms originally chambered for many obsolete cartridges, and which retain that original chambering.

Not antiques

(a) Shotguns and smooth-bored guns, including shot pistols, chambered for standard shotgun cartridges, .22″ and 9 mm rim-fire cartridges.
(b) Rifles and hand guns chambered for .22″ or 9 mm rim-fire ammunition.
(c) Revolvers, single-shot pistols and self-loading pistols which are chambered for, or will accept, popular centre-fire cartridges of the type .25″, .32″, .38″,

---

[1] The guidance in this Appendix is based on Chapter 8 of *Firearms Law: Guidance to the Police* (2002). For the full list of obsolete calibres see Appendix 5 of the *Guide*.

.380″, .44″, .45″, .450″, .455″ and .476″, or their metric equivalents including 6.35 mm, 7.62 mm, 7.63 mm, 7.65 mm, 8 mm and 9 mm.

(d) Modern reproduction firearms or old firearms which have been modified to allow the use of shotgun cartridges or certain other cartridges.

(e) Extensively modified weapons (e.g. sawn-off guns).

(f) Verey signalling pistols chambered for 1 and 1½ inch cartridges or 26.5/27 mm cartridges.

(g) Pump-action and self-loading centre-fire rifles, except that examples originally chambered for certain obsolete cartridges and retaining that original chambering may qualify for exemption as antiques.

Note (i): The exemption does not apply to ammunition, and the possession of ammunition suitable for use with an otherwise antique firearm will normally be taken to indicate that the firearm is not possessed as a curio or ornament.

Note (ii): The exemption does not apply to firearms of modern manufacture which otherwise conform to the description above. Thus modern firing replicas of obsolete breech-loading or of muzzle-loading firearms will require to be held on certificate. 'Modern manufacture' should be taken to mean 'manufactured since (or during) the Second World War'.

For firearms of historic interest, see Appendix I.

Appendix B

MUSEUMS FOR WHICH FIREARMS LICENCES MAY BE ISSUED[1]

The Armouries, HM Tower of London
The National Museum of Wales
The Science Museum
The Royal Marines Museum
The Royal Navy Museum
The British Museum
The National Maritime Museum
The National Museums and Galleries
    on Merseyside

The National Army Museum
The Royal Air Force Museum
The Victoria and Albert Museum
The Fleet Air Arm Museum
The Royal Navy Submarine
    Museum
The Imperial War Museum
The National Museums of Scotland
The Wallace Collection

A museum or similar institution which is for the time being fully registered with the Museums and Galleries Commission.[2]

Any other museum or similar institution in Great Britain[3] which has as its purpose, or one of its purposes, the preservation for the public benefit of a collection of historical, artistic or scientific interest which includes or is to include firearms and which is maintained wholly or mainly[4] out of money provided by Parliament or by a local authority.[5]

---

[1] F(A)A 1988, s 19 and Sch, paras 1(1), 5.

[2] F(A)A 1997, s 47; Firearms (Museums) Order 1997.

[3] 'Great Britain' means England, Wales and Scotland, and excludes the Channel Islands and the Isle of Man.

[4] The word 'mainly' probably means 'more than half' (*Fawcett Properties Ltd v Buckingham CC* [1960] 3 All ER 503 at 512, HL).

[5] Other museums or similar institutions may be added to this list by Home Office order (F(A)A 1997, s 47).

Appendix C

CLOSE SEASONS FOR SHOOTING GAME AND DEER[1]

The dates apply to the whole of Great Britain unless otherwise specified.

Section 1[2]

Black game	11 December to 19 August, except in Somerset, Devon and that part of the New Forest which lies in Hampshire where it is 11 December to 31 August
Bustard or wild turkey	1 March to 31 August
Grouse or red game	11 December to 11 August
Partridge	1 February to 31 August
Pheasant	1 February to 30 September

---

[1]   In the case of all the birds and animals in ss 1 and 2, shooting on Sunday and Christmas Day is forbidden (GA 1831, s 3).

All dates are inclusive.

The close seasons are not operative in cases where the Ministry of Agriculture imposes a requirement that game be killed to prevent damage to crops, pasture, foodstuffs, livestock, trees, hedges, banks or any works on land (AA 1947, s 98(1), (2)).

For close seasons for the purposes of the WCA 1981, see Appendix E2.

[2]   GA 1831, s 3.

Section 2

Hare   None[3]

Section 3[4]

Male red deer, fallow deer and sika deer	1 May to 31 July
Female red deer, fallow deer, roe deer and sika deer	1 April[5] to 31 October; Scotland: 16 February to 20 October
Male roe deer	1 November to 31 March; Scotland: 21 October to 31 March
Chinese water deer	1 April to 31 October; Scotland: no closed season
Muntjac	No closed season

---

[3] According to *Oke's Game Laws*, 5th Edition, p 8, the period is 1 March to 31 July. This book does not, however, indicate whether or not the dates are inclusive, nor quote any statutory authority for the period. On the other hand, *Oke* at p 118 takes the view, supported by *Halsbury's Laws of England*, 4th Edition Reissue, Vol 2, para 292, that there is no specified close season for hares, and this is thought to be the better view. Certainly, there is no period of the year during which it is an offence to kill hares, except for the restrictions on the rights of occupiers to shoot hares and rabbits on certain moorlands and unenclosed lands at certain times of the year. However, in Scotland pursuant to the Wildlife and Natural Environment (Scotland) Act 2011, s 6(2) creates close seasons in respect of the mountain hare and the brown hare. In the case of the mountain hare the close season is the period in any year beginning with 1 March and ending with 31 July. In the case of the brown hare the close season is the period in any year beginning with 1 February and ending with 30 September. Such close seasons may be varied by Scottish Ministers by Order.

[4] DA 1991, Sch 1. Other species of deer and close seasons for them may be added by order of the Home Office who may also vary or delete such additions.

[5] Changed from 1 March – Regulatory Reform (Deer) (England & Wales) Order 2007 (SI 2007/2183).

Appendix D

WILD BIRDS WHICH ARE PROTECTED BY SPECIAL PENALTIES[1]

Avocet

Bee-eater

Bittern

Bittern, Little

Bluethroat

Brambling

Bunting, Cirl

Bunting, Lapland

Bunting, Snow

Buzzard, Honey

Capercaillie[2]

Chough

Corncrake

Crake, Spotted

Crossbills (all species)

Curlew, Stone

Divers (all species)

Dotterel

Duck, Long-tailed

Eagle, Golden

Falcon, Gyr

Fieldfare

Firecrest

Garganey

Godwit, Black-tailed

Goldeneye

Goose, Greylag (in Outer Hebrides, Caithness, Sutherland and Wester Ross only)

Goshawk

Grebe, Black-necked

Grebe, Slavonian

Greenshank

Gull, Little

Gull, Mediterranean

Harriers (all species)

Heron, Purple

Hobby

Hoopoe

Kingfisher

Kite, Red

Merlin

Oriole, Golden

Osprey

Owl, Barn

Owl, Snowy

Peregrine

Petrel, Leach's

Phalarope, Red-necked

Pintail

Plover, Kentish

Plover, Little-Ringed

Quail, Common

Redstart, Black

---

[1]   WCA 1981, Sch 1.

[2]   Capercaillie cannot now be shot at any time.

Redwing
Ruff
Sandpiper, Purple
Scaup
Scoter, Velvet
Shorelark
Spoonbill
Stint, Temminck's
Swan, Hooper
Tern, Little
Tit, Bearded
Treecreeper, Short-toed
Warbler, Dartford
Warbler, Savi's

Rosefinch, Scarlet
Sandpiper, Green
Sandpiper, Wood
Scoter, Common
Serin
Shrike, Red-backed
Stilt, Black-winged
Swan, Bewick's
Tern, Black
Tern, Roseate
Tit, Crested
Warbler, Cetti's
Warbler, Marsh
Whimbrel

Appendix E1

WILD BIRDS WHICH MAY BE KILLED OR TAKEN OUTSIDE THE CLOSE SEASON[1]

Coot	Duck, Tufted
Gadwall	Goldeneye
Goose, Canada	Goose, Greylag
Goose, Pink-footed	Goose, White-fronted[2]
Mallard[3]	Moorhen[4]
Pintail	Plover, Golden
Pochard[5]	Shoveler
Snipe, Common	Teal
Wigeon	Woodcock

---

[1] WCA 1981, s 2(1), (3) and Sch 2, Part I. None of the birds listed above (with the exception of the White-fronted Goose) can be killed or taken in Scotland on Sundays or Christmas Day pursuant to WCA 1981, Sch 1A as inserted by the Wildlife and Natural Environment (Scotland) Act 2011, s 3(8).

[2] In England and Wales only.

[3] Before the term Mallard, pursuant to the Wildlife and Natural Environment (Scotland) Act 2011, s 3(7)(a) Black Grouse and Red Grouse are added in respect of Scotland.

[4] After the term Moorhen, pursuant to the Wildlife and Natural Environment (Scotland) Act 2011, s 3(7)(b) Grey Partridge, Red-legged Partridge and Common Pheasant are added in respect of Scotland.

[5] After the term Pochard, pursuant to the Wildlife and Natural Environment (Scotland) Act 2011, s 3(7)(c) Ptarmigan is added in respect of Scotland.

Appendix E2

CLOSE SEASONS OUTSIDE WHICH WILD BIRDS LISTED AT APPENDIX E1 ABOVE MAY BE KILLED, INJURED OR TAKEN[1]

Woodcock[2]	1 February to 30 September
Snipe	1 February to 11 August
Wild duck and wild geese in or over any area below high water mark of ordinary spring tides	21 February to 31 August
In any other case	1 February to 31 August

---

[1] WCA 1981, s 2(4). All dates are inclusive. These close seasons may be varied, and special protection for additional periods given, by government order (WCA 1981, s 2(5), (6)).

[2] This period does not apply to woodcock in Scotland which therefore in that country fall under the heading 'In any other case'.

Appendix F

LICENCES FOR SHOOTING WILD BIRDS[1] AND WILD ANIMALS[2]

Purpose for which licence may be granted	Type of wildlife to which it is applicable	Issuing authority
1. Scientific research or educational	Both	Natural England or the appropriate Secretary of State for birds; Natural England[3] in other cases
2. Conserving wild birds or wild animals	Both	Natural England or the appropriate Secretary of State for birds; Natural England in other cases
3. Protecting a collection of wild birds or a zoological collection	Both	The appropriate Secretary of State for birds. Natural England for wild animals

---

[1] In this context game birds are included. For their definition and that for wild birds, see WCA 1981, ss 16(1), 27(1). However, game birds will not be included in respect of Scotland pursuant to the Wildlife and Natural Environment (Scotland) Act 2011, s 2.

[2] WCA 1981, ss 16(1)–(3), (9), 27(1). Licences may be: general or specific; granted to persons of a class or to a particular person; subject to compliance with specified conditions; modified or revoked at any time by the issuing authority. A licence will be valid for the period (not exceeding 2 years) stated in it (if not previously modified or revoked), and a reasonable charge may be made for it (WCA 1981, s 16(5), (6)(b)).

[3] Details as to which department to apply to in England Scotland or Wales are available on the internet.

Purpose for which licence may be granted	Type of wildlife to which it is applicable	Issuing authority
4. Preserving public health or public safety and (for birds) air safety	Both	The Ministry of Agriculture or the appropriate Secretary of State
5. Taxidermy	Wild birds	The appropriate Secretary of State
6. Preventing the spread of disease	Both	The Ministry of Agriculture or the appropriate Secretary of State
7. Preventing serious damage to livestock, foodstuffs for livestock, crops, vegetables, fruit, growing timber or any other form of property or to fisheries	Both	The Ministry of Agriculture or the appropriate Secretary of State
8. Providing food for human consumption. Licences restricted to: (a) gulls' eggs (b) lapwings' eggs at any time before 15 April in any year	Wild birds	The appropriate Secretary of State

Appendix G

WILD ANIMALS WHICH MAY NOT BE KILLED OR TAKEN BY CERTAIN METHODS[1]

Badger
Bats, Typical (all species)*
Dolphin, Bottle-nosed*
Dormice (all species)*
Marten, Pine*
Polecat*

Shrews (all species)

Bats, Horseshoe (all species)*
Cat, Wild*
Dolphin, Common*
Hedgehog
Otter, Common*
Porpoise, Harbour (otherwise
known as Common porpoise)*
Squirrel, Red

---

[1] See WCA 1981, Sch 6 for references to this list of animals. Those marked by an asterisk are repealed in respect of Scotland pursuant to the Wildlife and Natural Environment (Scotland) Act 2011, s 19.

Appendix H

PARTICULARS TO BE ENTERED BY FIREARMS DEALER IN REGISTER OF TRANSACTIONS

(a) The quantities and description of firearms and ammunition manufactured and the dates thereof.

(b) The quantities and description of firearms and ammunition purchased or acquired with the names and addresses of the sellers or transferors and the dates of the several transactions.

(c) The quantities and description of firearms and ammunition accepted for sale, repair, test, proof, cleaning, storage, destruction or other purpose, with the names and addresses of the transferors and the dates of the several transactions.

(d) The quantities and description of firearms and ammunition sold or transferred with the names and addresses of the purchasers or transferees and (except in cases where the purchaser or transferee is a registered dealer) the areas in which the firearm certificates were issued, and the dates of the several transactions.

(e) The quantities and description of firearms and ammunition in possession for sale or transfer at the date of the last stocktaking or such other date in each year as may be specified in the register.[1]

(f) In the case of a firearm sold for export to a buyer without a firearm or shotgun certificate, the number and place of issue of any passport held by the buyer.[2]

Note: The VCRA 2006 made provision for the same details to be recorded in a register in relation to sale, repair and possession of air weapons and their components, and of 'metallic primers'.[3]

---

[1] FA 1968, Sch 4; Firearms Rules 1998, r 10(5).

[2] F(A)A 1988, s 18(4).

[3] FA 1968, Sch 4, Part 2.

Appendix I

FIREARMS OF HISTORIC INTEREST

Certain handguns, which would otherwise be treated as prohibited weapons, may be held under the authority of a conditional firearm certificate or a visitor's firearm permit[1] if fulfilling certain conditions. One condition is that these guns are not chambered for any of the following types of ammunition:[2]

.22″ rim-fire
.25″ ACP/6.35 mm
.25″ – 20
.32″ ACP/7.65 mm
.32″ – 20
.32″ Smith & Wesson Long
7.62 mm Soviet Tokarev
.38″ 40 Winchester
.380″ ACP 9 mm short
9 mm Luger/Parabellum/9 x 19 mm
.38″ Smith & Wesson
.38″ Special
.38″ – 200
.44″ Special
.44″ – 40 Winchester
.45″ ACP

---

[1] For visitors' firearm permits, see Chapter 7.

[2] F(A)A 1997, s 7; Firearms (Amendment) Act 1997 (Firearms of Historic Interest) Order 1997 (SI 1997/1537).

Index

References are to page numbers.